PROPHETIC JESUS, PROPHETIC CHURCH

PROPHETIC JESUS, PROPHETIC CHURCH

The Challenge of Luke-Acts
to Contemporary Christians

Luke Timothy Johnson

WILLIAM B. EERDMANS PUBLISHING COMPANY
GRAND RAPIDS, MICHIGAN / CAMBRIDGE, U.K.

Wm. B. Eerdmans Publishing Co.
2140 Oak Industrial Drive N.E., Grand Rapids, Michigan 49505 /
P.O. Box 163, Cambridge CB3 9PU U.K.

Printed in the United States of America

17 16 15 14 13 12 11   7 6 5 4 3 2 1

Library of Congress Cataloging-in-Publication Data

Johnson, Luke Timothy.
Prophetic Jesus, prophetic church:
the challenge of Luke-Acts to contemporary Christians /
Luke Timothy Johnson.
p.   cm.
ISBN 978-0-8028-0390-0 (pbk.: alk. paper)
1. Bible. N.T. Luke — Theology.   2. Bible. N.T. Acts — Theology.
3. Prophecy (Christianity) — Biblical teaching.
4. Jesus Christ — Prophetic office — Biblical teaching.
5. Church — Biblical teaching.   I. Title.

BS2595.6.P72J64   2011
232'.8 — dc22

2011007214

Contents

Preface

The need for prophecy is stated succinctly by the book of Proverbs 29:18: "Without a vision (or, 'without prophecy'), the people perish." Prophets are the human beings who speak to their fellow humans from the perspective of God and, by so speaking, enable others to envision a way of being human more in conformity with God's own vision for the world.

Humans chronically and desperately need prophetic visions. Without them the world runs all too smoothly on the basis of programs and politics formed exclusively by human reason — and human reason severed from God's saving word tends to become simply a kind of cunning. Without prophetic challenge, the world quickly becomes structured along the lines of expediency and self-interest.

There probably has never been a time when at least some Christians did not long for the voice of prophecy that could challenge the usual assumptions and accustomed practices in the world (and in the church itself) and could jolt people into new insight and empower them with new energy. Our age is no exception. We need prophecy. The church today particularly needs to hear the voice of prophecy in order to carry out its own prophetic mission.

For prophets to arise, however, their imaginations also need to be shaped and energized. Prophets do not have magic access to God's way of seeing and speaking. The sight and speech of prophets need to be formed — and have always been formed — by the words and deeds of earlier prophets. The ancient visions provide symbols that can be reinvigorated by new experiences of God in the world.

I have written this book precisely as an effort to stimulate such prophetic vision for the church today. My argument is straightforward and has three parts. First, when the New Testament composition commonly designated by scholars as Luke-Acts (the Gospel of Luke and the Acts of the Apostles) is read as a literary unity, it reveals a prophetic vision of both Jesus and the church. Indeed, the church of Acts is, if anything, even more radically prophetic than Jesus in the Gospel. Second, as part of canonical Scripture, the voice and vision of Luke-Acts has a prophetic function for the church in every age. It does not simply report past events; it imagines a world that challenges the one that humans in every age construct on their own terms. Third, if we in the church today choose to heed Luke's challenge, we shall need to think of the church in more explicitly prophetic terms and find ways of embodying and enacting God's vision for humans.

Some readers of this book will notice a family resemblance to a book I wrote some years ago, *Scripture and Discernment: Decision Making in the Church* (Abingdon, 1996). Luke-Acts also inspired that effort and was the source for the model of decision-making as theological process that I proposed for the church's consideration. The present work, however, elevates the argument about the prophetic character of Luke-Acts to another level. My interest here is not simply the discovery of a narrative exemplar for a single dimension of the church's life so much as a scriptural vision for the life and mission of the church as such — a life and mission grounded in the prophetic ministry of Jesus Christ. Consequently, although readers will find in these pages the same emphasis on the living God working in human lives through the Holy Spirit, the scope broadens to include an overall sense of how the church, through the power of the Holy Spirit, can continue and extend Jesus' prophetic work in the world.

As a professional New Testament scholar, I have some interest in showing the consequences of a thorough-going literary reading of Luke-Acts as a compositional unity, but this book is entirely directed to readers within the faith community. It began as a series of presentations to ecclesial groups, notably the clergy conference of the Indiana Archdiocese and the Mile-High Scripture Institute in Denver, as well as classes in Emory University's Candler School of Theology and in Notre Dame University's Summer Theology program. Responses from these groups encouraged me to think that this approach would be appreciated by others as well. I am particularly grateful for the imaginative ways that students at Candler and Notre Dame employed Luke's prophetic vision as a lens for analyzing specific ecclesial situations in the present. Michael Thomson of Wm. B. Eerdmans Publishing Company has been patient and constant in his support of this project. And, as in everything I have written, my most heartfelt and tender gratitude is to Joy, whose own witness to God has always been, for me, prophetic.

Scripture references are based on the New American Bible translation © 1986 by the Confraternity of Christian Doctrine (CCD), with occasional modifications in light of the Greek.

Introduction

When Luke the evangelist completed his two-volume narrative in the late first century and wrote a short prologue to his patron Theophilus explaining his reason for writing, he could not have imagined the strange future facing his composition. He could not have foreseen that an account written for the assurance of contemporary Gentile members of a new Mediterranean cult would become part of the sacred Scripture of a world religion based on and extending the texts of Torah derived from Judaism. He could not have imagined that the process of making his composition part of the New Testament canon would separate the two parts of his single story, so that his account of "what Jesus said and did" would appear with the other Gospels, while his account of what Jesus' witnesses did and said would serve to introduce the letters of Paul. He could not have believed that this canonical separation would lead in turn to the reading of the two parts of the narrative in isolation from each other (and their author's literary intention), in a centuries-long history of interpretation that considered "the Gospel of Luke" as another version of the "good news" with those offered by Mark, Matthew, and John and considered "the Acts of the Apostles" as the first history of the church.

But all this did happen, and the consequences have been momentous. The full effect of Luke's literary achievement and the full power of his theological imagination have seldom if ever been appreciated in the long history of New Testament interpretation. Before the modern period, biblical compositions were hardly ever read in terms of their respective "voices" — they were read as repositories of divine logia; human authorship was acknowledged but seldom truly computed. The Gospel of Luke and the

1

Acts of the Apostles were mined separately for what they could teach about God and the path of discipleship. An engagement with the discrete canonical witnesses was not the prevailing principle of interpretation, but the assertion of their harmonious teaching.

As the historical-critical approach espoused by modernity became the dominant mode of investigating the New Testament, Luke and Acts continued to be read separately in the search for answers to new questions. In this approach, the differences between the two volumes came to be emphasized more than their points of commonality. Each was valued — or not valued — as a historical source for discrete topics: the Gospel in the quest for the historical Jesus, Acts in the history of nascent Christianity. Each was thought to fail the stern test of historical reliability: the Gospel was viewed with the others as a work overly theological in character, so that only pieces of it could be used for serious historical reconstruction of Jesus; Acts was considered secondary and inferior as a source for reconstructing Paul's ministry and thought.

Oddly, though, both parts of Luke's writing continue to provide an implicit and mostly unacknowledged role in present-day historical reconstructions. Virtually all versions of the "historical Jesus" on offer at bookstores derive their construal from Luke's portrayal of Jesus as a political and prophetic messiah. And attempts to construct a "life of Paul" find it impossible to do it on the basis of Paul's letters alone; willy-nilly, Acts provides the chronological framework that organizes the evidence of the letters.

Theologically, the two volumes have received quite different reviews from critics. Insofar as most contemporary reconstructions of the historical Jesus rely fundamentally on Luke's Gospel, and insofar as such historical reconstructions have a theological more than a properly historical goal, it can be said that Luke's theological outlook receives massive approbation. Indeed, the vaunted criteria for determining the "authentic" words of Jesus tend not to matter when it comes to the treasured Lukan parables (the Prodigal Son, the Good Samaritan) or to the understanding of Jesus' ministry as one of "open commensality."

In contrast, Acts tends to receive a negative theological judgment no matter what the season. When New Testament scholars measured theological worth from the perspective of Paul's letters, above all his teaching on righteousness through faith and his theology of the cross, Acts was regarded as a theological disaster area. It represented a form of "early Catholicism," meaning that it portrayed Christianity in triumphalistic terms. Because of its emphasis on miracles, Acts was seen as a "theology of glory" rather than a faithful version of Paul's "theology of the cross." Even more strikingly, those who laud the portrait of Jesus in the Gospel of Luke as the prophetic impetus of the "Jesus movement" or of an "unbrokered kingdom" find in Acts the sure signs of the betrayal of the radical movement and understanding of the kingdom: Acts, they assert, turns the movement into an institution; its prophetic character is lost.

My argument in this book goes in the complete opposite direction. I follow the best in critical gospel study deriving in large measure from the pioneering work of H. J. Cadbury (*The Making of Luke-Acts,* 1927), by reading Luke and Acts as a single literary composition with coherence as a literary work and consistency in its religious outlook. The application of literary and narrative criticism to Luke-Acts has shown the fundamental correctness of reading the two volumes as a literary unity, and a variety of studies have demonstrated the exegetical value of this approach.

I therefore consider recent efforts to re-segment the two volumes — whether done in the name of canon and reception history or in the name of thematic inconsistency — to be wrongheaded. Canonical arrangement does not determine how canonical compositions are to be read. We are not obliged to read Hebrews as a letter written by Paul simply because many early Christians so regarded it and some ancient manuscripts place it among Paul's letters. Nor does the canonical placement of James or Revelation demand that we read them as either later or lesser than Paul. The accidents of canonical arrangement do not constrain interpretation.

Neither does the way ancient or modern readers construed canonical compositions compel contemporary readers. We would not say that present-day interpreters of Paul, for example, are constrained by the readings of Augustine and Luther. While respecting the theological insights that former interpreters had into Paul's Letter to the Romans, we would agree, I think, that better knowledge of Paul's historical and social context as well as of his rhetoric enables a reading that comes closer to the way Paul would have been heard by those Roman Christ-believers who first heard it proclaimed. If Paul's rhetoric in Romans shows us that his argument extends all the way through the letter, with each section playing its distinct and necessary rhetorical role, we would rightly seek to understand that argument as a whole, however much Augustine or Luther or Calvin — fine readers all — failed to read it that way.

While not disputing the legitimacy of reading Luke and Acts separately — there are, after all, many ways of approaching texts ancient and modern — I choose in this book to read Luke-Acts according to the best historical and literary judgment concerning its original composition and therefore closest to what we can consider the text's first intentionality, that is, what the composition sought to communicate and accomplish. Such a reading demands consideration precisely of the literary shape Luke gave to his work. The first part of my argument, then, invites the reader to see the ways in which Luke has constructed a certain kind of meaning through the structure and style of his story. Specifically, I show how Luke makes particular use of prophecy as a way of giving coherence to his account — connecting the story of Jesus and the church to that of Israel in a specific way, as the continuation of God's saving activity through prophetic utterance and deed.

But prophecy is not simply a literary technique for Luke. The heart of my examination of Luke-Acts is the analysis of the portrayal both of Jesus and of the apostles in terms of prophecy. Luke characterizes Jesus and the movement that bears his name in ways that anyone familiar with the biblical tradition should recognize as having the marks of the prophet: being inspired by the Holy Spirit, speaking God's word, embodying God's vision for humans, enacting that vision through signs and wonders, and bearing witness to God in the world. Reading Luke-Acts in this fashion demonstrates the profound degree of continuity between the two parts of Luke's story: it is from beginning to end a story about God's prophets. Indeed, if there is a difference between the Gospel and Acts, it is not that Luke portrays the church as an institutional betrayal of the radical Jesus movement. Quite the contrary; Luke shows the church in Acts to be even more radical than the prophet Jesus. Scholars have erred in this matter above all because they have failed to read Luke-Acts as a literary unity and have failed to reckon adequately with the implications of Luke's prophetic characterization.

In fact, Luke's characterization of the first-generation church in terms of a prophetic manner of life — being led by the spirit, sharing possessions, engaging in an itinerant mission, exercising servant leadership, bearing powerful witness before religious and state authorities — takes on an added edge when we remember that Luke composed his work considerably after the events and shaped them with a purpose. The Christian writings that emerged from that first period of nascent Christianity, the letters of Paul, already suppose in the decades of the 50s and 60s a church that is located primarily in urban centers and in households and that struggles to resolve the egalitarian impulses associated with baptism into Christ within the hierarchical structures of the Hellenistic household.

The first readers of Luke's narrative would perhaps not have seen his story as a nostalgic recollection of a time past but rather as a summons to an ideal that might be in danger of being lost, not as a work of bland historiography but as a thrilling act of utopian imagination, less a neutral report on how things were than as a normative prescription for how things ought to be. Luke's two-volume work, in short, may well itself have had a prophetic character for its earliest readers, who could see his depiction of Jesus' ministry and the work of Jesus' prophetic successors as a challenge to the present condition of the church in the late first century.

Whether or not Luke's first readers heard his words as prophetic, present-day readers are both able and required so to read them. This is because Luke's readers today read Luke-Acts as part of the canonical Scripture of the Christian church. The act of canonization bore with it the implication that the discrete writings from Christianity's first days had a permanent normative value, that they are inspired by God, that they speak God's word — that, in short, they are prophetic for every age of the church, challenging it and calling it into question. Such, at least, has been the conviction of Christians through the centuries who have these (and only these) compositions proclaimed to them in the liturgical assembly, accompanied by the declaration "this is the word of God."

When Paul's letters are read in worship, the church hears them as the stimulus to self-examination, both individually and communally. The congregation does not ask in such a setting whether Paul is accurately reporting the events in Galatia or Corinth, but rather how Paul's response to his historical situation — as found in the specific rhetoric of his letters — might have significance for believers today. It does not matter whether the ancient Pauline churches in Galatia were harassed by Jewish missionaries or by status-seeking insiders; what matters is Paul's teaching on the ultimacy of faith and love. It does not matter whether Corinthian believers were speaking in foreign languages or in speechlike babble; what matters is Paul's insistence that all expressions of the spirit serve to build up the assembly in faith. We can borrow Paul's own words concerning ancient Israel's story in Scripture: "these things happened to them as an example, and they have been written down as a warning to us" (1 Cor 10:11). Whatever the event of the past might have been, it is the actual scriptural story that instructs and warns. Paul states similarly in Romans 15:4: "Whatever was written previously was written for our instruction, that by endurance and by the encouragement of the scriptures we might have hope."

The same sort of reading applies to Luke-Acts when it is read by the believing community. Luke's Jesus is not a simple reportage of the historical figure, but an imaginative construction — guided by the inspiring spirit and the faith of the community — of a prophet who announces and enacts God's visitation of the people Israel. Luke's depiction of the church may or may not be based on facts from the past; it also is an imaginative construction — guided by the inspiring spirit at work in the author's words — of a prophetic community that extends that prophetic visitation to all the peoples of the world. The pertinent question for believing readers is not "Is Luke's rendering of Jesus historically accurate?" but rather, "How does Luke's imaginative construal challenge the values of the world?" The pertinent question is not "Was the early church as Luke describes it?" but rather, "How does Luke's portrayal of the early church challenge the church in every age?"

My purpose in this book is to present the prophetic challenge in as sharp a fashion as possible for readers in the church today. I do this, not by imposing some extraneous framework on Luke's literary endeavor, but by taking the literary dimensions of Luke's text with utmost seriousness and teasing out what I regard as the legitimate implications to be drawn from his literary work. By no means do I suggest that Luke-Acts is the only witness to which the church should attend today. A genuine theological reading of the New Testament engages all of the canonical compositions in a complex conversation involving not only the diverse texts of Scripture but, as well, the continuing experience of the Holy Spirit in human lives, the use of reason shaped by the mind of Christ, and the traditions of the community communicated by liturgical and creedal forms as well as by the witness of the saints. The church's reading of Luke's prophetic witness should, by all means, be a dialectical one. My argument here, however, is that if Luke's voice is not heard today and engaged in its prophetic fullness, then it may be that the actual voice of Luke-Acts is not being heard and engaged at all.

I have been speaking of "the church" reading and engaging Luke-Acts in its prophetic witness. Such a proposal is itself at least a slightly utopian vision. Two great and obvious difficulties stand in the way of its realization. The first is that the very concept of church is deeply controverted among contemporary Christians. Christianity today is divided more on the basis of ecclesiastical polity than it is on the basis of doctrine or morality. Disagreements about conditions of membership, the structure of authority, and the shape of worship are all manifest signs of Christianity's disunity. Even more troubling is the fact that the individualistic tendencies fostered by modernity have weakened participation in the shared practices of any form of church.

Although I am a life-long Roman Catholic and continue to be a loyal Catholic layperson, I do not envisage "church" as necessarily conforming to the hierarchical structure of Catholicism. I recognize as authentic realizations of church any community where two or three gather in the name of the risen Lord Jesus and both speak and act the truth of the gospel in love. Indeed, as I speak of "church" in these pages, I have in mind most of all local congregations within any denomination that actually gather in the name to worship, study, and practice the works of faith. And when, on the basis of Luke's challenge, I pose questions concerning the use of possessions or the practice of authority, I pose these with respect to all public and organized forms of Christianity, not simply my own denomination. Since Luke-Acts does not advocate or address any specific form of ecclesiastical polity, my assumption is that Luke's prophetic challenge can and should be heard by every form of Christian church.

The second difficulty is that faith communities have little experience of or commitment to "reading and engaging" canonical witnesses *as* church. The dominant forms of reading among Christians are individualistic: the New Testament is read for what it says to "me" rather than to "us." This is, to be sure, an exaggeration; tradition has been built up, after all, by the ways in which communities found in Scripture support for their creeds and practices. But to read together for the sake of engaging the prophetic challenge posed by a writing to the church as such, this is something that communities seldom do. Yet there is the greatest need for the church — in whatever form it takes — to read precisely as church and, reading as church, to hear how scriptural witnesses speak to the nature and practices of the church as such. Perhaps this is also a utopian expectation. Yet imaginative leaps into utopian visions have a way of becoming real when actually put into practice. The church can become transformed as church by reading together as church. Reading Luke-Acts in this fashion, I think, particularly offers the opportunity for such transformation.

To enable such a reading of Luke-Acts, I begin with a consideration of the literary form Luke gave to his two-volume work and then develop what I perceive to be elements of prophecy in his writing. I then take each of the constitutive elements of prophetic character and show how they are developed respectively by each volume. When each of these characteristics is developed, I turn to a reflection on how that specific quality might generate useful self-reflection by the church today.

CHAPTER ONE

The Literary Shape of Luke-Acts

In order to hear the distinctive witness of Luke-Acts as a unitary literary composition, it is necessary to gain a firm sense of how it is put together and how its form helps shape its meaning. The best preparation for following the argument of this book is a repeated reading of Luke-Acts in its entirety and in sequence — the way Luke wrote it to be read (see Luke 1:3) — before entering into my examination of specific passages and themes.

This first chapter can serve as a companion for such preliminary reading. It briefly sketches what biblical scholar H. J. Cadbury memorably called "the making of Luke-Acts." The point of this presentation is not to develop hypotheses about Luke's possible sources, but to use synoptic comparison — that is, analyze Luke over against Mark and Matthew — as a way of sharpening our perception of how Luke tells his story. I begin with the most rudimentary sort of *material* analysis, showing what pieces Luke includes and how he fits them together. I move then to a *stylistic* analysis, in order to alert readers to the implications of Luke's ability to speak in several dictions. I then consider the question of the *genre* of the two-volume work and what it suggests about Luke's purposes, before turning finally to one of the ways in which Luke provides specific *structural* shape to his narrative.

Material Analysis

The most obvious source that Luke uses for the first part of his story is the Gospel of Mark. Like Matthew, he uses the basic Markan plot line, extending from the baptism of Jesus by John to the burial and empty tomb. Luke therefore presents Jesus' ministry in the same basic sequence that we find in Mark: he begins in Galilee, travels to Judea, and experiences his passion and death in Jerusalem. We do not know how a copy of Mark reached Luke. But it is clear that he treated Mark with considerable respect; where he follows Mark, he follows him more closely than does Matthew. Because Mark is extant, present-day readers can observe the way that Luke uses this source. More than that, we can compare Luke's usage to that of Matthew, and this added dimension of comparison sharpens our perception of Luke's particular literary and religious interests. If Mark were not extant, however, it is also the case that we could not reconstruct his source with precision. Luke uses his source respectfully but camouflages it thoroughly through his editing. He also alters Mark's account through subtraction and addition of material.

Luke's most impressive subtraction is found in his "great omission" of the material that is found in Mark 6:45–8:26. Although it has sometimes been suggested that Luke may have used a copy of Mark lacking that section, the more likely explanation is that Luke deliberately excluded it because of a concern for the contents. Three aspects of this part of Mark may have caused Luke concern: (1) it contains doublets (such as the feeding of the four thousand (Mark 8:1-9) in addition to the feeding of the five thousand (6:34-44) and Luke tends to avoid such obvious repetition; (2) it tells two stories (the healing of the deaf man in 7:31-37 and the blind man in 8:22-26) in which Jesus displays techniques that might be associated with magic, and Luke wants to draw a clear distinction between the powerful deeds done by Jesus and his followers and magic; (3) it portrays Jesus' disciples in strongly negative terms (as in 7:17-19; 8:14-21), while Luke's presentation of them tends to be more positive.

Like Matthew, though in a distinctive fashion, Luke extends Mark's story by adding narrative material at the beginning and end of the Gospel account. By their construction of an infancy narrative, both Matthew and Luke connect the story of Jesus more explicitly to the story of Israel. Matthew does this through a genealogy and a series of scenes with Joseph as hero, showing how the events of Jesus' birth, escape to Egypt, and return to Nazareth all were "in fulfillment" of specific prophetic texts. Luke connects Jesus to Israel in a more complex fashion, with a series of scenes that juxtapose John (and his family) and Jesus (with his family), using canticles recited by characters to provide the interpretation of events as the continuation of God's loving care towards his people.

9

By telling of explicit resurrection appearances, the two evangelists also connect the story of Jesus to the life of the church. In Matthew, the flight of the women from the empty tomb finds its term in an encounter with the risen Lord, and Matthew's final scene has Jesus commanding the eleven to make disciples of all nations, "teaching them all that I have commanded you" (Matt 28:20). Luke has a more elaborate set of appearance accounts, together with reports of other sightings of the Lord. The risen Jesus comes among his followers and interprets Scripture with reference to his suffering and death (Luke 24:25, 44) and promises them a powerful gift of the spirit (24:47-49). He concludes the narrative with a short account of Jesus' departure from his followers into heaven (24:51).

Matthew and Luke both insert substantial amounts of discourse material — passages that provide explicit sayings of Jesus — within the Markan story line. They do this, however, in distinctive ways. Matthew constructs discrete "sermons" by Jesus (in chs. 5–7, 10, 13, 18, 23–25) that interrupt the narrative flow and enhance the portrayal of Jesus as the teacher of the church. The amount of this material in Matthew can be appreciated when we realize that the contrast between sixteen chapters in Mark and twenty-eight chapters in Matthew is only part of the story: Matthew systematically reduces the number of words used to tell the stories he shares with Mark. This narrative reduction increases the perception of Matthew's Gospel as dominated by the speeches of Jesus. Luke also inserts large amount of discourse material into the story of Jesus. Much of this discourse material is found also in Matthew and is conventionally designated as "Q" material (from the German word "Quelle," or "source"). But a substantial amount of discourse — including the most distinctive and beloved of Jesus' parables — is found only in Luke (and is designated as L material).

Luke follows a different approach to the inclusion of this mass of material than does Matthew. He does not construct formal and internally-organized discourses. Instead, he inserts Jesus' sayings into biographically more plausible situations: Jesus speaks as he walks, as he performs deeds, as he eats with others. There was not room for all Luke's additional material within Mark's framework, however, so Luke fits it into the story by expanding the hints of Jesus' travelling from Galilee to Jerusalem in Mark 10:17, 32, 46, into a full-fledged and formal journey, extending from Luke 9:51 to 19:44. This ten-chapter journey narrative plays an important role in Luke's narrative. It serves to portray both the character and destiny of Jesus, as well as his distinctive mode of teaching to disciples, calls of discipleship to the crowds, and parables of rejection of those who reject his message.

Luke's most dramatic narrative extension is found in a complete second volume that picks up the story where the Gospel left off and continues with an account of the birth of the church in Jerusalem (Acts 1–7), its expansion through Samaria and Judea (8–10), and its spread across the Mediterranean (11–28), all this enacting the prediction of the risen Lord in Acts 1:8, "You will receive power when the Holy Spirit comes upon you, and you shall be my witnesses in Jerusalem, throughout Judea and Samaria, and to the ends of the earth." Although many efforts have been made to find specific sources that Luke might have used for this portion of his composition, none have been successful. The narrative in Acts certainly made use of materials available to the author — whether small or large, oral or written — but so skillful is Luke in rewriting such materials (as we can see in the case of Mark) — that everything appears to come directly from him.

Two implications of Luke's narrative continuation can be noted at once. The first is literary: by continuing the story of Jesus into the story of the apostles, Luke provides the first authoritative interpretation of the Gospel narrative. Our interpretation of Luke's Gospel, consequently, requires of us not only attention to the way in which Luke maintains or alters his Markan source, not only attention to the diverse way in which Luke treats Mark in contrast to Matthew, but above all the way in which his second volume drops or develops the themes of the Gospel. This is especially the case because Luke has more literary freedom in the second volume than in the first volume, since, so far as we know, he is the first one to extend the story of Jesus in this fashion and was therefore less constrained by a respect for earlier sources.

The second implication is theological: Luke writes his narrative concerning the church as the continuation of the story of Jesus. He need not have fashioned the account at all — no one had before him — and if he wrote it, he could have shaped it in a variety of ways. His composition reflects a deliberate literary and theological choice. And he has so convincingly connected his account of the apostles to that of Jesus that many readers are convinced that this is the way things happened, indeed had to have happened. A fuller appreciation of his literary and theological choice is developed throughout the book, but it must be noted at once as something startlingly new in nascent Christian literature.

Finally, Luke explicitly connects the two parts of his story — for it is a single story — by means of a prologue to each volume. The very short prologue to Acts (1:1-3) recalls to the intended reader, Theophilus (in all likelihood, Luke's literary patron), the basic elements of the first volume. The longer prologue to the Gospel (Luke 1:1-4), also addressed to Theophilus, actually serves as an introduction to the composition as a whole. The two prologues together make Luke's literary intentions absolutely clear: he wants the two volumes to be read in sequence as parts of a single story.

Stylistic Analysis

When Luke follows a source, he treats it with considerable respect. His version of the healing of the Gerasene demoniac (Luke 8:26-39), derived from Mark 5:1-20, indicates the marked degree to which he adheres to his source, and the characteristic elements he chooses to alter. The passage is particularly instructive because we can contrast Luke's delicate touch with Matthew's more radical redaction. Matthew 8:28-34 is visibly shorter. The evangelist has removed all incidental detail dealing with the condition of the demoniac and his destiny. Rather than a single man with many demons, Matthew has Jesus encounter two demoniacs. Matthew focuses attention not on them but solely on the power of Jesus, so that the exorcism becomes another demonstration of Jesus' power rather than, as in Mark and Luke, a poignant story that draws the reader into a contemplation of the one whom Jesus liberates.

Luke's respect for his source does not mean that he does not seek to improve Mark's version stylistically. He corrects what he regards as inaccuracies: Mark's "sea" becomes for the more cosmopolitan Luke a "lake" (8:22). He seeks clarity, making sure the reader understands that Jesus reaches shore before he steps from the boat (8:27) and that after the exorcism the man was no longer a "demoniac" but "the man from whom demons had come out" (8:38). He also is concerned for consecutiveness: Mark has people come from a city without establishing that the man lived in the tombs outside a city; Luke establishes the location at the beginning of his account (8:27).

Luke's own stylistic tendencies are more evident in passages for which he has no source. In some parts of his narrative — most of all in the infancy account — Luke clearly imitates the Septuagint, the Greek translation of the Hebrew Bible carried out ca. 250 B.C.E. The scenes of annunciation and birth, as well as the several canticles spoken by the characters, resonate with septuagintal diction and follow the patterns of biblical prototypes: the annunciation to Mary is a pastiche of biblical annunciation accounts and prophetic language; Mary's Magnificat echoes Hannah's triumphant song. So dense is Luke's biblical diction in his first two chapters that they can accurately be described as a kind of haggadic midrash based on the Septuagint.

It is not only in the infancy accounts that we find biblical imitation or septuagintal language. Luke has shaped the sequence of stories in 7:1-17 to resemble the respective healing stories of Elisha and Elijah (see 2 Kgs 5:1-15; 1 Kgs 17:17-24). The second report of Jesus' ascension in Acts 1:9-11 recalls the ascent of the prophet Elijah (2 Kgs 2:9-12). The language used for the deaths of Ananias and Sapphira in Acts 5:1-11 resonates with the account of the punishment of Achan in Joshua 7:10-26. Stephen's lengthy speech in Acts 7:2-50 uses the specific diction of the Septuagint even as it provides a fresh structure to the biblical story.

Luke is equally adept, however, at appropriating the rhetorical devices of Hellenistic literature. The prologue to the entire composition (Luke 1:1-4) is written in a style and form that identify the author as a writer familiar with Greco-Roman conventions. Luke writes speeches for his characters in the manner of Hellenistic historians and composes concise summaries that provide a sense of amplitude to the sparse details he has to relate. Paul's defense speeches in the last part of Acts follow precisely the form prescribed for forensic rhetoric. Especially in Acts, Luke's narrative makes use of the full repertoire of Greco-Roman romances, with trials, prison escapes, sea voyages, storms at sea, and shipwrecks.

In short, Luke shows himself to be a writer of unusual stylistic range, fully capable of producing scenes and speeches according to the ancient rhetorical ideal of *prosōpopoiia,* or writing in character, speaking as if another person. When Paul addresses the synagogue audience in Acts 13, Luke makes him sound just like Peter when he preaches to Jews in Jerusalem, but when in Acts 17 Paul addresses a crowd including Stoic and Epicurean philosophers in Athens, Luke makes him sound like a wandering Greco-Roman philosopher, and when Paul addresses the elders of the city of Ephesus in Acts 20, Luke makes him sound every bit the pastor of the flock. The opening prologue, together with such stylistic versatility, suggests that Luke was, among early Christian writers, the most literarily self-conscious and deliberate, and that in his composition, we see Christianity's deliberate entry into the Greco-Roman world as a form of Judaism.

Genre Analysis

There is every reason to think that Luke's two-volume work, which according to conventions would be called simply *To Theophilus,* constituted the author's version of "the good news." In response to the question, "What is Luke's Gospel?" then, our literary analysis suggests that the correct answer is "the two volumes called Luke-Acts." It is not inappropriate, however, to inquire into the specific genre within which the two volumes together would fit, according to the standards of antiquity. If Luke is literarily self-conscious and deliberate, then how did he craft his work in order to create a specific impression and response among readers? Asking about the genre of a literary work is asking about authorial intentionality and reader expectation. Determining genre does not by any means exhaust the process of interpretation, but it sets interpretation within a realistic framework. To some extent, genre analysis is a process of elimination. Luke-Acts is clearly not epic or lyric poetry, nor is it gnomic wisdom instruction. It is a story. We begin, then, by seeking to place Luke-Acts among types of ancient narrative.

I have already pointed out how the Acts portion of the narrative is replete with standard Hellenistic literary conventions, so that there is some resemblance between Acts and Greco-Roman novels (such as Chariton of Aphrodisias's *Chaereas and Callirhoe*). The comparison fails, however, on several grounds. First, it applies only to the Acts portion and not at all to the Gospel portion of Luke's work. Second, Hellenistic novels invariably have a strong component of romance in the proper sense, that is, a certain degree of eroticism. There is not a trace of the erotic in Luke-Acts. Third, while Greek and Roman novels often have a religious interest (the outstanding example is Apuleius's *Metamorphoses*), such interest tends to be incidental and subordinate to the desire to entertain. Luke-Acts entertains only coincidentally, while its religious interest is central and constant.

Some scholars have suggested that Luke-Acts fits within the genre of Hellenistic biographies, another widely-attested form of ancient narrative. Many *bioi* ("lives") were composed to celebrate great soldiers (Alexander the Great), philosophers (Plato), and religious leaders (Moses). Certainly, Luke's narrative bears some resemblance to such biographies. Luke locates Jesus in a specific family and traces stages of his growth. As I have already noted, Luke places the sayings of Jesus in biographically plausible settings. But does the book of Acts fit within this genre? In fact, the *bioi* of certain philosophers resemble Luke-Acts in the way they depict first the life and teachings of a philosophical founder and then trace the careers of the philosopher's successors, or school. The attention that Acts gives to the apostles as Jesus' representatives could be seen in this light.

The resemblance to philosophical lives grows greater when we appreciate the way in which Luke shades his portrait of Jesus and the apostles. In contrast to Matthew and Mark, Luke's Jesus faces his suffering and death with philosophical equanimity rather than terror; he instructs his disciples at the Last Supper in the manner of the Greek symposium and at the end both forgives his enemies and peacefully entrusts his spirit to God. The first community of believers is described in terms that strongly recall descriptions of philosophical schools, which also "held all things in common." The apostles, in turn, witness to the truth before courts and kings with philosophical *parrhēsia* ("boldness"), declaring with Socrates that they must obey God rather than humans. Paul even delivers the good news to the philosophers at Athens in terms that they would understand.

There are, however, several important ways in which Luke-Acts does not fit the genre of philosophical biography. First, although the followers of Jesus are indeed *mathētai* ("students," "disciples"), it is difficult to think of the proclamation of the risen Jesus by the apostles in Acts as falling into the pattern of a philosophical school's "teaching." Second, to consider Luke-Acts as a *bios* of Jesus and his followers is to narrow the focus of the narrative and leave out two characters that give Luke-Acts its distinctive character. The God of Israel is more off-stage than on, but is a constantly assumed presence in Luke's story and intervenes often and decisively. And Israel itself, as the people of God, is also a central character, whose acceptance or rejection of God's visitation dominates Luke's story from beginning to end. Finally, those elements of characterization that are appropriately designated as "philosophical" can also be termed as "prophetic," for witnessing to the truth in obedience to God is surely as much a prophetic as a philosophical trait.

The manner in which Luke "opens up" the story of Jesus and his followers to include the story of Israel within the still broader story of the cultures of the Mediterranean world — he has Paul declare to the procurator Festus, "this was not done in a corner" — suggests that the genre best fitting Luke-Acts is historiography. The prologue to the composition (Luke 1:1-4) indicates a historian's concerns: Luke uses earlier written sources; he has carried out his own careful research; he is concerned to relate the story in the proper sequence. I have pointed out earlier how Luke's style betrays a concern for consecutiveness; this concern extends across his entire narrative: he has a historian's instinct not only for chronological sequence but also for causality. Alone among the evangelists, moreover, he takes pains to connect the story of Jesus and his followers to the larger story: he notes the political rulers and realities under and within which the good news was born and grew (see 1:5; 2:1-2; 3:1-4; 13:31; 23:1-12; Acts 18:1-2; 19:23-40; 25:1-12). In both volumes, Luke uses summaries and speeches in the manner of Hellenistic historians, namely to expand on the facts at his disposal and provide interpretation of the story he is telling.

Ancient historians wrote not merely to report facts about the past, but to shape a past that provided moral examples or made an argument in behalf of the characters. A number of Greco-Roman and Jewish histories are extant that are rightly considered *apologetic:* they make an argument in behalf of Greek and Roman culture or in behalf of Judaism. Luke-Acts appears as just such a form of historiography. But in defense of what does he write? An answer must cover both volumes, both parts of the story. The traditional answer has been "the Christian movement," and there is a sense in which this is true: Luke tries to show how the Jesus movement is not dangerously misanthropic but rather benignly philanthropic, but this suggestion covers Acts much more explicitly than it does the Gospel. The same objection applies even more forcefully to the opinions that Acts was written as a defense of Paul before his trial (or of Paul against Jewish detractors), or even as a defense of the Roman Empire for Christians tempted to apocalypticism.

The best understanding of Luke-Acts as an apologetic history takes into account both volumes and the stories of both Jesus and his followers, as well as Luke's persistent attention to God and Israel. The best clues as to what kind of apology Luke is writing, in fact, come from his own statement of his intentions in the prologue to the entire composition in Luke 1:1-4.

If we push through the boilerplate language of a historical prologue — that the author has used earlier accounts and his own research — three elements of Luke 1:1-4 are of particular importance for understanding Luke's literary and religious purpose. The first is the phrase "the things that have been fulfilled among us," which itself deserves several comments: (a) the use of the biblical "divine passive" suggests that it is God who has brought things to fulfillment; the narrative from beginning to end is about what God has done; (b) the notion of "fulfillment" points to the way in which events in the story of Jesus and the church "accomplish" or "give the full significance of" the prophetic texts of Scripture in which God spoke promises to his people; (c) the phrase "among us" suggests that Luke perceives the story of God's fidelity to his promises as occurring not simply in the past story of Jesus but also in the story of Jesus' followers, up to the generation of the author and his audience.

The second significant phrase in the prologue is unfortunately camouflaged by virtually all contemporary translations. In 1:4, Luke states that he is writing so that Theophilus "might have *asphaleia* concerning the things in which you were instructed." When an author provides an explicit motive for composition, it is necessary both to pay it close attention and to make sure it is properly understood. In this case, we learn that Luke's reader(s) have already been instructed in the Christian way, through those who were eyewitnesses and became ministers of the word and also through earlier narratives. Like the other evangelists, Luke shapes his version of the good news against the backdrop of versions already held by readers. In this case, Luke regards his shaping of the story as a means of providing *asphaleia* to such readers. Now, here is where most English translations miss the point, by stating "that you may know the *truth* concerning the things in which you were instructed." But Luke does not use the Greek word for truth *(alētheia)*. He is not writing to provide a correct or truthful version in opposition to false versions of the good news. He uses the term *asphaleia,* which has the sense of "assurance" or "confidence" as opposed to doubt or insecurity. Luke seeks to accomplish a volitional rather than a purely epistemic result. But if he is writing in order to provide assurance or confidence, what is there about earlier versions of the good news that could have created a condition of uncertainty or doubt among Luke's readers?

Before taking up that question, we need to look at the third significant phrase in the prologue. Luke distinguishes his account from earlier "narratives" *(diēgēsis)* by declaring that he has written "in sequence" *(kathexēs)*. It is precisely this manner of writing — tracing the sequence of events as they fulfill God's promises to Israel through the story of Jesus and the church — that Luke thinks will provide his readers with confidence rather than doubt. Luke has explicitly and deliberately alerted his readers — his earliest audience as well as all subsequent ones — to the ordering of his narrative as its most important, that is, convincing, feature.

What readers would be in a state of insecurity concerning the things in which they had been instructed, so that an account written in sequence could relieve their doubts? Here, the narrative shape of Luke-Acts as a whole helps us understand the prologue's statement of purpose. There can be little doubt that Luke's readers were among Gentile believers. The most obvious theme of Luke's two-volume work is that God's promises have reached the Gentiles. Luke's Gospel account is distinctive for the hints it provides concerning Gentile inclusion. Jesus is to be a "light to the Gentiles" (Luke 2:32). Luke extends the quotation from Isaiah 40:3-4 at John's preaching to include the words "all flesh shall see God's salvation" (3:6). Luke's version of Jesus' genealogy traces his origins not just to Abraham but to Adam, the father of all humanity (3:38). Jesus speaks of people coming "from east and west and north and south" and sitting at table in the kingdom of God (13:29). The resurrected Lord tells his disciples that repentance will be preached "to all nations" (24:47).

That promise is enacted in Acts when the witness "to the ends of the earth" (Acts 1:8) is shown to involve the proclamation to the Gentiles, first as a small event (10:1-48) and then, guided by the Holy Spirit, a major effort (11:19-26; 14:27). Indeed, Luke marks a "turn to the Gentiles" in three formal statements made to Jews. Paul tells the synagogue in Antioch, "Behold we turn to the Gentiles, for so the Lord has commanded us, saying, 'I have set you to be a light for the Gentiles, that you may bring salvation to the uttermost parts of the earth'" (13:46-47). In 18:6 he declares, "From now on I will go to the Gentiles," and at the very end of the composition he announces, "This salvation of God has been sent to the Gentiles; they will listen" (28:28). The struggle over the inclusion of the Gentiles and the terms of their reception occupies the central portion of the Acts narrative (from chs. 10-15), and leads to the perception that "God has visited the Gentiles, to take out of them a people for his name" (15:14), a divine initiative that brings to fulfillment a prophetic utterance of Amos 9:11-12: "the rest of men may seek the Lord, and all the Gentiles who are called by my name" (Acts 15:17).

It makes good sense to suppose that Luke is writing such good news to those who, in the person of Theophilus, are themselves among the Gentiles who have joined this new version of Judaism. They are among those who have listened and believed. But why should they experience uncertainty? It is because the good news to the Gentiles is shadowed by what appears to be bad news for God's first people, the Jews. According to tradition, the Jews of Jerusalem rejected Jesus as Messiah and persecuted the first followers in Judea (see 1 Thess 2:14-15). Acts itself reflects the reality that the spread of the message to the Gentiles was at least partly due to its rejection among Jews of the Diaspora. We notice that each of Paul's formal declarations of turning to the Gentiles follows a statement that speaks of the rejection of the good news by the Jews (Acts 13:46; 18:6; 28:26-27). At the time of Luke's writing — even if as early as 85 c.e., well after the destruction of the temple in 70 — the hope for a successful Jewish mission seemed to be over; the future of the messianic movement was with the Gentiles.

Such a turn of events was bound to cause a certain amount of uncertainty among Gentile believers, for this reason: the God of Israel made his promises to the people of Israel, the Jews. The promise (of the land, of progeny, of success and security) was for them and their children. If the Jews have missed out on the promise revealed through Jesus the Messiah, and if by the rejection of Jesus they have been replaced by the Gentiles, then the most serious sort of question arises concerning the truthfulness and fidelity of God. It will not do to say that someone else now has the promise. A promise is meaningless if it can be so arbitrarily shifted. The question of God's truthfulness is a question of theodicy. It matters not only to Jews but especially to Gentiles: if they are now the clients of the God of Israel, what confidence can they have in that God, if he has proven capable of such fickleness?

We know for a fact that the combination of Gentile belief and Jewish rejection of the gospel threatened confidence in God's faithfulness already in the time of Paul, who asks whether God's word had failed (Rom 9:6) or whether God has proven unjust (9:14) or rejected his people (11:1). Paul answers these questions with an understanding of history that sees the Jewish rejection of the gospel as a single moment in a dialectic of grace that would lead to "all Israel being saved" (11:26). Luke addresses a remarkably similar theological issue through narrative. The three key phrases of Luke's prologue (Luke 1:1-4) directly address the situation I have tried to reconstruct: he writes (a) of the fulfillment of God's promises among his readers, (b) to reassure his Gentile audience concerning God's faithfulness, (c) choosing the medium of a narrative that traces events "in sequence." In short, Luke's two-volume work can be considered as a species of apologetic history, which makes a defense of God's work in history. It is, in the proper sense of the term, a work of theodicy.

Structural Analysis

I have suggested the importance of sequence in Luke's narrative: he seeks to accomplish his goal of providing security precisely by the way in which he orders the events he recounts. The concern is that of the historian, but it is also the concern of the theologian who wishes to have narrative yield meaning concerning the God who acts in the world. The interpretive principle with respect to Luke-Acts, then, is that *where* something occurs in his narrative is as significant as *what* is reported. Luke also uses two other literary devices to give structure to his story; attention to geography and use of prophecy. The first is generally recognized, though its interpretive import sometimes is not; the second leads us directly into the heart of Luke's literary and theological purposes.

Geography

Everyone perceives that Luke pays particular attention to geography. In the Gospel part of the story, everything tends *toward* Jerusalem. The infancy account reaches its climax when Jesus is presented in the temple and is proclaimed as "a light of revelation to the Gentiles and glory for your people Israel" (Luke 2:32). The story of the boy Jesus in the temple returns him to Jerusalem to be "about my father's affairs" (2:49). Luke reverses the sequence of the final two testings of Jesus as found in Matthew, so that the climactic temptation occurs on the parapet of the temple in Jerusalem (4:9-12; compare Matt 4:1-11). Only in Luke's version of the transfiguration are we told that Jesus was conversing with Elijah and Moses "of his exodus that he was going to accomplish in Jerusalem" (Luke 9:31).

Most of all, Luke makes the journey of Jesus to Jerusalem a major element in his story. The journey has a solemn opening: "When the days for his being taken up were fulfilled, he resolutely determined to journey to Jerusalem" (9:51). Repeatedly over the next ten chapters, he reminds readers that Jesus was "on the way" (9:57; 10:1, 38; 13:22), specifically to Jerusalem (13:31-35; 17:11; 18:31; 19:28). Jesus declares that "it is impossible that a prophet should die outside of Jerusalem" (13:33), and when he arrives at the city, he mourns over it because "you did not recognize the time of your visitation" (19:44).

Like the other evangelists, Luke locates Jesus' final teaching ministry in the city of Jerusalem (20:1-38), as well as his passion, death, and burial (22:1-23:56). Unlike them, however, Luke also locates the resurrection appearances exclusively in the immediate environs of the city (24:13-49) rather than also in Galilee. And at the last of these appearances, he instructs his followers to "stay in the city until you are clothed with power from on high" (24:49). It is from Bethany (on the outskirts of the city; see 19:29) that Jesus ascends into heaven, after which the disciples "returned to Jerusalem with great joy, and they were continually in the temple praising God" (24:52-53). In short, Luke structures the first part of his story so that everything moves toward and stays in the ancient cult center — and symbolic heart — of the Jewish people.

The fact that Luke could exercise even more literary control in his second volume makes the geographical structure he gives this part of his narrative more impressive. His second account of Jesus' ascension occurs on the outskirts of the city on the Mount of Olives (Acts 1:12). Before his departure, Jesus tells his disciples that they will receive power when the Holy Spirit comes upon them and that they will be his witnesses "in Jerusalem, throughout Judea and Samaria, and to the ends of the earth" (1:8). Luke's geographical emphasis could scarcely be clearer. The subsequent narrative of Acts carries out this geographical program, as Luke describes first the community established by the Holy Spirit at Pentecost, up to the scattering of the followers — except the apostles — caused by the execution of Stephen (8:1-3), then shows the spread of the good news through Samaria and Judea (8:4-39; 9:31-43). With the conversion of Paul (9:1-19), Luke prepares for the final geographical expansion "to the ends of the earth," reached symbolically when Paul arrives in Rome (28:14). The basic geographical movement of Acts, then, is outward.

But Luke introduces an important variation in this simple inward-outward geographical pattern. He shows how each outward impulse is followed by a circle back to the city of Jerusalem: the mission to Samaria is confirmed by John and Peter from Jerusalem (8:14); Saul returns to the city after his call, only to be sent out again (9:23-30); the baptism of the household of Cornelius is defended before the leadership in Jerusalem (11:1-18); the church in Jerusalem sends Barnabas to confirm the mission to Gentiles in Antioch (11:19-24); Paul's mission to the Gentiles in debated then confirmed by the apostolic council in Jerusalem (15:1-35); Paul journeys to Jerusalem and confers with James (21:15-26) before he is arrested and ends finally in Rome. Even as he moves the good news to other nations and other peoples, Luke keeps reminding the reader of the city of Jerusalem and its place at the center of his story.

The effect of Luke's geographical structure is in fact to secure the place of Jerusalem at the heart of his narrative. We observe that all of the pivotal events take place there: the first rejection of Jesus as Messiah; his passion and death; his resurrection appearances; his ascension; his outpouring of the Spirit on his followers; the birth of the church; its first expansion; and its suffering of persecution at the hands of Jewish leaders. The full significance of this centering of the story will only become clear in the next chapter, as we consider the way in which Luke makes literary use of prophecy within his narrative.

CHAPTER TWO

The Prophetic Shape of Luke-Acts

The analysis of Luke-Acts as a single literary work has revealed that it is carefully and intentionally crafted. Not only Luke's use of prologues, but as well his sophisticated use of style and narrative structure point to a high degree of literary self-consciousness. The most distinctive element in Luke's fashioning of his story, however, is his use of prophecy. In this chapter, I consider the several dimensions of prophecy as a literary feature within Luke-Acts, by way of preparation for a close consideration of the prophetic character of Luke's message.

The Fulfillment of Torah

A consistent element in the writings of the New Testament — as in fact, in the writings from the Jewish sect at Qumran — is the conviction that things said in Torah reach a "fulfillment," or realization, or actualization, in the events and experiences of believers. Indeed, such a conviction is of fundamental importance in the composition of Christianity's earliest writings, all of which interpret the experience of the death and resurrection of Jesus — as well as the continuing experiences in the community — through the words of Scripture, above all through the specific texts of the Septuagint (LXX), the Greek translation of the Jewish Scripture.

Speaking of the events of the exodus, Paul tells the Corinthians, "These things happened to them as an example, and they have been written down as a warning to us, upon whom the end of the ages has come" (1 Cor 10:11). And in Romans, he states as a matter of principle, "Whatever was written previously was written for our instruction, that by endurance and by the encouragement of the scriptures we might have hope" (Rom 15:4). In the same letter, he speaks of the good news from God as "promised previously through his prophets in the holy scriptures" (Rom 1:2; see also Heb 1:1-2). In this understanding, the words of Scripture themselves have a prophetic character — spoken by God in the past, they lie open to a realization through God's work in the present.

Like the other evangelists, Luke shares this same conviction and uses the "fulfillment of prophecy" in Scripture as a major part of his apology for God's fidelity; as I have pointed out, the opening words of his prologue concern "the things brought to fulfillment among us." The way he employs this apologetic motif differs considerably, however, from that found in the Gospel of Matthew. Matthew characteristically introduces specific citations from Scripture with a set formula, "this happened in order to fulfill . . ." (e.g., Matt 1:22; 2:17; 8:17; 12:17). Such citations function as a kind of authorial commentary within Matthew's narrative in which the evangelist directly addresses the reader, "telling," and not merely "showing." Matthew attaches such explicit biblical citations to every moment in the career of the Messiah, from his birth to his betrayal and death. He thus demonstrates to the reader that Jesus "fulfilled" Torah in every respect.

Luke's way of showing that Torah is fulfilled is distinctive in five ways. First, as I suggested in my stylistic analysis in the first chapter, when Luke's diction and scene-construction echo the language of the Septuagint, the reader cognizant of Scripture inevitably "hears" the event depicted by Luke as one that actualizes in the present God's word in the past. The annunciation of Jesus' birth has such scene-construction and verbal echoes. The scene recalls the annunciation to the mother of Samson in Judges 13:3-7; Gabriel's greeting to Mary echoes the language of Zephaniah 3:14-17.

Second, Luke extends the fulfillment of Scripture beyond the story of Jesus and applies it equally to "the events among us" in the story of the church. The narrative of Acts is studded with specific citations from the Septuagint as well as echoes of its language. Indeed, one of the longer explicit citations in Luke's two-volume work occurs at the end of Acts (28:26-27), when Paul applies to the unbelieving Jews of Rome the passage from Isaiah 6:9-10 that speaks of Israel's refusal to hear the prophetic word — a passage to which Luke only briefly alludes in his Gospel (Luke 8:10). Luke's entire story, extending across both volumes, stands as the fulfillment of God's prophetic word.

Third, Luke considerably refines the manner in which he communicates the fulfillment of prophecy, especially in contrast to Matthew's mechanical alignment of specific texts and events. He does not use a specific formula for introducing citations and, in fact, is capable of more sweeping generalizations concerning the fulfillment of Scripture, as when he has Jesus tell the disciples after the resurrection, "Oh, how foolish you are! How slow of heart to believe all that the prophets spoke! Was it not necessary that the Messiah should suffer these things and enter into his glory?" Luke adds, "Then beginning with Moses and all the prophets, he interpreted to them what referred to him in all the scriptures" (Luke 24:25-27). Similarly, at the Last Supper, Jesus tells his disciples, "For I tell you that this scripture must be fulfilled in me, namely, 'He was counted among the wicked' [Isa 53:12]; and indeed what was written about me is coming to fulfillment" (Luke 22:37).

Fourth, Luke places the explicit citation and interpretation of Scripture almost exclusively within the speeches of his characters. This is the case both with Jesus (see Luke 4:1-19) and with the disciples, who proclaim him after his resurrection (Acts 2:17-21; 4:25-26; 13:33-35). The practice is consistent with the technique of Hellenistic historians, who used speeches to interpret the significance of their narratives. The fact that Luke places the citation and explication of Scripture at the heart of these interpretive discourses speaks eloquently of the importance of the fulfillment of prophecy for his literary and religious project. It also identifies the disciples as persons capable of discerning the deeper meaning of God's words within the events of the present.

Fifth, the speeches in Acts demonstrate both Luke's Hellenistic sensibilities — he uses speeches in the manner of historiographers, and he has his characters interpret the Greek version of Scripture — and his immersion in contemporary Judaism: his manner of interpreting the Septuagint finds parallels in the practice of Palestinian Jews who interpreted the Hebrew Scripture. In Stephen's speech (Acts 7:2-53), we find an example of biblical retellings such as are found also in the book of *Jubilees* or the Qumran *Genesis Apocryphon*. In the prayer of the apostles in Acts 4:23-30, we find the explicit citation of LXX Psalm 2:1-2, followed by a point-by-point interpretation such as is found in the style of *pesher* interpretation used by the Qumran community. And across the speeches of Peter and Paul in Acts 2, 3, and 13, we find a form of haggadic midrash on the Psalms such as that deployed by the early Pharisaic movement.

Literary Prophecy

Luke is particularly distinctive in the way he makes prophecy a literary technique. Here it is not texts from antiquity that find a "fulfillment" in the story of Jesus and the disciples, but statements of characters within the narrative that find a fulfillment within the subsequent story. Luke uses this device so frequently that it suggests not only a literary instinct but as well a distinct religious sensibility. This author thinks, and therefore writes, in terms of prophecy.

Sometimes the prophecy is followed immediately by its fulfillment, often with a certain degree of irony. Thus, the spirit-filled prophetic Messiah Jesus declares before his townspeople in Nazareth that "no prophet is accepted in his own native place" (Luke 4:24), and on hearing of the way his prophetic predecessors had reached outside Israel to heal (4:25-27), his townspeople reject him and seek to kill him (4:28-29). Similarly, the spirit-filled Stephen concludes his long recital of the biblical story by charging the members of the Sanhedrin before whom he speaks, "You always oppose the Holy Spirit; you are just like your ancestors. Which of the prophets did your ancestors not persecute?" (Acts 7:51-52), and although Luke repeats that Stephen was "filled with the Holy Spirit," his listeners are filled with fury and put him to death (7:54-58). A final example: when Paul is preaching in the synagogue at Antioch, he warns his hearers against letting "what was said in the prophets come about," namely that they reject the words of the prophet (Acts 13:40-41; see Hab 1:5); But when Paul announces that because of their rejection God has sent the message to the Gentiles, the Jews of the city stir up a persecution against Paul and Barnabas (13:50).

Luke also has characters in the story make pronouncements that find a realization much later in the narrative. Among the many striking examples are the cases when Jesus says something within the first volume that finds its "fulfillment" in the second. Thus, for example, in Luke 10:10-11 Jesus instructs the seventy-two that he sends ahead of them that if a town rejects them, they should say, "The dust of your town that clings to our feet, even that we shake off against you." And in Acts 13:51, when Paul and Barnabas are rejected by the Jews of Antioch in Pisidia, Luke notes that "they shook the dust from their feet in protest against them and went to Iconium." Jesus forewarns his disciples that they will be persecuted, handed over to the synagogues and prisons, brought before kings and governors because of his name, and that they will give witness "that your adversaries will be powerless to resist or refute" (Luke 21:12-15). In the story of Acts, Luke shows the apostles repeatedly being brought to trial and confounding those who arrest them (Acts 4:5-17; 5:17-42), and the adversaries of Stephen "could not withstand the wisdom and the spirit with which he spoke" (6:10).

Similarly, at the Last Supper, Jesus tells his disciples, "I confer a kingdom *(basileia)* on you, just as my father has conferred one on me, that you may eat and drink at my table in my kingdom, and you will sit on thrones judging the twelve tribes of Israel" (Luke 22:29-30). In Matthew's parallel passage (Matt 19:28), the declaration necessarily has an eschatological reference: Jesus' followers have their reward in the future kingdom. But Luke has a second volume in which to show how Jesus' statements find realization within the story of the disciples, and in the first part of Acts he does in fact show how the apostles "rule over Israel" among the people restored through the spirit and serve at tables in the name of the risen Lord (Acts 4–6).

A final example, among many others: when Jesus speaks of an unforgivable sin that is blaspheming against the Holy Spirit in Mark 3:29 and Matthew 12:31, the precise meaning is obscure. But in Luke's version (Luke 12:10-12), the reference is perfectly clear to anyone who reads both volumes, for Luke has Jesus himself explicate the difference between a word against the Son of Man and blasphemy against the Holy Spirit: "When they take you before synagogues and before rulers and authorities, do not worry about how or what your defense will be or about what you are to say. For the Holy Spirit will teach you at that moment what you should say" (Luke 12:11-12). And when the apostles are brought before the Sanhedrin, Luke makes the fulfillment of Jesus' prophecy explicit: "Then Peter, filled with the Holy Spirit, answered them" (Acts 4:8). The resistance to the work of the Holy Spirit through the apostles is, for Luke, the blasphemy that cannot be forgiven (see Acts 5:29-32).

Even more striking are the instances when characters make declarations at the beginning and end of each part of Luke's two-volume work. These serve as "programmatic prophecies" that govern entire stretches of the narrative, instructing the reader to understand the story's unfolding as the fulfillment of prophecy. The infancy account is understandably rich in such pronouncements, as characters (Gabriel, Zechariah, Mary, Simeon) make statements concerning John and Jesus that the reader finds fulfilled only by reading through the narrative.

Gabriel alerts the reader to see John as one going before the Lord "in the spirit and power of Elijah" to "prepare a people fit for the Lord" (Luke

1:17), and Zechariah prompts the reader to see in John a "prophet of the Most High" going before the Lord "to prepare his ways" (1:76). Gabriel similarly tells the reader that the child born of Mary through the overshadowing of the Holy Spirit will be both son of David to rule over Israel and Son of God whose kingdom will have no end (1:31-35), and it is Mary's song of praise that first alerts the reader to God's prophetic program of overturning the rich and powerful and exalting the lowly (1:46-55). And it is the spirit-filled Simeon who identifies Jesus for the reader as God's salvation, a light of revelation to the Gentiles and also a glory of the people Israel (2:30-32), as well as a "sign of contradiction" who will cause the "fall and rise of many in Israel" (2:34). When the reader of the Gospel story finds all of these statements worked out thematically through the narrative, the story appears inevitably as the "fulfillment of prophecy" spoken by the very characters within the narrative.

The programmatic function is plainly exhibited by the statement of Jesus at the very end of the first volume, when he declares that Scripture shows how "repentance for the forgiveness of sins would be preached in his name to all the nations, beginning from Jerusalem" (Luke 24:46-47), and similarly at the beginning of the second volume, when Jesus tells his followers that they are to be his witnesses "in Jerusalem, throughout Judea and Samaria, and to the ends of the earth" (Acts 1:8). I have already observed how this last statement serves as a geographical guide to the narrative development of Acts; we should note also that it is a prophecy that finds its fulfillment in the subsequent story told by Luke. The last statement in Acts has the same programmatic character, when Paul announces, "This salvation of God has been sent to the Gentiles; they will listen" (Acts 28:28). In this case, the prophecy is not fulfilled within Luke's narrative, but since his narrative has shown that all such prophecies are fulfilled, the reader is instructed to find its fulfillment in the continued success of the message of the good news among Gentiles.

The effects of Luke's use of literary prophecy are several and significant.

1. He suggests that "the things brought to fulfillment among us" refer not merely to the way the words and deeds of Jesus and his followers "fill out" ancient texts, but equally to the way things said by characters in the story — especially the things said by Jesus — find realization in the experience of the church.

2. The constant use of prophecy-fulfillment serves to connect parts of the story, above all the narratives found in the first and second vol-

umes. The technique helps shape the perception that everything in the story of Jesus points ahead to the story of the church and everything in the story of the church continues the story of Jesus.

3. Most obviously, Luke's use of literary prophecy makes the emphatic point that his characters — above all Jesus and the apostles — are prophets, filled with the spirit of God, whose words find fulfillment in God's work in the world.

Prophetic Characterization

The discussion to this point has focused on prophecy-as-prediction: either texts from Torah or statements of characters find a fulfillment within the story. But Luke also uses prophecy as a means of characterization. Here, the emphasis shifts from prophecy-as-prediction to prophecy-as-a-way-of-being-in-the-world (or story). Since this aspect will form the topic that I will argue through the rest of this book, I need to lay the foundation with particular care. There are four initial lines of evidence to review.

1. The Use of the Title "Prophet" (prophētēs)

Luke does not restrict the designation of prophet to Jesus, but his use of it for Jesus is particularly important. He has Jesus speak of the prophets of old (1:70; 3:4; 4:17, 27; 9:8, 19; 10:24; 13:28, 34; 16:16, 29, 31; 18:31; 24:25, 27, 44) and compare his followers to them (6:23; 10:24; 11:47, 49, 50); he also explicitly designates John the Baptist as a prophet (1:76; 7:26-28). In Acts, Luke speaks often of the ancient prophets (2:16; 3:18, 21, 24; 7:42, 48; 8:28, 30, 34; 10:43; 13:15, 20, 27, 40; 15:15; 24:14; 26:22, 27; 28:23, 25) — including David (2:30) — and speaks of the believers as children of the prophets (3:25). He also speaks of specific believers as "prophets" (11:27; 13:1; 15:32; 21:10). Luke's use of the title with reference to Jesus, however, is strategically significant. Thus, the first occurrence is in Jesus' opening sermon in Nazareth, a scene that Luke found as bare bones in his Markan source (see Mark 6: 1-6) but expanded and moved to the beginning of Jesus' ministry, immediately after asserting repeatedly that Jesus is filled with the Holy Spirit. After announcing that Isaiah's words about a spirit-filled anointed one are fulfilled in him (Luke 4:21), Jesus refers to himself the proverb that a prophet is not accepted in his native place (4:24).

In a section of the Gospel account that is redolent of prophetic imagery (7:1-50), Luke has the crowd greet the raising of the widow of Nain's son: "A great prophet has arisen in our midst" and "God has visited his people" (7:16). Luke furthermore twice aligns the question concerning Jesus' messianic identity with speculation that "one of the ancient prophets has arisen" (9:8; 9:19). This connection to the ancient prophets is strengthened when Jesus declares, in a context that points toward his future suffering, "it is impossible that a prophet should die outside of Jerusalem" (13:33). Finally, in the appearance of the risen Jesus to the disciples on the road to Emmaus, his followers identify him as a "man who was a prophet mighty in deed and word before God and all the people" (24:19).

2. The Imitation of Biblical Prophets

I have noted how Luke uses diction drawn from the Septuagint and constructs scenes based on biblical exemplars. A significant number of his stories about Jesus are shaped to echo the biblical accounts concerning Moses and the two prophets whose exploits in Scripture are themselves loosely modeled on Moses, namely Elijah and Elisha. I will develop the Moses connection below. For now, I concentrate on the way Luke uses the figures of Elijah and Elisha to portray Jesus as a prophet. In Jesus' inaugural sermon in Nazareth (Luke 4:16-30), Luke has Jesus use the figures of Elijah and Elisha as prophetic antecedents for his own mission to the outcast: although there were many widows in Israel, Elijah went to the assistance of the widow of Zarephath, and although there were many lepers in Israel, the prophet Elisha healed the foreign soldier Naaman rather than them (Luke 4:25-27; see 1 Kgs 17:8-16; 2 Kgs 5:1-14).

Luke shows Jesus working two wonders in 7:1-15. Everyone recognizes that the second, the raising of the widow's son in 7:11-15, echoes the scriptural account of Elijah's raising of the widow of Zarephath's son in 1 Kings 17:17-24, an echo made explicit by Luke's using the precise phrasing of the LXX in 7:15, "he gave him to his mother." Once this is recognized, it is possible to observe as well that Luke has shaded the story of the healing of the centurion's slave (Luke 7:1-10) so as to more clearly echo the story of the healing of Naaman; we notice in particular the role played by Jewish intermediaries (see 2 Kgs 5:1-14). These wonders cause the crowd to proclaim Jesus as a great prophet and God's visitation (Luke 7:16), and they initiate a discussion of John and Jesus as God's emissaries (7:18-35) and a concluding story concerning the forgiveness of a sinful woman, which revolves around the question whether Jesus is "really a prophet" (7:39).

In Luke's transfiguration account (9:28-36), Elijah appears with Moses and Jesus in his glory, speaking "of his exodus that he was going to accomplish ('fulfill') in Jerusalem." The Greek term *exodus*, or "passage," clearly recalls the leadership of Moses in liberating the people (see also Acts 7:35), but ancient readers also knew traditions associating both Moses and Elijah with ascents to the presence of God. Having established such an explicit connection among these three great prophets, Luke leaves ambiguous further possible allusions to them. The reader might with some justification, for example, think of an allusion to Moses and Elijah when Luke speaks of "two men in dazzling clothes" who appear to the women seeking Jesus in the tomb (Luke 24:1-8; see the "dazzling white" garments at the transfiguration). Even more plausibly, the reader might find an allusion to the two prophets Elijah and Elisha in Luke's second ascension scene, when "two men dressed in white garments" address those gazing into the sky after the departing Jesus (Acts 1:9-11). Some among them might even have remembered the tale relating how Elisha received a double portion of Elijah's prophetic spirit because he saw him ascending (2 Kgs 2:9-12).

The point of using such prophetic imagery is not to suggest that Luke thinks of Jesus as Elijah or Elisha *redivivus* — any more than the many literary connections Luke makes between Jesus and David (see, e.g., Luke 1:27, 32, 69; 2:4, 11; 3:31; 6:3; 18:38-39; 20:41-44; Acts 2:25, 29, 34; 4:25; 7:45; 13:22, 34, 36; 15:16) suggest that Jesus is David *redivivus*. It is John, after all, whose prophetic career is "in the spirit and power of Elijah" (Luke 1:17). It is, rather, to suggest that Jesus embodies — "fulfills," if one desires — the qualities of a very specific sort of prophetic figure. Readers are to understand Jesus not as a court advisor or person of letters, like an Isaiah or Jeremiah, but as a leader of the people who works wonders through the power of the Holy Spirit. For this reason, Luke draws the strongest connection between Jesus, his followers, and the figure who was the first and greatest of the prophets of this type, Moses.

3. Literary Characterization in Acts

The evidence here is particularly significant because of the greater degree of literary control Luke was able to exercise in the Acts account. The evidence points to a way of characterizing Jesus and the apostles as prophets like Moses. The place to start the analysis is Luke's Pentecost account, specifically his quotation from the prophet Joel (Acts 2:17-21; see Joel 3:1-5 LXX[Eng. 2:28-32]), whom he has Peter invoke as a way of interpreting the outpouring of the Holy Spirit and the speaking in many tongues by the followers of Jesus (Acts 2:1-13).

The scriptural text cited by Peter already makes clear that the spirit poured out on "all flesh" — both men and women — is the spirit of prophecy (Joel 3:1 LXX). It will be manifested by dreams and visions, but even more visibly by "wonders in the heavens and on the earth" (Joel 3:3). Luke, however, makes three small but critical alterations in the text of the Septuagint. He changes the original "after these things" to "in the last days" (Acts 2:17), thereby indicating that the outpouring of the Holy Spirit is an eschatological event. He emphasizes the prophetic nature of the spirit by adding an additional "and they shall prophesy" in 2:18. And he adds the words "signs" *(sēmeia)* to "wonders" *(terata)* to form the phrase "wonders in the heavens above and signs on the earth below" (Acts 2:19).

By these alterations Luke accomplishes three things: (a) he connects prophecy explicitly to the work of God through the Holy Spirit; (b) he establishes a means by which prophecy can be identified — it is manifested through signs and wonders; (c) he draws an implied connection between the prophecy exercised by Jesus and the spirit-gifted community and that of Moses. The last two points need some immediate development.

Because the working of "signs and wonders" is the manifestation of prophecy, Luke is able to use a kind of literary shorthand to identify his characters as prophets, even when that term is not used. Thus, in the speech that follows this citation, Peter immediately if indirectly identifies Jesus as a prophet: "Jesus the Nazorean was a man commended to you by God with mighty deeds, wonders, and signs, which God worked through him in your midst, as you yourselves know" (2:22). Then, after recounting Jesus' crucifixion and resurrection, Peter states: "Exalted at the right hand of God, he received the promise of the Holy Spirit from the Father, and poured it forth as you see and hear" (2:33). The one who in his life was a prophet is the source of the prophetic spirit that is now manifested in signs and wonders ("as you see and hear").

Luke subsequently uses this same literary shorthand as a way of characterizing Jesus' followers as prophetic figures throughout the narrative of Acts: they are each full of the Holy Spirit, speak God's word, work signs and wonders among the people, and as witnesses generate a divided response. These attributes are ascribed in turn to Peter and John (Acts 2:29, 32, 41, 43; 4:4, 8, 29, 31, 33; 5:12, 32; 6:2), to Stephen (6:3, 8, 10; 7:55; 22:20), to Philip (6:3; 8:4, 6, 13, 14, 29, 35, 39, 40), to Barnabas and Paul (11:24; 13:4, 5, 32; 14:3-4, 7; 15:12, 35; 16:6, 10, 32), as well as to Paul alone (13:4, 9; 16:6-7; 17:11, 13, 18; 18:11; 19:11; 20:22, 32; 22:15; 26:16; 28:31). From such literary stereotyping, the reader is easily able to connect the spirit-filled ministry of the apostles to that of Jesus and to understand both as essentially prophetic in character, empowered and directed by the Holy Spirit.

The phrase "wonders and signs," however, also draws a literary connection to the first and greatest of Israel's prophets. Virtually every use of the phrase in the LXX refers to the events of the exodus, when Moses led the people from Egypt and through the desert (see, e.g. Exod 4:8, 9, 17, 28, 30; 7:3, 9; 10:1, 2; 11:9-10; Num 14:11-12; Deut 4:34; 6:22; 7:19; 11:3; 26:8; 29:3; Pss LXX 77[Eng. 78]:43; 104[105]:27; 134[135]:9). Of particular importance is the final statement made about Moses in Deuteronomy: "Since then no prophet has arisen in Israel like Moses, whom the Lord knew face to face. He had no equal in all the signs and wonders the LORD sent him to perform in the land of Egypt against Pharaoh and all his servants and all his land, and for the might and terrifying power that Moses exhibited in the sight of all Israel" (Deut 34:10-12). The statement joins "signs and wonders" explicitly to Moses' role as a prophet, notes the public character of his mighty deeds "in the sight of all Israel," and sets an expectation for a prophet who might "arise" like Moses. We note immediately the similarity to the language that Luke has Peter use for Jesus: he was commended by God to them with mighty deeds, wonders, and signs in their midst (Acts 2:22), and he was "raised up" (2:32).

That Luke intends his readers to draw such a connection between Moses and Jesus (and his disciples) is shown clearly by Peter's second speech in Acts (3:12-26). After speaking of the death and resurrection of Jesus and the "times of refreshment" offered by the Messiah, Peter quotes the words of Moses in Deuteronomy 18:15, 18: "A prophet like me will the Lord, your God, raise up for you from among your own kinsmen; to him you shall listen in all that he may say to you," and combines with this a modification of Leviticus 23:29: "everyone who does not listen to that prophet will be cut off from the people" (Acts 3:22-23). Luke wants the reader to understand that Jesus is this prophet whom God "raised up," not in the sense of selection, but in the sense of resurrection and exaltation: the spirit of the risen Jesus working signs and wonders through the apostles is the final and fateful call to the people who rejected him the first time.

4. The Story of Moses

Luke's invitation to regard Jesus as "the prophet like Moses" is unmistakable in his version of the Moses story provided by the speech of Stephen in Acts 7:2-53. As noted earlier, this "biblical retelling" is entirely Luke's handiwork. It is not simply the biblical account; it is, rather, an intentional and careful reshaping of the biblical account to serve a rhetorical purpose. As a Hellenistic historiographer, he places speeches in his characters' mouths in order to provide interpretation of his own narrative. In this case, the speaker Stephen has already been identified as a prophetic figure who has the Holy Spirit and works signs and wonders. It is the way Luke has him structure the story of Moses in 7:17-53 that is of special interest.

Luke signals the resemblance between Moses' story and that of Jesus immediately in Acts 7:17, when he connects Moses to "the fulfillment of the promise that God pledged to Abraham" (see 7:3, 7, as well as Luke 1:55 and 1:73). Moses' infancy likewise resembles that of Jesus through the mention of his being "educated in all the wisdom of the Egyptians, and . . . powerful in his words and deeds" (7:22; see Luke 2:47, 52). More striking, Moses' adult mission is cast in the form of two "visitations" (or interventions) to Israel (7:23; compare Luke 1:68; 7:16; 19:44).

The first visitation was when Moses intervened to kill an Egyptian who was oppressing an Israelite (Acts 7:24). But his fellow Jews rejected him when he tried to intervene further as a mediator of peace between them, and threatened him (7:26-28). Moses was forced to flee into exile (7:29). Luke has Stephen interject a revealing interpretation. Moses considered that they would understand that God was offering deliverance (salvation) through him. But they did not understand (7:25). The failure to understand Moses' mission leads to his rejection, and his rejection leads to his being forced into exile. Moses' exile, however, turns into an encounter with God (7:30-33) and his commission to return to deliver the people: "I have come down to rescue them. Come now, I will send you to Egypt" (7:34).

The second visitation, then, was in power. Luke has Stephen extol Moses' prophetic work among the people in terms that echo the terms used for the rejection of Jesus by the people and his subsequent vindication and empowerment by God (see Acts 2:22-36; 3:13-15):

> This Moses, whom they had rejected with the words, "Who appointed you ruler and judge?" God sent as both ruler and deliverer, through the

angel who appeared to him in the bush. This man led them out, performing wonders and signs in the land of Egypt, at the Red Sea, and in the desert for forty years. (7:35-36)

Then, Stephen connects Moses to Jesus in this most obvious way, by referring to the same prophecy from Deut 18:15 that Peter had used in Acts 3:22:

It was this Moses who said to the Israelites, "God will raise up for you, from among your own kinsfolk, a prophet like me." (7:37)

Even Stephen's statement concerning Moses' giving of the law echoes Peter's statement concerning Jesus' bestowal of the Spirit in Acts 2:33: "he received living utterances to hand on to us" (7:38).

The second visitation of the prophet Moses, alas, also ended in rejection. The people turned from those living words to the worship of an idol (7:39-41). The result of this second rejection, however, was not the exile of the prophet, but the exile of the people themselves: "I shall take you into exile beyond Babylon" (7:42-43). Thus Stephen, himself described as a prophet, accuses his listeners of rejecting all of God's prophets, including Jesus: "Which of the prophets did your ancestors not persecute? They put to death those who foretold the coming of the Righteous One, whose betrayers and murderers you have now become" (7:52). Then they put the prophet Stephen to death by stoning (7:58).

It is impossible to know how much his understanding of Jesus shaped Luke's retelling of Moses' story, and how much his understanding of Moses shaped his portrait of Jesus and his followers. What is certain is that the account of the prophet Moses in Acts 7:17-53 together with the double citation of Deut 18:15 supports the suggestion that Luke himself reads the two stories as mutually informing. We are thus better able to grasp why the risen Jesus begins with "Moses and all the prophets" as he interprets for his disciples "what referred to him in all the scriptures" (Luke 24:27) and why the risen Jesus also says to them, "everything written about me in the law of Moses and in the prophets and psalms must be fulfilled" (24:44). Indeed, on the basis of this analysis, we are led to a better appreciation of the prophetic structure of Luke's entire two-volume work and how it serves to provide "assurance" to his Gentile readers.

Prophetic Narrative Structure

The analysis of Luke's use of geography led to the conclusion that he deliberately centered everything important in the city of Jerusalem. It is the center, the place of pivot, within the two-volume work. Now, understanding how Luke saw Jesus' story in terms of the prophet like Moses, we can see how this geographical centering serves a key function within Luke's apology for God's ways in the world.

The Gospel portion of Luke's work clearly corresponds to the "first visitation" in fulfillment of God's promises to Israel. Thus, already in Luke's infancy account we have an emphasis on the same themes found in Stephen's recital concerning Moses. God has visited the people to bring them redemption (1:68), in fulfillment of the promises to Abraham (1:55), and to bring good news of peace (1:79). In Luke's account of Jesus' ministry, we find first his establishment of Jesus as the prophetic Messiah (chs. 3–7), who gathers a people defined by faith from within Israel (chs. 8-9), and prepares a new leadership over that people through the training of the disciples (ch. 9).

Then, from chapters 9 through 19, he shows the prophet Jesus on his way toward Jerusalem and the inevitable fate of true prophets (6:22-23). Jesus teaches constantly on the road. To the crowds, he issues summons to discipleship, and once they join with the prophet, he teaches them explicitly the demands of discipleship in terms of prayer, the use of possessions and power, and perseverance. But Simeon had prophesied that Jesus would be a sign of contradiction for the fall and rise of many in Israel (2:34), and as the prophet makes his way to his death, as many reject his message as accept it. The poor and lowly are those who receive the prophet, but the leaders and religious elite reject him (7:29-30; 15:1-2). When Jesus arrives at the city, therefore, he pronounces woes over it, for not recognizing the time of its visitation (19:44).

When Jesus enters the city, he cleanses the temple and takes virtual possession of it as a place for his teaching of the people, day after day (20:1, 9; 21:37-38). The people gather to hear him, but the religious leaders challenge him and seek his death (20:1-8, 26, 40; 22:1-6). Luke leads the reader through the events of the first rejection of the prophet: his betrayal, arrest, trial, and crucifixion (22:7–23:49). Throughout this account, Luke works to distinguish the responses of the ordinary people and the leaders. He emphasizes the responsibility of the leadership for the rejection and death of the Messiah (see 22:2, 52, 54, 66; 23:1-5, 35). Yet even on this point, we see the similarity to the Moses story. We saw that in Moses' first visitation, the people "did not understand" that he was to bring them deliverance. Luke mitigates the first rejection of Jesus in the same way. In Acts 3:17, Peter says to the crowd in Jerusalem, "Now I know, brothers, that you acted out of ignorance, just as your leaders did." And among the last words of Jesus are, "Father, forgive them; they know not what they do" (Luke 23:34).

The first rejection of the prophet's visitation is not, for Luke, the end of the story. Because of ignorance, that rejection could be forgiven. And God will offer the people another chance. Luke prepares for that second offer by keeping the ordinary people on the sidelines (except for 23:13) during the process of Jesus' *exodus* in Jerusalem: they appear as passive observers at the crucifixion (23:35), as people gathered for a spectacle (23:48). But when they see what happened, "they returned home, beating their breasts" (23:48). Luke shows a people ready for the repentance when they are offered a second chance.

The "departure" *(exodus)* of Jesus through his ascension (Luke 24:51; Acts 1:9-11) is in fact an exaltation and empowerment: he is "exalted at the right hand of God" (Acts 2:33). The story of Pentecost — interpreted through Peter's speech — is, in turn, the empowerment of Jesus' followers: "having received the promise of the Holy Spirit from the Father, [he] poured it forth" (2:33). The prophetic spirit poured out on the disciples (2:18) is in fact the "raising" of the prophet like Moses and the second visitation of God to the people. Those who bear witness to the resurrection of Jesus (4:33) and work signs and wonders in his name (5:12) represent the offer of a second chance of repentance to Israel (2:38; 3:19).

Luke shows all of this happening in Jerusalem. In Jerusalem also is posed the fundamental plot question: will the pattern of the Mosaic prophet prove inexorable? Will the people as a whole reject God's visitation a second time and, as the Scripture stated, be "cut off from the people"? The question is fundamental to the issue of God's fidelity. He has offered a second chance, but if the chance is not taken, then the promise has not actually been fulfilled. There must be a faithful Israel if the Gentile believers can have any sense of assurance about their commitment to him.

The opposition to the apostles' ministry is the same as to Jesus. The rulers and authorities, the members of the Jewish court, resist the message and persecute those who proclaim it (Acts 4:1-22; 5:17-42). Their rejection of the "prophet whom God raised up" reaches a climax with the stoning of Stephen (6:12-15; 7:54-59). These are the ones Luke wants the reader to see as "cut off from the people" (3:23). Among the ordinary people, however, the apostles' message receives a glad response: thousands hear the word, repent, are baptized, and join the prophetic people the Holy Spirit is forming around the risen Lord Jesus (2:41, 47; 4:4; 5:14; 6:7). Luke deliberately portrays the believers as the restored Israel that is enjoying the "times of refreshment" brought by the Spirit (3:20): they pray, share their possessions, and enjoy favor with the people (2:41-47; 4:32-37). The apostles assume their role of exercising "rule" *(basileia)* over this restored Israel in place of those whose rejection of the prophet has led to their rejection from the people.

Luke therefore shows in the Jerusalem portion of his story that God's fidelity trumps even the infidelity of the people; that the first rejection of Jesus was forgiven because it was based on ignorance; that a second and more powerful offer of salvation was made through the spirit-filled emissaries of the prophet whom God raised up; and that only the rejection of this second offer led to a severing from the people God was forming. Despite the continuing rejection of the good news by Jews in the Diaspora, therefore, Gentile believers understood that God had proven effectively faithful, that there was a realization of the promise to Abraham in the spirit-filled community among the Jewish followers of Christ, and that the Gentile church was not a replacement of Israel but rather an extension of it (see Acts 15:15-18).

Yet the final prophecy uttered by Paul in Acts has a double edge. "This salvation of God has been sent to the Gentiles," he declares; "they will listen" (Acts 28:28). Luke has shown the Gentiles that by "listening" they have found a place within the prophetic people. But now, they must also look to "see how they hear" (Luke 8:18). The Gentile readers of old — and readers in the church today — need to see how they actually listen to and live by Luke's prophetic message. But the entire style and structure of Luke's work, I hope I have shown, has prepared ancient and contemporary readers to think precisely in such terms.

CHAPTER THREE

The Character of the Prophet

I have shown how prophecy plays a key role in Luke's construction of his two-volume work. The story of Jesus and his disciples fulfills the texts of Scripture, and the prophecies spoken by characters within the story are fulfilled by the narrative that follows them. Individual incidents concerning Jesus and his disciples imitate stories about the prophets Elijah and Elisha. And the portrayal of both Jesus and his followers is shaped by Luke to conform to the image of "the prophet like Moses": they are all filled with the Holy Spirit, speak God's word, work signs and wonders before the people, and bear a witness that divides their hearers. Luke has even structured his two-volume work to correspond to Moses' story recited by Stephen: God sends his prophet a first time to visit the people for their salvation; they do not understand and reject the prophet; God then empowers the prophet by "raising him up" and, through his spirit-filled emissaries, visits the people a second time with the offer of repentance and salvation.

As a literary device, then, prophecy enables Luke to connect the two parts of his own narrative and connect these, in turn, to the biblical story, so that the mission to the Gentiles appears not as a replacement for Israel but its extension, and so that the fidelity of God to his promises is demonstrated, thus giving "assurance" to Luke's Gentile readers who have come to faith.

The prophetic dimension of Luke-Acts, however, extends well beyond these surface effects and rhetorical effect. In order to appreciate the way in which "prophecy" provides a remarkably comprehensive understanding of the content of Luke's two-volume work, it is necessary to take a step back and consider the meaning of prophecy within the biblical tradition, for it is clear that Luke appropriates and makes his own the full richness of this scriptural theme. I begin with the importance of prophecy-as-prediction and then move to the more powerful aspect of the theme, prophecy-as-way-of-life.

Prophecy as Prediction

Having things said by God in Torah fulfilled in the story of Jesus and his followers and having things spoken by Jesus and his followers fulfilled in the course of his narrative is, as I have suggested, a powerful literary means by which Luke establishes continuity among Israel, Jesus, and the Christian movement. But it also expresses profound religious convictions concerning God and the world that have roots in both Greco-Roman and Jewish religious traditions.

The first conviction is that the deity communicates with humans through oracles spoken by prophets, words that are often obscure to those first hearing them and requiring interpretation. In Greco-Roman religion, the Sibylline and Delphic oracles were important sources for the decipherment of the gods' will within the history of the peoples who sought their direction. These oracles retained a certain open-ended quality precisely because the form of their expression prevented full and immediate comprehension. Professional interpreters dedicated themselves to the decipherment of such divine oracles. In Israel likewise, the sayings of the prophets — especially those that were written in the prophetic books as difficult and allusive Hebrew poetry — were regarded as "divine oracles" whose meaning was open-ended and required interpretation. A large part of the task of scribes as a professional class, both within the Pharisaic and Essene sects, was the decipherment of the ancient prophets' meaning as it pertained to the present.

The second conviction is that the god who thus discloses truth to humans also controls human history. Among Greco-Roman philosophers, the conviction — denied by the Epicureans but affirmed strenuously by Platonists and Stoics — was called "providence." Prophecy, in this view, was one of the ways in which God's benevolent and righteous direction of history was exercised. At the heart of the Jewish and early Christian investment in the fulfillment of prophecy was the same understanding of human history as directed by God, with an even greater emphasis than in the Greco-Roman world on the saving intention and merciful fidelity of the

God who guided human affairs to the ends that God desired. For Luke, as I have shown, the demonstration of "the things fulfilled among us" proves that the God to whom Gentiles have committed their lives is faithful and reliable.

The sort of argument from the fulfillment of prophecy that we find made for Jesus as Messiah in the other evangelists and in Luke-Acts for the Christian movement as well was employed vigorously in early Christian apology after the New Testament period. For apologists such as Justin, Origen, and Tertullian, historical events appeared to prove the truth of Christian claims precisely because it could be shown how they corresponded to texts written long ago in Scripture or, even more impressively — as in the case of the destruction of the temple and the conversion of the Gentiles — to words spoken by the human Jesus before his death. Scripture itself had established the principle that the authenticity of a prophetic oracle is determined by its being fulfilled (Deut 18:22). Apologetic arguments based on the fulfillment of prophecy have less appeal to present-day Christians. Indeed, more recent historical events point away from the triumphalism based on such arguments: Christianity does not appear obviously or unequivocally as God's favorite. But it is important to remember that for most religious people of antiquity, these arguments possessed considerable force. Prophecy as prediction, then, is a critical aspect of Luke's rhetoric, but prediction does not by any means exhaust the significance of prophecy within his work.

Prophecy as Way of Life

The more important dimension of prophecy in Luke-Acts is also rooted in the biblical tradition, and it is this dimension that the remainder of my argument concerns, for it is this dimension that very much concerns present-day readers and calls them and their communities into question. Prophecy is not merely a matter of words spoken, but a way of being in the world: it brings God's will into human history through the words, yes, but also the deeds and character of the prophet.

The meaning of prophecy here is not "speaking beforehand" as in prediction, but "speaking for," as in representation. This role of the prophet is intimated in the story of Moses. When Moses is sent to Pharaoh, he complains that he is deficient in speech. So God appoints his brother Aaron to be Moses' spokesperson. The Lord tells Moses, "You are to speak to him, then, and put the words in his mouth. I will assist both you and him in speaking and will teach the two of you what you are to do. He shall speak to the people for you: he shall be your spokesman, and you shall be as God to him" (Exod 4:15-16). And later, "See, I have made you as God to Pharaoh, and Aaron your brother shall act as your prophet. You shall tell him all that I command you. In turn, your brother Aaron shall tell Pharaoh to let the Israelites leave his land" (Exod 7:1-2).

The several aspects of the prophetic character form the basis of my continuing analysis of Luke-Acts and of the questions such analysis poses to Christian communities today. These dimensions of the prophetic character are drawn not only from the prophetic writings, but also from the depictions of prophetic figures (like Moses, Elijah, Elisha, and Nathan) in the narratives of the Old Testament.

1. The Prophet Is Led by the Spirit of God

The spirit *(pneuma)* and spirit of God *(pneuma tou theou)* appear throughout the Greek translation of Scripture that Luke and his readers used. Spirit is the symbol for God's presence and power at work through humans and human agency. In the ancient tales of Israel's judges, for example, we find the phrase "the spirit of the Lord was upon him" as the energy that drove Othniel (Judg 3:10), Gideon (6:34), Jephthah (11:29), Samson (13:25; 14:6, 19; 15:14), Saul (1 Sam 10:6, 10; 11:6; 19:23), and David (1 Sam 16:13; 2 Sam 23:2), as they worked their heroic deeds among the people.

The connection with prophecy is made already with Moses, whom we have already seen designated as a prophet in Deuteronomy 18:15 and 34:10. In response to discontent among the people in the wilderness, the Lord instructs Moses to choose seventy elders from among the Israelites: "I will come down and speak with you there. I will also take some of the spirit that is on you and will bestow it on them, that they may share the burden of the people with you" (Num 11:16-17). Then, "as the spirit came to rest on them, they prophesied" (Num 11:25). When a complaint is made about two men who prophesied under the power of the spirit who had not been in the original gathering, Moses declares, "Would that all the people of the LORD were prophets! Would that the LORD might bestow his spirit on them" (Num 11:29). The same biblical book ascribes the prophecies of Balaam to the coming of the spirit upon him (Num 24:2) and refers to Joshua, Moses' successor, as a "man of the spirit" (Num 27:18).

A dramatic account of spirit-possession leading to prophecy is provided by the story of Samuel (the seer/prophet, 1 Sam 9:9) sending Saul to encounter "a band of prophets" whose prophetic condition is accompanied by musical instruments. Samuel tells Saul, "The spirit of the LORD will rush upon you, and you will join them in their prophetic state and will be changed into another man. When you see these signs fulfilled, do whatever you judge feasible, because God is with you" (1 Sam 10:5-7). It happens as Samuel has said, and the spirit draws Saul into a prophetic condition, making people ask, "Is Saul also among the prophets?" (1 Sam 10:9-13). The prophetic spirit continues to operate in the band of prophets over whom Samuel presides (1 Sam 19:20-21) and to fall on Saul (19:23-24). The spirit of the Lord moves Elijah from place to place (1 Kgs 18:12). And when Elijah ascends to heaven, his disciple Elisha receives a double portion of the prophetic spirit (2 Kgs 2:9, 15).

Among the writing prophets, it is in Ezekiel that the spirit is most often associated with the prophet himself, whose visions and actions are directed by the spirit that "comes into him" (Ezek 2:2; 3:24; 11:5) or "lifts him up" (3:12, 14; 8:3; 11:1; 37:1), and in one instance even causes Ezekiel to "prophesy to the spirit" that he sees in his vision of the dry bones (37:9). Otherwise, language about the spirit is more often connected to a prophet's vision for a future anointed figure (see LXX Isa 4:4; 11:2; 42:1) — as in the passage quoted in Luke 4:16-18 and applied to Jesus (Isa 61:1) — or to a future renewal of the people as such (Isa 32:15; 44:3; 59:21). Thus, in Ezekiel's vision of the dry bones, he is told to prophesy so that the spirit gives life to the dead remnants of Israel (37:1-14; see also 11:19; 18:31; 36:26-27); Zechariah 12:10 has a vision of an outpouring of a spirit of grace and petition on the house of David, when "they look on him whom they have pierced," a text echoed by John 19:37; and Joel has a vision of the outpouring of the spirit on all flesh so that they might prophesy (Joel 3:1-5) — the text appropriated by Luke to interpret the event of Pentecost (Acts 2:17-21).

The language concerning the Holy Spirit as the effective cause of prophecy — the spirit is the one who fills or lifts up or comes to the prophet — serves to make several important implicit affirmations. (1) The spirit is the divine force that expresses in physical beings the presence and power of "the living God." (2) The living God moves ahead of humans in history and uses the bodies of prophets to discern and identify how the living God is at work in the world. (3) Prophecy is therefore not derived simply from human cunning or insight, but arises from an elevation of human capacity caused by God. (4) "Inspiration" is shorthand for the many ways in which

God as spirit works through human bodies to make God's presence and power and, above all, God's vision for humans available to them. (5) Inspiration can fail in at least two ways, making prophecy a less-than-obvious enterprise: humans can simply fail in their efforts to serve as instruments for God (see 1 Sam 28:15), and "an evil spirit" can make them lie in the name of God rather than bear true witness (1 Kgs 22:1-28). But even these distortions bear testimony to the conviction that authentic prophecy is empowered by the spirit of God.

2. The Prophet Speaks God's Word to Humans

The prophet is not only empowered by God; the prophet speaks for God. The prophet sees what other humans see, but also sees something more; the prophet hears the words others speak but within them hears a further word. The prophet is a fellow human being who speaks to other human beings in a fully human language that somehow represents God. How can this be? Part of it is the claim of inspiration: God leads the prophet to speak in this manner by first having empowered the prophet to hear a deeper word within the ordinary speech of human life and by empowering the prophet to see in what everyone else sees some further reality that they do not seem to see. But what about the content of the prophet's speech? The human words spoken by the prophet can be called "God's word" because they communicate to other humans God's perspective on the human situations they share, communicating as well God's vision for humanity that the present circumstances impede.

In this sense, Moses is the perfect prototype of the prophet. Moses "knew the LORD face to face" (Deut 34:10); he heard all the words that the Lord wanted the people to hear (Exod 19:7-8) and delivered them to the people (20:1) for them to do (24:3-8). The legislation that Moses announces, the covenant between God and the people that Moses establishes, contains God's vision for a people that is to be set apart among all nations (Deut 29:9-14; 31:9-13). The word that Moses speaks in behalf of God sets out a program of behavior (as in the "ten words" of the Decalogue, Exod 20:2-17; Deut 5:6-21) and a vision of society, a true "politics" that includes norms for social justice and worship. To "hear the prophet" Moses means turning from the worship of other gods (Deut 5:6-10) — and the norms of other nations (Lev 18:24-30) — to the worship of the Lord alone, which includes living by the norms for life that Moses delivered from the Lord.

That the prophet receives the word of God (e.g., Hos 1:1; Joel 1:1; Zeph 1:1; Hag 1:1; Zech 1:1; Jer 1:11; Ezek 1:3) and speaks the word of God to the people is axiomatic in the writings of the prophets (see Amos 3:1; 5:1; 7:16; Hos 4:1; Mic 6:1; Zech 4:6; 7:8; Isa 1:10; 28:14; 38:4; Jer 1:2, 4; 7:2; 10:1; 43:1; 49:7; Ezek 3:4; 6:1; 11:14; 13:1; 37:4). The claim to speak the word of God served not only to command a hearing. But as in the case of Moses, the "word" also had genuine content. The prophets called the people back to the observance of the Mosaic covenant, the worship of the Lord alone, and the keeping of the ritual and social legislation spoken by Moses. Thus, the prophets railed against idolatrous worship (see Hos 8:1-4; Zeph 1:5-6; Mal 2:10; Jer 1:16; 2:11-13; Ezek 20:1-8: Isa 44:6-20), but they also consistently attacked economic oppression (Amos 3:10; 8:4-6) and heedless luxury (Amos 6:1; Mic 2:1-2; Isa 3:16; 5:8; Jer 22:13), stealing (Hos 4:2; 7:1), the perversion of injustice (Hos 10:13; 12:1; Mic 3:9-12; Zeph 3:3-7), and the neglect of the poor in the land (Amos 2:6-8; Hos 12:7-9; Mic 3:1-3; Mal 3:5; Isa 3:5, 14-15; 5:7-10; Jer 5:25-29). The word of the Lord expresses God's vision for humanity: "Keep justice and do righteousness," says Isaiah (56:1), and this is spelled out fully by Zechariah 7:9-10:

> Render true judgments, show kindness and mercy each to his brother, do not oppress the widow, the fatherless, the alien, or the poor; and let none of you devise evil against his brother in your heart.

Similarly, Jeremiah 22:3 declares the Lord's will:

> Do justice and righteousness, and deliver from the hand of the oppressor him who has been robbed. And do no wrong or violence to the alien, the fatherless, and the widow, nor shed innocent blood in this place.

3. The Prophet Embodies God's Word

The word of God is not only spoken by the prophet verbally; it is often also expressed through the symbolism of the body. What could more powerfully express Moses' commitment to God's word than his writing them on two stone tablets (Exod 31:18; 32:15-16) and then, when he saw the golden calf that had been built by Aaron in response to the apostasy of the people, smashing the tablets (32:19) and destroying the idolatrous statue (32:20)?

Moses similarly lifted the staff as symbol of God's power at the crossing of the Red Sea (14:15-21) and raised his arms to sustain the Israelites in battle against Amalek (17:11). At God's command, he erected the bronze serpent in the wilderness as an effective sign of the Lord's power to heal from deadly illness (Num 21:4-9).

Later prophets also expressed the prophetic message through bodily gesture. Samuel tore the robe of Saul and declared, "the LORD has torn the kingdom of Israel from you this day" (1 Sam 15:27-28). Elijah stretched himself three times over the dead son of the widow of Zarephath as he cried out, "O LORD my God, let this child's soul come into him again" (1 Kgs 17:21). Ahijah tore his own garment into twelve pieces, saying to Jeroboam, "Take for yourself ten pieces; for thus says the LORD, the God of Israel, 'Behold, I am about to tear the kingdom from the hand of Solomon, and will give you ten tribes'" (1 Kgs 11:30-31).

Similar words spoken through bodily gesture are found in the writing prophets. Hosea spoke God's word with his body when at the Lord's command he took a harlot to be his wife, "for the land commits great harlotry by forsaking the LORD" (Hos 1:2). Jeremiah buried a soiled waistband by the bank of the Euphrates river; when he dug it up and saw that it was rotted, he declared, "Thus says the LORD: Even so I will spoil the pride of Judah and the great pride of Jerusalem" (Jer 13:1-9). He takes a flask from a potter and breaks it as a sign of the city's fate: "Thus will I smash this people and this city" (Jer 19:10-11). When the city of Jerusalem was under siege by the Chaldeans, Jeremiah ceremoniously bought a field in Anathoth, stating, "Thus says the LORD of hosts, the God of Israel: Houses and fields and vineyards shall again be bought in this land" (Jer 32:6-15).

Ezekiel was particularly extravagant in his use of body language. He symbolized the disaster befalling Jerusalem by lying on his side bound with cords before a model of Jerusalem besieged; ate the food of fasting; cut his hair in batches, striking some with the sword and scattering some to the wind (Ezek 4:1–5:12). He clapped his hands and stamped his foot, as he cried, "Alas, because of all the evil abominations of the house of Israel" (Ezek 6:11). He presented his body to the people as the symbol of God's word: "I am a sign for you" (Ezek 12:11).

Prophetic embodiment can be thought of in another way as well: the spirit-led person's own character conforms to the word of God, meaning the prophet lives out bodily the vision for humanity that God intends. Thus, Moses' entire life can be seen as an embodied faithfulness to God and the people. He saves a fellow Israelite despite being misunderstood

(Exod 2:11-12); he obeys God's summons to go to Pharaoh (3:4–4:9); he leads the people to freedom (12:37–14:31); he accepts the punishment for his one act of disobedience (Num 20:10-12; Deut 32:48-52). Moses' personal character, likewise, was one that embodied the vision of God spelled out in Torah. He was "the meekest of men" (Num 12:3). He ascended to God's presence (Exod 24:18) and spoke to God face to face in the tent (33:1-17); he was God's intimate friend (33:12). He saw the backside of God on the mountain and heard him declare his identity (34:5-9). He showed his utter devotion to the people by his willingness to be written out of God's book for their sake (32:32).

Elijah similarly obeyed God's every command, as when he drank from the stream and was fed by ravens in the time of famine (1 Kgs 17:1-6) and when he journeyed to Mount Horeb seeking God's presence and experienced it in the still small voice (19:1-18). He showed his contempt for royal luxury by his manner of clothing (2 Kgs 1:8). In the call of the prophet Isaiah (Isa 6:1-13), the prophet's wickedness and sin are cleansed by the burning ember put to his lips by the angel, and he is able to serve as God's spokesperson to the people. The prophets Jeremiah and Ezekiel, as I have shown, used their bodies to express God's word symbolically. Each of them also "embodied" that word in their own experience. Jeremiah's call as a youth (Jer 1:4-10) led to the agonies of a life dedicated totally to God (see 15:10-21; 20:7-18), and God explicitly tells him to make his very life a warning to the people: he is not to marry (16:2) or go into a house of mourning (16:5) or enter a place of celebration (16:8). After his initial vision (Ezek 1:1-28), the prophet Ezekiel is given a scroll to eat, to symbolize the Lord's demand that he "obey me when I speak to you; be not rebellious like this house of rebellion, but open your mouth and eat what I shall give you" (2:8). Ezekiel is struck dumb to signify his utter dependence on what the Lord directs him to speak (3:26-27); he must experience personally the famine and the uncleanness that are to come on the people (4:1-15); he must act out the people's exile (12:1-6); even the death of his wife, "the delight of your eyes," must be experienced as a personal sign of the fate of the people (24:15-23).

The most obvious, but therefore easily overlooked, way in which the prophets embody God's word is in their complete devotion to the one who called them. They see what God causes them to see, and they report such visions to their fellow Israelites as the truth. They hear a word undiscernable to others, and they report it as "from the Lord" to their fellows. They act in ways strange even to themselves, perform gestures deeply against the grain of simple humanity, in obedience to God's desire that they serve as a sign to the people. They embody the word of the covenant by putting no false gods before the Lord who calls them to their extraordinary and difficult task. It is this dimension of embodiedness that above all defines prophecy as a "way of being in the world."

4. The Prophet Enacts God's Vision

There is an obvious overlap between the last characteristic (embodiment) and this one. Insofar as the prophet expresses God's vision for humanity in his or her own life, that is already a form of enactment. But the distinctive aspect of this characteristic is the way in which the prophet works for the realization of God's vision in the larger world of human culture and politics. Moses once more provides the model. He works tirelessly to form a people that can distinctively live according to God's vision for all humanity. Through God's commission and power, Moses strikes Egypt with the plagues (Exod 7:14–11:10) and liberates this people from its bondage in Egypt (14:10–15:21). In the wilderness, he provides them with the "living words" by which they can live as God's special people (19:1–23:33). Moses helps the people survive the wilderness experience by mediating the bestowal of food (quail and manna) and water that keep them alive (Exod 16:4–17:7) — gifts that also teach them to depend on the Lord. He appoints elders to help administer the people (Exod 18:13-27). He receives from the Lord detailed instructions for the construction of the sanctuary and the worship that will set this people aside as holy (Exod 24:12–31:18) and then carries out those instructions (Exod 35:1–40:32): "thus Moses finished all the work" (40:33).

The narrative descriptions of Elijah and Elisha show them actively working to shape a people obedient to the Lord. That the narratives want readers to see them as working in the spirit of Moses is shown by having each of them cross through water on dry land (2 Kgs 2:8, 14). By supplying the widow and her son with provisions during a time of famine, Elijah enacts the vision of Torah for the care of the widows and orphans (1 Kgs 17:8-16). His raising the widow of Zarephath's son from the dead demonstrates that he is "a man of God" and that "the word of God comes truly from [his] mouth" (1 Kgs 17:24). He does battle with the priests of Baal and brings down fire on the altar dedicated to the Lord in order to demonstrate "the LORD is God" (18:1-39); then he has the priests opposed to the Lord killed

(18:40). Elijah calls down fire to destroy the messengers of Ahaziah as a demonstration against following gods other than the Lord (2 Kgs 1:1-12).

The portrait of Elisha is meant to mirror that of Elijah, except that, as one with a double portion of the spirit driving his master, his works in behalf of the Lord are even more numerous. Like Elijah, he enacts Torah's program for the care of orphans and widows by supplying the needs of a widow and her child (2 Kgs 4:1-36). But he also "heals" food for the band of the prophets when it had gone bad (4:38-41), and he multiplies twenty loaves of bread into food for a hundred (4:42-44). In answer to Elisha's prayer, the Lord strikes the attacking Arameans blind (2 Kgs 6:13-23). Both Elijah and Elisha are closely associated with the "band" or "guild" of prophets (see 1 Kgs 20:35-42; 2 Kgs 2:15; 6:1-2; 9:1), almost as an alternative kingdom totally dedicated to the rule of God over against human rulers. On the orders of Elisha, indeed, the guild prophets anoint the reformer Jehu as the king of Israel (2 Kgs 9:1-10).

The prophet Isaiah was active in the affairs of state, trying to support the righteous King Hezekiah (2 Kgs 18:1–20:21). When the words he spoke to King Ahaz were neglected, Isaiah turned to the shaping of a band of disciples to preserve his teaching and to support his resistance to a kingdom not obedient to the word of the Lord (Isa 8:1-20). Jeremiah challenges the people of Judah as they worship in the Jerusalem temple, because they put their trust in such ritual rather than in keeping the covenant:

> Only if you thoroughly reform your ways and your deeds; if each of you deals justly with his neighbor; if you no longer oppress the resident alien, the orphan, and the widow; if you no longer shed innocent blood in this place, or follow strange gods to your own harm, will I remain with you in this place. (Jer 7:5-7)

Like the prophetess Huldah (2 Kgs 22:14-17), Jeremiah supports the reforms of King Josiah (see 2 Chr 35:25). But like Isaiah, Jeremiah also writes his prophecies in a book and entrusts them to disciples, when his efforts to influence royal adherence to the covenant are frustrated (Jer 36:1-32).

5. The Prophet Bears Witness in the Face of Opposition

The final characteristic of the prophet in the biblical tradition derives from the fact that God's vision for humanity is not always — or even frequently

— popular with everyone. Indeed, the word of God must often be spoken in the face of oppression and persecution. The authentic prophet, then, is not one who seeks popularity or acceptance, but one who speaks boldly before powers perfectly capable of destroying the prophet, who bears witness to the truth of God's vision for humans even in the face of those who represent visions hostile to God's.

Moses exemplifies such witness when he obeys God's command and confronts Pharaoh with the demand, "Let my people go" (Exod 5:1). After the series of plagues that afflicted Egypt, Pharaoh was still obdurate, and threatened Moses: "Leave my presence, and see that you do not appear before me again! The day you appear before me, you shall die!" (Exod 10:28). Samuel the seer bore such witness before the people when he warned them concerning their desire for a king (1 Sam 12:1-18), and he confronted Saul when the king disobeyed God's command through the prophet, telling him the kingship would go to another (15:1-23). Nathan the prophet promised David an enduring throne (2 Sam 7:1-16), but when the king sinned with Bathsheba, Nathan confronted him with the deed and demanded his repentance (2 Sam 12:1-25).

Elijah the Tishbite challenged Ahab, the king of Israel, when at the urging of Jezebel the king was about to take unlawful possession of Naboth's vineyard (1 Kgs 21:17-29). Even earlier, Ahab ran afoul of the guild prophets for disobeying the Lord's direction concerning the fate of Israel's adversary (1 Kgs 20:13-42). Together with the king of Judah, Ahab was also challenged by the prophet Micaiah, who, unlike the court prophets who predicted only good things, refused to speak anything except what the Lord commanded him and predicted disaster, receiving for his efforts physical abuse and imprisonment (1 Kgs 22:9-28). Although threatened with death for his interference with the royal wish, Elijah denounces King Ahaziah for seeking an oracle from Baal-zebub (2 Kgs 1:1-15). Elisha speaks boldly (if not contemptuously) to the kings of Israel and Judah (2 Kgs 3:9-15). He provides detailed advice to the king of Israel in battles against the king of Aramea (2 Kgs 6:8-10), leading that king to seek to capture the prophet (6:13). The king of Israel, in turn, also sought to kill the prophet for the bad turn events took in his kingdom (6:31-33). The historical recital concerning the infidelity of both Israel and Judah in 2 Kings 17 notes that "although the LORD warned Israel and Judah by every prophet and seer, 'Give up your evil ways and keep my commandments and statutes in accord with the entire law which I enjoined on your fathers and which I sent you by my servants the prophets,' they did not listen" (17:13-14; see also 17:23). The prophet Isaiah spoke words of both comfort and threat to King Hezekiah (19:1–20:19), and the Lord spoke "through his servants the prophets" against the evil deeds of Manasseh, the king of Judah (2 Kgs 21:10-11).

Such witness in the face of raw and hostile power was dangerous and led, as these texts show, to resistance and even suffering. The treatment of Jeremiah under Jehoiakim and Zedekiah was severe: his writings were burned; he was put in a dungeon, and finally into a cistern, where he sank into the mud (Jer 36:1–37:16). The tradition that Isaiah was savagely murdered by Manassah found expression in an apocryphal writing *(The Ascension of Isaiah)*. The conviction that true prophets suffered while false prophets prospered is found in the words of Jesus reported by Luke: those who are excluded and insulted and denounced because of their association with the Son of Man should rejoice, "for their ancestors treated the prophets in the same way," while a woe is addressed to those of whom people speak well, "for their ancestors treated the false prophets in the same way" (Luke 6:23, 26). Similarly, Luke has Jesus condemn the teachers of the law: "You build the memorials of the prophets whom your ancestors killed . . . this generation [will be] charged with the blood of all the prophets shed since the foundation of the world" (Luke 11:47-50).

Conclusion

This review of the characteristics of prophecy in Scripture reveals the repertoire of images and traits available to Luke as he narratively depicted Jesus and his followers. By no means is the significance of prophecy within his work exhausted by the theme of the fulfillment of texts from Torah. It is the way he delineates the ministry of Jesus and his followers in terms of prophecy-as-way-of-being-in-the-world that demands the closest attention. In the chapters that follow, I take each of the elements of the prophetic character and show how Luke develops them in each part of his two-volume work. The demonstration will show that far from deviating from the prophetic character and program of Jesus in the Gospel, the followers of Jesus are shown by Luke to be as fully, and perhaps even more radically, prophetic than Jesus himself. The Jesus movement does not conclude with the death of Jesus, but continues with even greater energy and power in his spirit-filled successors. The challenge that this portrayal presents to the church in our world will be considered with respect to each distinct element of the prophetic character.

CHAPTER FOUR

The Prophetic Spirit

The most obvious indicator that Luke conceives of Jesus and his followers as prophetic figures is the prominent role played by the Holy Spirit throughout his two-volume work. The last chapter showed how the biblical portrait of the prophet provided Luke with a rich set of antecedents for speaking of humans led, driven, and inspired by the Holy Spirit as they represented God's vision to other humans. Before showing how Luke develops this aspect of prophecy, however, it is helpful to begin with some introductory remarks concerning language about spirit and Holy Spirit in the New Testament more generally.

Readers do well not to project on the New Testament's language the later, more highly developed doctrine concerning the Holy Spirit within Trinitarian theology. The doctrine that the Holy Spirit is the "third person" of the triune God in ontological terms legitimately develops out of the New Testament language but is not to be found as such within it. There are certainly elements of "person" in some New Testament passages that make the Holy Spirit the subject of sentences, especially those involving actions such as choosing or willing (John 15:26; 1 Cor 12:11). Such language is found also in Luke-Acts, which contributes not a little to the perception of the Holy Spirit as "personal" (see, e.g., Acts 13:2; 16:6-7).

The dominant characteristic of *pneuma* in the New Testament is its association with power (see Rom 1:4; 8:2-26; 15:19; 1 Cor 2:4; 12:3-13; 2 Cor 3:17-18; Gal 3:5; 5:25), a power that elevates human capacities for knowing and speaking, touches humans in their capacities of thinking and willing, and transforms humans into the image of Christ (2 Cor 3:17-18). Thus, Jesus promises his followers at the end of Luke's Gospel that they will receive

"power from on high" (Luke 24:49; see also Acts 1:8), and that empowerment is depicted in Acts in terms of the outpouring of the Holy Spirit (Acts
2:1-4). The term "holy" *(hagios)* in the term "Holy Spirit" *(pneuma hagion)*
expresses the conviction that such empowerment is not self-generated, but
comes from another. It is holy because this empowerment comes from the
Holy One, God, and is the medium for the communication of the presence
and power of God. Specifically, the Holy Spirit is associated in the New Testament with the resurrection of Christ. The possession of the Holy Spirit is
the premise for the confession that Jesus is Lord (that is, the resurrected, exalted one; see 1 Cor 12:1-3); and the resurrected Lord is universally regarded
as the source of the Holy Spirit that "dwells in" believers (Gal 4:6; Rom 8:11).

The presence of the Holy Spirit among believers is also associated
with the fulfillment of the promise *(epangelia)* made by God to Abraham.
This connection simultaneously asserts continuity between the work of
God in the prior covenant and that established through the death and resurrection of Christ and implies an equal discontinuity. The promises to
Abraham, after all, were entirely connected with the land, with progeny
and prosperity. They were promises precisely for those who were "children
of Abraham" through physical lineage. In Galatians 3:14-29, however, Paul
argues that Gentiles who had received the outpouring of the spirit (Gal 3:1-
5) were also children of Abraham and heirs of the promise (Gal 4:6-7; see
also Heb 6:1-20). This is a dramatic recasting of the very terms of the
promise and enables Paul to envisage both believing Jews and Gentiles to
make up "the Israel of God" (Gal 6:16), which is constituted, not by physical descent, but by the spirit (Rom 9-11; Eph 2:11-22).

Luke has exactly the same understanding of the Spirit's role in fulfilling the promises to Abraham. At the end of the Gospel narrative, Jesus tells
his disciples, "Behold, I am sending the promise of my Father upon you"
(Luke 24:49), and in the beginning of Acts, he has the risen Jesus remind
them to wait for "the promise of the Father about which you have heard
me speak" (Acts 1:4). When Peter subsequently interprets the outpouring
of the spirit on those gathered, he declares of Jesus: "Exalted at the right
hand of God, he received the promise of the Holy Spirit [or: 'promise that
is the Holy Spirit'] and poured it forth, as you both see and hear" (Acts
2:33). And at the end of this Pentecost speech, Peter invites the repentance
of his listeners, "for the promise is made to you and to your children and to
all those far off, whomever the Lord our God will call" (Acts 2:39). That
this is exactly the connection Luke wants his readers to perceive is evident
also from Peter's second speech in Acts:

All the prophets who spoke, from Samuel and those afterwards, also announced these days. You are the children of the prophets and of the covenant that God made with your ancestors when he said to Abraham, "in your offspring all the families of the earth shall be blessed." For to you first, God raised up his servant and sent him to bless you by turning each of you from your evil ways. (Acts 3:24-26)

The fact that thousands of Jews within Jerusalem heard and responded to this call, were baptized into the Jesus movement, and received the Holy Spirit (Acts 2:38-41) was critical, we have seen, for Luke's apologetic argument concerning God's fidelity. The offer of the promise was made, and it was accepted. Later believers from among the Gentiles could have confidence in the God of Israel.

Of all the New Testament writings, however, none so thoroughly develops the understanding of the Holy Spirit as the spirit of prophecy as does Luke-Acts, for this is a theme that runs consistently through the two volumes of Luke's narrative and forms the first element in his characterization of Jesus and the church as prophetic.

Jesus' Childhood: The Prophetic Heritage

Luke's extended infancy account gives his Gospel a more genuinely biographical character. Jesus appears as a real human being with a family (mother, father, uncle, aunt, and cousin) and enmeshed in Jewish culture. At the historical level, Luke provides a convincing portrait of simple folk living in villages — Zechariah belongs to the order of priests, though not at an exalted level — much as ancient Israelites had lived in the days of the Judges, without giving away the fact that the Hellenistic city of Sepphoris was only a few miles away from Jesus' boyhood home. Indeed, the names of the family suggest a deliberate connection to biblical Israel: Joshua, Miriam, Zechariah, Elizabeth.

The shaping of this part of Luke's narrative is, however, entirely prophetic: Jesus' family is a family of prophets, and Luke's Israel is one according to the spirit and not simply according to the flesh. He provides the basic historical facts of the conception and birth of John (1:5-25, 57-66) and Jesus (1:26-38; 2:1-20), as well as the presentation of Jesus (2:22-24) and his youthful teaching in the temple (2:41-52); he states names (1:5, 19, 27, 63; 2:25, 36), dates (1:5; 2:1-2, 21-22), places (1:9, 26, 39, 65; 2:4, 22, 41, 51). The history Luke relates, though, is one directed by the spirit of God and interpreted prophetically through the gift of the Spirit. The specific scenes, as I stated in Chapter One, imitate biblical exemplars (see especially the annunciation to Mary, 1:26-38). And the meaning of the historical facts is provided by prophetic pronouncement and poetry (1:13-20, 28-37, 42, 46-55, 68-79; 2:11-12, 29-32, 34-35).

Most of all, Luke portrays each of the characters in the infancy as directed by God's spirit. Thus, Luke notes that when Jesus' uncle Zechariah's tongue is loosened at the birth of John, "his father, filled with the Holy Spirit, prophesied" (Luke 1:67). In the words of Zechariah's prophecy (the "Benedictus"), he states concerning his son that he will "be called prophet of the Most High, for you will go before the Lord to prepare his ways, to give his people knowledge of salvation through the forgiveness of their sins" (1:76-77). Jesus' aunt Elizabeth is also prophetic: when she hears Mary's greeting, the child John leaps in her womb, and Elizabeth, "filled with the Holy Spirit," recognizes Mary as "the mother of my Lord" (1:41-43).

When the angel Gabriel tells Mary that she will bear a son named Jesus (1:31) and she asks how this can be (1:34), the angel replies, "The Holy Spirit will come upon you, and the power of the Most High will overshadow you" (1:35). Now, the obvious point of reference for this statement is the birth of the child, for Gabriel continues, "Therefore the child to be born will be called holy, the Son of God" (1:35). I believe that it is also legitimate to see in the Holy Spirit's "overshadowing" of Mary her prophetic investment. Two developments support this suggestion: first, in the Acts narrative, Luke deliberately places Mary at the center of those "male and female servants" who receive the Spirit and prophesy at Pentecost (see Acts 1:13-14; 2:1-13) — notice here that she terms herself "servant of the Lord" (Luke 1:38); second, in the presence of her prophetic relative Elizabeth, Mary utters the prophetic canticle that anticipates the ministry of her son (Luke 1:46-55).

Luke clearly establishes John's identity as a prophet from the beginning of his narrative. Gabriel declares that "he will be filled with the Holy Spirit even from his mother's womb" (Luke 1:15) and that he will go before the Lord "in the spirit and power of Elijah . . . to prepare a people fit for the Lord" (1:17). The narrative subsequently notes that the boy John "grew and became strong in the spirit, and he was in the desert until the day of his manifestation to Israel" (1:80). The reader of Luke's Gospel is therefore fully prepared to recognize the John to whom "the word of God came in the desert" as a prophet (3:2). Luke terms the repentance that he proclaims to the people who come to be baptized as "preaching the good news" (3:18).

Like Matthew's Gospel, Luke includes John's statements concerning God's ability to raise up children to Abraham "from these stones" (3:8; see Matt 3:9) and the promise that the mightier one coming after him will baptize "with the Holy Spirit and fire" (Luke 3:16; Matt 3:11). Luke develops this last statement thematically, however, by having the risen Jesus restate the distinction in Acts 1:5: "For John baptized with water, but in a few days you will be baptized with the Holy Spirit," and then having Peter recollect this statement of Jesus when he relates the baptism of Cornelius to the Jerusalem elders: "John baptized with water, but you will be baptized with the Holy Spirit" (Acts 11:16). Luke further amplifies John's prophetic ministry by supplying him with teaching that anticipates Jesus' own (Luke 3:10-14). Given all this narrative development, Jesus' own testimony to John as "a prophet and more than a prophet" (Luke 7:25-26) has even more impact than the parallel statements found in Matt 11:7-15.

Simeon and Anna are not part of Jesus' family, but they fill out the prophetic tone of Luke's opening chapters. Luke gives particular attention to Simeon's possession of the prophetic spirit: he describes him as righteous and devout as he awaited the consolation of Israel, "and the Holy Spirit was upon him" (Luke 2:25). It was the Holy Spirit that revealed to him that he would see the Messiah before he died (2:26). Finally, "he came in the Holy Spirit" to the temple, where he received the child in his arms and uttered the prophetic pronouncements that serve as programmatic for the subsequent narrative (2:29-35). And although Luke does not speak of her receiving the Holy Spirit, Anna is described as a prophet "who spoke about the child to all who were awaiting the redemption of Jerusalem" (2:38).

By his use of the language of the Holy Spirit in the first pages of his two-volume work, Luke communicates to the reader three things: (1) Everything that happens throughout his story traces its origins to the presence and power of God at work among humans — God "visits" the people for their salvation. (2) The Israel out of which the early church is to grow is, from the start, an Israel "according to the spirit," a people defined by their response to God's intervention in their midst. (3) The prophet Jesus grew up in the context of prophecy; he was shaped by a family that was itself led by the spirit and that by speech and act declared "let it be done to me according to your word" (1:38).

The Spirit-Filled Messiah

Luke's treatment of John reveals his literary technique. He uses the material over which he has maximum control early in his narrative to establish themes; once they are unmistakably imprinted into the narrative, he can afford to be less explicit in his characterization. Thus, having established in the infancy account that John was a prophet in the spirit and power of Elijah, he could allow the reader to draw the appropriate inferences from his receiving "the word of God" and "preaching the good news" in the ministry section of the Gospel; the reference to John as a prophet and more than a prophet in 7:26 is simply for good measure. We find the same technique in the case of Jesus: the fact that he is spirit-filled Messiah and prophet is established early and can be assumed by the reader for the rest of the narrative.

We have seen that Luke also associates Jesus with the Holy Spirit already in the infancy account. Mary his mother is told, "The Holy Spirit will come upon you and the power of the Most High will overshadow you" (Luke 1:35). I suggested earlier that the statement could imply the prophetic investment of Mary, but I also acknowledged that the text makes an explicit connection to the divine agency involved in Jesus' conception and his identity as God's son: "Therefore, the child to be born will be called holy, the Son of God" (1:35). Luke's concern to show Jesus as the spirit-filled Messiah is most evident, however, in the way he alters his Markan source in the narrative of Jesus' baptism and its sequel.

Luke's editing of Mark's version of the baptism of Jesus by John accomplishes four things: (1) by using three participial constructions — after the people had been baptized, and Jesus was baptized, and was praying — Luke establishes distance between Jesus and John, so that their prophetic missions are seen as successive rather than simultaneous, and so that Jesus' anointing by the Spirit can be seen as God's agency; (2) by showing that Jesus receives the Spirit while praying, he establishes an important theme about prophetic embodiment that will be examined in the next chapter: the prophet is one who attends to God; (3) by adding the word "bodily" in the description of the Spirit's descent, Luke emphasizes its permanent rather than transient presence to Jesus; (4) the designation of Jesus as "Beloved Son" both echoes the language Luke had used about the overshadowing of the Spirit in 1:35 and points forward immediately to the genealogy. The reader is to understand from this point forward that the power at work in Jesus as God's son is the power of God's spirit.

In contrast to Matthew's Gospel, which begins with a genealogy that traces Jesus back to Abraham (Matt 1:1-17), Luke supplies quite a different version immediately after the baptism that has asserted the spirit-filled Jesus as God's son (Luke 3:23-38). Luke's genealogy runs in the opposite direction from Matthew's — not from the past to the present, but from the present to the past. It does not connect Jesus only to the start of the Jewish people, but to the start of humanity — it ends with the figure of Adam. And it finds its climax in the assertion that Jesus is God's son, even though he was "thought to be" the son of Joseph (3:23). That his status as God's son is, for Luke, a matter of spirit-possession is confirmed by his editing of the temptation account that he shares with Matt 4:1-11. Matthew had already changed Mark's harsh characterization of Jesus as "driven" into the wilderness by the spirit (Mark 1:12) to state that he "was led by the Spirit" (Matt 4:1). Luke begins his account, however, by stating that Jesus was "filled with the Holy Spirit" as well as being "led by the Spirit" (Luke 4:1). More significantly, Luke reports that Jesus returned from the wilderness "in the power of the Spirit," as he began his ministry of preaching in the synagogues of Galilee (4:14).

This narrative sequence is important for grasping the significance of Luke's construction of the next scene "in order," namely Jesus' inaugural sermon in his hometown of Nazareth. Luke found the makings of this story in Mark 6:1-6, where it appears as a simple rejection of the hometown boy because his origins are too well known. But Luke also found in that account the words of Jesus concerning the rejection of a prophet in his own country (Mark 6:4), and this combination of elements enabled him to make strategic use of the story. The distinctiveness of Luke's treatment is all the more clear because the parallel in Matthew 13:54-58 maintains the same place in the narrative and offers only slight emendation. In contrast, Luke shifts the story to the very beginning of Jesus' ministry: this is his first public appearance (Luke 4:16-30). He also considerably expands the story, creating an account that unmistakably identifies Jesus as the prophetic Messiah.

Readers now hearing of Jesus standing in the synagogue to read from the scroll of the prophet Isaiah have just heard that the Spirit came bodily on Jesus, that he was full of the Spirit, that he was led into the desert by the Spirit, and that he was in the power of the Spirit. The narrative prepares for the words of Isaiah 61:1-2, "The spirit of the Lord is upon me, because he as anointed me, to bring good news to the poor . . ." (Luke 4:18). The full content of this citation I will consider when analyzing the prophetic agenda in Chapter Six. For now, I note only the way in which Luke understands Messiah/Christ literally in terms of being "anointed" by the Spirit of the Lord. It is this citation that Luke has Jesus apply directly to himself: "today this scripture passage is fulfilled in your hearing" (4:21). Luke sharpens this characterization by having Jesus compare himself to the earlier spirit-led prophets, Elijah and Elisha, which in turn is set up the statement that Luke took from Mark, that no prophet is accepted in his own native place (4:23-27). These statements, finally, lead to the rejection of the prophet Jesus by the people of Nazareth, who, hearing of God's visitation of people outside Israel, seek to kill Jesus (4:28-30).

The Nazareth pericope is a classic instance of Luke's using stories as "programmatic prophecy": it shows how Jesus is a sign of contradiction for the fall and rise of many in Israel (as Simeon had prophesied in 2:34), and it enables readers to perceive everything subsequently done by Jesus as the works of a spirit-filled prophet. Thus, immediately before Jesus pronounces the blessings on the poor (in fulfillment of 4:18) in 6:20, we read that "everyone in the crowd sought to touch him because power came forth from him and healed them all" (6:19). When, after working healings that recall Elisha and Elijah in Luke 7:1-15, readers understand why the crowd declares, "A great prophet has arisen in our midst, and God has visited his people" (7:16). Readers grasp as well the point of Jesus responding to John's query whether he was the one to come, that John should look at the deeds Jesus is doing, above all preaching good news to the poor (7:22), and when Jesus declares John to be a prophet and more than a prophet (7:26), readers perceive that the declaration is made in the context in which Jesus' own prophetic identity is confirmed (7:36-50).

Luke finds no need to reinforce the point that Jesus is directed by the Spirit; indeed, for the remainder of the Gospel narrative, there is only one more clear reference to the Holy Spirit with reference to Jesus himself. In 10:21, Luke has Jesus rejoice at the return of the seventy-two he had sent out to preach: "At that very moment he rejoiced in the Holy Spirit." The parallel in Matt 11:25 lacks the mention of the Holy Spirit in this place. We are reminded of the way Luke combined the Holy Spirit and prayer also in Jesus' baptism (Luke 3:21-22). Luke omits mention of the Spirit in another passage where Matthew has it. In conflict with Pharisees over the casting out of demons, Jesus says in Matt 12:28, "If it is by the Spirit of God that I drive out demons, then the kingdom of God has come upon you." In contrast, Luke has Jesus say, "If it is by the finger of God that I drive out demons, then the kingdom of God has come upon you" (Luke 11:20). The phrase "finger of God" is a deliberate allusion to Moses' confrontation with Pharaoh in Exodus 8:19.

Preparing the Disciples

Distinctive to Luke's two-volume work is the way the teaching of the disciples has implications for the narrative development of Acts. Thus, Luke shares with Matthew 10:1-15 a sending out of the Twelve (9:1-6) but adds another sending of seventy-two in 10:1-12. I will analyze the content of these commissions at a later point. For now, it is necessary only to note that such passages form, for Luke, part of Jesus' deliberate process of preparation of his followers for the prophetic work that they will do, and that will be described, in the second volume. It is no surprise, then, to find the Gospel's remaining passages mentioning the Holy Spirit applied to the later experience of the disciples.

Thus, shortly after praising God "in the Holy Spirit" for God's revelation to the childlike (10:21-22), Jesus teaches his disciples concerning prayer (11:1-13), in the process assuring his followers concerning the efficacy of prayer to the Father: "If you, then, who are wicked, know how to give good gifts to your children, how much more will the Father in heaven give the Holy Spirit to those who ask him!" (11:13). Luke's language is the more striking here because in Matthew's parallel passage Jesus speaks of the Father giving "good things" rather than "the Holy Spirit" (Matt 7:11). Equally striking is Luke's shaping of another passage that he shares with Matthew. In the context of the dispute with the Pharisees concerning casting out demons by Beelzebul, Matthew has Jesus declare, "Every sin and blasphemy will be forgiven people, but blasphemy against the Spirit will not be forgiven; and whoever speaks a word against the Son of Man will be forgiven; but whoever speaks against the Holy Spirit will not be forgiven, either in this age or in the age to come" (Matt 12:31-32).

Luke tellingly shifts the saying to a discussion concerning perseverance during persecution (Luke 12:2-8) and adds reference to that future condition of disciples within Jesus' saying:

> Whoever speaks a word against the Son of Man will be forgiven, but the one who blasphemes against the Holy Spirit will not be forgiven. When they take you before synagogues and authorities, do not worry how or what your defense will be or about what you are to say. For the

Holy Spirit will teach you at that moment what you should say. (Luke 12:10-12)

Luke distinguishes between speaking against the Son of Man (Jesus) in the Gospel narrative (the time of the first visitation) and blasphemy against the Holy Spirit in the Acts narrative (the time of the second visitation). He similarly prepares for the experience of the disciples in another passage — this time not using the explicit language of the Holy Spirit but of wisdom. Speaking of their being dragged before synagogues, kings, and governors, he tells them:

> Remember you are not to prepare your defense beforehand, for I myself shall give you a wisdom in speaking that all your adversaries will be powerless to resist or refute. (Luke 21:13-15)

Finally, the risen Jesus tells his disciples, "Behold I am sending the promise of my Father upon you; but stay in the city until you are clothed with power from on high" (24:49). All of these passages point forward to the role the Holy Spirit will play in Acts.

The Prophetic Spirit in Acts

Luke's account of the bestowal of the Holy Spirit on the followers of Jesus at the Jewish feast of Pentecost (the "birth of the church") combines all three aspects of the Holy Spirit in the New Testament. First, it is an *empowerment:* Jesus told them twice before the ascension that they would receive "power from on high" (Luke 24:49; Acts 1:8), which is demonstrated by the spectacular "signs and wonders" of the disciples speaking of the "mighty acts of God," heard in all the languages of those listening (2:4-11).

Second, Pentecost is Luke's climactic *resurrection* story. Luke does his theology through narrative, and the sequence of his stories after Jesus' death can be seen as an interpretation of Jesus' resurrection in terms of a dialectic of absence and presence. His empty tomb account (Luke 24:1-12) makes clear that "the living one" is not among the dead. The stories of Jesus' appearances to followers (24:13-49) show that the resurrected one is to be found among his followers — although in a way that is not entirely obvious. The double account of the ascension (Luke 24:51; Acts 1:9-11) removes Jesus from an empirical presence among his disciples — he is exalted to the full presence and power of God. The outpouring of the Spirit (Acts 2:1-4), finally, reveals the new mode of Jesus' presence among them. We note that the event of Pentecost is interpreted by Peter in terms of Jesus' resurrection: "God raised this Jesus, of this we are all witnesses. Exalted at the right hand of God, he received the promise of the Holy Spirit from the Father and poured it forth, as you both see and hear" (Acts 2:32-33).

Third, the gift of the Spirit is the fulfillment of God's *promise* to Abraham and establishes the restored Israel. This is indicated by the language of "promise" in connection with the gift of the Spirit (Luke 24:49; Acts 1:4; 2:33, 39); by Luke's distinctive account of the election of Matthias (Acts 1:15-26), which restores the circle of the Twelve and symbolically expresses that Israel receives this gift; and by the depiction of the first community of believers in terms that evoke an Israel according to the spirit (Acts 2:41-47; 4:32-37).

Of most interest to our investigation, however, is the distinctive Lukan interpretation of the outpouring of the spirit as *prophetic*. The evidence for this has been offered earlier and can be summarized quickly here. (1) Luke's shaping of the ascension account — the two men (representing Elisha and Elijah?), the message about the disciples "seeing him" as he goes into heaven — recalls for the biblically literate reader the story of Elisha's reception of a "double portion" of the prophetic spirit because he can see Elijah as that prophet ascends into heaven in a whirlwind with flaming horses. (2) In Acts 2:14-21, Luke has Peter use the citation from Joel 3:1-5 to interpret the outpouring of the spirit, maintaining Joel's identification of the spirit as prophetic, and emphasizing it by adding the words "and they shall prophesy" (2:18). (3) By modifying Joel's language to form the phrase "wonders and signs" as the indicator of the prophetic spirit, Luke draws the gift of the spirit close to the depiction of the prophet Moses who worked "signs and wonders" in Israel. (4) Immediately after this citation, Luke has Peter describe the ministry of Jesus in prophetic terms: "Jesus the Nazorean was a man commended to you by God with mighty deeds, wonders, and signs, which God worked through him in your midst, as you know" (Acts 2:22). (5) In his second speech, Peter draws an explicit connection between the resurrection of Jesus and "the prophet like Moses"; the refusal to obey leads to rejection from the people — a connection made even more explicitly by Stephen's speech (Acts 7:35-37).

In literary terms, Peter's speech at Pentecost functions for the Acts narrative much the way in which Jesus' inaugural speech at Nazareth functions in the Gospel narrative. The Gospel made clear that Jesus was full of the spirit, his citation of the Isaiah passage provided an interpretation, and Jesus' subsequent words made clear the prophetic character of his messianic identity (Luke 4:14-30). Here, the outpouring of the spirit on the disciples is equally emphatic, the citation from Joel interprets the spirit as the spirit of prophecy, and Peter's subsequent words draw an explicit connection between this prophetic spirit, the prophet Jesus, and the prophet Moses. The Nazareth story serves as a programmatic prophecy for the entire Gospel narrative that follows: the reader recognizes Jesus as the spirit-filled prophet without Luke needing to make this explicit. The Pentecost story similarly serves as a programmatic prophecy for the subsequent narrative. In Acts, however, Luke has considerably more literary freedom, and he chooses not to make the prophetic character of the spirit at work in the disciples entirely implicit.

In the narrative following Pentecost, Luke emphasizes the role of the Spirit in three ways. First, as I showed in an earlier analysis, Luke characterizes his main characters in a stereotypical fashion to identify them as prophetic men of the Spirit: Peter and John (4:8; 5:12, 32), Stephen (6:5, 8; 7:55), Philip (6:5; 8:6), Paul and Barnabas (11:24; 13:9; 14:1-7), are all filled with the Holy Spirit, bear witness by speaking God's word and proclaiming good news, work signs and wonders, and stimulate responses of acceptance and rejection among the people.

Second, Luke constructs a scene following the first persecution of the apostles in which they interpret Psalm 2:1-2 in a fashion that connects their suffering to that of Jesus — as spoken by "the Holy Spirit through the mouth of our father David" — and pray that they might "speak your word with all boldness, as you stretch forth your hand to heal, and signs and wonders are done through the name of your holy servant Jesus," a prayer that is answered immediately by the shaking of the building in which they were, "and they were all filled with the Holy Spirit and continued to speak the word of God with boldness" (Acts 4:23-31). Of particular importance here is not only the connection between the Spirit at work in Jesus and in them, but above all the continuing character of the Spirit's work through them.

Third, Luke shows throughout the rest of Acts how the Holy Spirit is an active force in the Christian mission. When the apostles in Jerusalem hear that Samaria accepted the word of God, they went to pray for them that they might receive the Holy Spirit (8:15), and when they laid hands on them, the Samaritans received the Holy Spirit (8:17). After Philip preaches Jesus to the Ethiopian eunuch from the prophet Isaiah and the proselyte is baptized, "the Spirit of the Lord snatched Philip away and the eunuch saw him no more" (8:39). When Peter preached the good news of Jesus to the household of the Gentile Cornelius, "the Holy Spirit fell on those who were listening" (10:44), astonishing the Jewish believers "that the gift of the Holy Spirit should have been poured on the Gentiles also" (10:45) and leading Peter to ask why the Gentiles should not be baptized, since they "have received the Holy Spirit even as we have" (10:47). When Peter reports these events to the Jerusalem elders, he says, "The Holy Spirit fell on them as it had upon us in the beginning, and I remembered the word of the Lord, how he had said, 'John baptized with water, but you will be baptized with the Holy Spirit'" (11:15-16).

In the church at Antioch where prophets and teachers were gathered in prayer and worship, the Holy Spirit directs them to send Barnabas and Paul on mission (13:1-4). When the number of Gentile converts presses the issue of the terms of their acceptance into the people — should they be circumcised and be required to observe Torah or not? — the testimony of the Holy Spirit's work is invoked as evidence for the equality of Jews and Gentiles: "God, who knows the heart, bore witness by granting them the Holy Spirit just as he did us. He made no distinction between us and them, for by faith he purified their hearts" (15:8-9). The decision to accept Gentiles without requiring circumcision and law-observance is stated as "the decision of the Holy Spirit and of us" (15:28).

The Holy Spirit prevents Paul and Silas from preaching in Asia (16:6), and the "Spirit of Jesus" similarly closes off a mission to Bithynia (16:7). Paul's preaching to disciples of John in Ephesus leads to an outpouring of the Holy Spirit like that at Pentecost, again leading them to speak in tongues and prophesy (19:2-7). Paul is compelled by the Spirit to go on his last fateful trip to Jerusalem (20:22), and in each city the Holy Spirit warns him of his impending imprisonment and hardships (20:23). Paul declares that it is the Holy Spirit that has placed overseers to tend the church of God (20:28). The disciples in Tyre implore Paul "in the Spirit" not to go to Jerusalem (21:4), and in Ptolemais the prophet Agabus declares, "Thus says the Holy Spirit," when predicting Paul's suffering (21:11). Finally, Paul declares to the unbelieving Jews in Rome that "well did the Holy Spirit speak to your ancestors through the prophet Isaiah," when he applies to them the texts of Isaiah 6:9-10 (28:25). From the beginning of the Acts narrative to the end, Luke makes clear that Jesus' prophetic successors are directed and empowered by the same Holy Spirit that was at work in the prophet Jesus.

Challenge to the Contemporary Church

An important part of my argument is not simply that Luke-Acts is liter-arily "prophetic," but that as part of canonical Scripture, it also speaks pro-phetically to the church in every age. I have even suggested that, writing around the year 85 C.E., Luke's portrayal of Jesus and the first believers was meant to be prophetic for its first readers, offering, not a romantic vision of Christian beginnings, but a utopian vision of Christian possibilities. It is possible to imagine that Luke's sense of the church as essentially prophetic may have been heard as at least slightly disruptive by communities already finding an institutional "place in the world" through households.

The way that Luke deploys language about the Holy Spirit through-out Luke-Acts certainly provides a number of points for serious self-examination by Christian communities today. As I stated in the Introduc-tion, Luke-Acts is not the only canonical witness to which the church must listen, and it is simplistic to suggest that this composition is normative for the church's life in a way that other New Testament compositions are not. But if readers are to take the New Testament writings seriously in their thinking, then they must take each of them straight, avoiding above all an easy harmonization that serves to suppress witnesses that pose a challenge.

The Living God

Luke's language about the Holy Spirit demands a perception of reality as fundamentally shaped by the power of God at every moment. "Holy Spirit" is another way of speaking about "the Living God" — not the ab-stract conclusion of a logical argument but the living premise of all exis-tence and all activity. To speak of God as Spirit in the way Luke does is to say that God's creative activity continues in the world and that, conse-quently, God continues to disclose Godself in the world. God as Holy Spirit moves ahead of human action and calculation and is capable of do-ing new things that are beyond human capacity or understanding. The Holy Spirit brings a son of God to birth from a young virgin and raises from the dead the crucified Messiah; the Holy Spirit raises up children to Abraham from the stones of Gentile populations. Within Luke's narrative, these new, unexpected, and in human terms "impossible" things are ac-complished by God's Holy Spirit.

Such a portrayal does not in the least suggest that the "signs and wonders" accomplished by the Holy Spirit were for one time only, as though the living God became a *Deus Otiosus,* a god "idle" or "retired" once the administrative machinery of the church was in place. There is no suggestion in Luke-Acts of such a supplanting, for there is no hint of ecclesial machinery; indeed, the logic of Luke's narrative is that the work of the Holy Spirit continues in the church: it is the Holy Spirit, Paul tells the elders in Ephesus, who has appointed overseers in communities (Acts 20:28). Rather, Luke's narrative leads us to conceive of the Spirit's work as continuing in the world today, continuing to empower humans with capacities beyond their comprehension, continuing to press upon humans with the presence of the risen Christ, continuing to fulfill God's promise of old to bless all nations.

Some charismatic or pentecostal expressions of Christianity have kept aspects of such perceptions alive and, to the degree they have, provide rich resources for other Christians, who have allowed the Holy Spirit to become a creedal afterthought and come dangerously close in their ecclesial life to acting as though God were not life-giving spirit active in all that acts, but one doctrine among others in a religious ideology. Inasmuch as charismatic Christians truly perceive the world as spirit-saturated and themselves as spirit-defined, they are faithful to the witness of Luke-Acts. Many Christians within these traditions, however, know that even for them, the gifts of the spirit tend to be restricted to the cultic expressions of tongues and prophecy and serve to support private piety. But at least these Christians keep alive for others the possibility of seeing "enthusiasm" as something other than something eccentric or even dangerous.

It is not immediately clear how conceiving of the church first of all as spirit-defined would affect the practical matters of life in the assembly. Further analysis of prophetic embodiment, enactment, and witness will suggest some possibilities. But none of these are likely without first there being the perception of Holy Spirit as symbol for the living God. At the most basic level, this perception leads the church — and every individual within the assembly — to grasp that the church is not answerable to itself or to its traditions, but to the presence and power that presses upon it at every moment. To deny this is to refuse to acknowledge the witness of Luke-Acts, first of all, but it is also to play a dangerous game. The story of Ananias and Sapphira (Acts 5:1-11) shows disastrous results from "falsifying" the Holy Spirit and "testing the Holy Spirit" (5:3, 9) by pretending to live according to the spirit of sharing while holding back individual interests. Even more impressive, Peter and John tell their own religious leaders (the Sanhedrin) who — on the advice of Gamaliel — want to play a political waiting game concerning the prophetic message of the apostles that not only the apostles are witnesses of these things, but also "the Holy Spirit that God has given to those who obey him" (5:32). The subsequent rejection of this message by the Sanhedrin in the stoning of Stephen is identified by that prophet in these terms: "You stiff-necked people, uncircumcised in heart and ears, you always oppose the Holy Spirit, just like your ancestors" (7:51). If paying attention to the Holy Spirit's work in the world is risk-filled, the failure to recognize the work of God in the world is more dangerous by far.

The Voice of Prophets

The witness of Luke-Acts is that God's preferred mode of communication with the world is through prophets, human beings who speak and act for God to other humans. The chain of prophets in Luke-Acts is impressive: Moses, Samuel, David, Elijah, Elisha, Isaiah, Zechariah, Elizabeth, Mary, John, Simeon, Anna, John, Jesus, and those followers of Jesus through whom the spirit of the resurrected one did signs and wonders. For Luke, it is the living God (the "Holy Spirit") who "spoke" through all of them, not only in words but also in their deeds. Grasping the central role of prophecy in Luke-Acts is essential for avoiding two common misconceptions of this writing.

It is sometimes thought that Luke has an insufficiently elevated Christology when compared to John, Paul, or Hebrews. But this is to a great extent due to the prophetic model. It is not that Jesus is "raised up" in exactly the way Moses was: Jesus is "raised up" as exalted Lord through resurrection and is the source of the prophetic spirit for others. Moses was a lovely child; Jesus is born "Son of God." Luke's point, however, is that God works through human agents, discloses his will through human spokespersons, finds expression for God's spirit through human bodies. The spirit of Jesus at work in the apostles is distinctive, but it is no more the spirit of the living God than that at work in the prophets of old.

Similarly, Luke's choice of "wonders and signs" as the evidence for the presence of the Holy Spirit — drawn, as we have seen, from the biblical traditions associated with Moses — is sometimes taken as a form of "theology of glory," pointing to the triumph of Christianity over other religions and an emphasis on success rather than suffering. But it is inaccurate to suggest that Luke lacks a sense of prophetic suffering. In fact, the rejection of the prophet is an essential part of the prophetic model he uses: Luke insists that "it is necessary" for the Messiah to suffer (Luke 24:26), and "it is necessary" to undergo hardships for the kingdom of God (Acts 14:22). The function of signs and wonders — the nature of which, by the way, still needs to be examined — is simply to point to the presence and power of God at work through the prophet. The effect is not to elevate the ministers but to give honor to God, since the same spirit is at work in them all.

The critical challenge to the church in the contemporary world has to do with the willingness to recognize the prophets that God raises up in our own age. If the spirit of God continues to work in every time, and if the spirit's chosen instrument is the human body, then prophets are in fact in the world as God's agents now. But because prophets are human like us, they always present the scandal of particularity. They are too much like us to be emissaries from God. Thus, Stephen reports Moses' fellow Israelite as saying, "Who appointed you ruler and judge over us?" (Acts 7:27), and Jesus' townsfolk in Nazareth say of him, "Isn't this the son of Joseph?"(Luke 4:22). The very humanity of the prophet makes even those supposedly open to God's spirit think twice about acknowledging that spirit working through a neighbor.

The challenge is even more acute because of the Holy Spirit's freedom and creativity in raising up prophets outside of expected circles. We might expect priests like Zechariah to prophesy, but we are surprised to hear a young woman of lowly status speak prophetically (Luke 1:46-79). We might recognize a John as a prophet in the spirit and power of Elijah, especially because of his ascetical life; but would we recognize as a prophet Jesus, the one who "comes eating and drinking," who can be called a "glutton and a drunkard, a friend of tax-collectors and sinners" (Luke 7:24-34)? We might acknowledge a Peter, chosen by Jesus, as a prophet, but would we also acknowledge a Paul as prophet, a man who sought to destroy the church (Acts 8:1-3; 9:23-30)? The hearing of prophets is as risky an undertaking as is listening for the Spirit.

The Character of Theology

If God's Holy Spirit — and the spirit of the risen and exalted Lord Jesus — continue to be active in the world, then theology within the church can never be fully "systematic" in the sense that all the data is in and needs only to be organized, can never be deductive in the sense that everything can be derived from first principles. Theology, Luke shows us, must be both inductive and nonsystematic, for the living God continues to reveal through the prophets as well as more broadly through human experience. Theology so understood is not a specialized activity of academically-trained persons in the church, but rather an activity in which all the faithful participate as they seek to articulate the shape and the meaning of their faith in the living God. Theology as response to the living God is necessarily revisionist, as Luke indicates particularly in two ways.

First, Luke shows how new insight into God derives from actual human experience. The beginning sections of each volume provide the obvious examples. It is Zechariah's experience of Gabriel's announcement, his wife's conception, his own muteness, and the birth of John that leads him to declare that "God has visited and brought redemption to his people" (Luke 1:68). It is Mary's experience of Gabriel's announcement and the greeting of her cousin Elizabeth that make her cry out that God "has looked upon his handmaid's lowliness" (1:48). Similarly, it is after seeing the risen Lord after his death, seeing him depart into heaven, and having the wind and fire of the Spirit give him ecstatic speech that Peter can declare, "God raised this Jesus; of this we are all witnesses" (Acts 2:32). And it is the experience of the Holy Spirit poured out on the household of Cornelius that leads Peter eventually to the realization, not only that God "gave them the Holy Spirit just as he did us" (15:8) but, more dramatically, that "we are saved through the grace of the Lord Jesus, in the same way as they" (Acts 15:11).

Second, Luke shows how such experience of the Holy Spirit also leads to new understandings of Scripture. The risen Lord teaches his disciples "what referred to him in all the scriptures" (Luke 24:27). The gift of the Holy Spirit at Pentecost enabled Peter to understand that "this is what was spoken through the prophet Joel" (Acts 2:16). The Ethiopian eunuch asks Philip concerning the text of Isaiah 53:7-8 that he was reading, "About whom is the prophet saying this? About himself or some other?" and Philip, "beginning with this scripture passage, proclaimed Jesus to him" (Acts 8:34-35). It is the experience of the Gentiles encountering the signs and wonders given by the Holy Spirit that enables James to discover new meaning in the prophet Amos (9:11-12) and declare that "the words of the prophets agree with this" (Acts 15:15-18).

If Christian communities today would take the witness of Luke-Acts concerning the Holy Spirit seriously, they would gain a livelier appreciation for theology as an essential dimension of life within the church, as it seeks to hear and respond to God's prophetic call in every circumstance of life.

The Character of the Church

Luke-Acts does not challenge the contemporary church at the level of polity, or institutional arrangement. Acts assumes the simple sort of local leadership for assemblies that were found also in Hellenistic synagogues: boards of elders with supervisors, who managed the financial and forensic affairs of the community (11:30; 14:23; 15:2-23; 16:4; 20:17-18). We find no sign of hierarchy, of sacramental system, or of a theological rationalization for ecclesial structure — apart from the note that the Holy Spirit had appointed overseers (20:28). Acts assumes the simple synagogal structure but does not make an argument for it. Luke's concerns challenge any and all institutional forms of the church.

Luke's interests lie elsewhere than in institutional arrangement, and his challenge to the church has less to do with the way the assembly structures itself than with the character of the assembly's response to the Holy Spirit at work in the world. Thus, Peter and his fellows responded appropriately when they saw the Holy Spirit descend on the household of the Gentile Cornelius: "Can anyone withhold the water for baptizing these people, who have received the Holy Spirit just as we have?" (Acts 10:47). And Peter rebukes those who would impose the burden of full law-observance on Gentiles who had received the Holy Spirit: "Why, then, are you now putting God to the test by placing on the shoulders of the disciples a yoke that neither our ancestors nor we have been able to bear?" (15:10).

What would make a church prophetic in Luke's view is its total dedication to responding to the call of God in every circumstance, more than to cultivating institutional self-interest. To the degree that "church" becomes a complex, worldwide organization, the danger of institutional maintenance and self-preservation is more acute. The more the "church" is a local body of believers gathered in the name of Jesus, the greater the chance that it can respond to the movements of the spirit in its immediate context. But whether small or large, simple or complex, local or universal, the essential character of the church must be the desire to answer to the living God. Otherwise, why does it exist?

In terms of its internal life, such commitment to the Holy Spirit is expressed by the cultivation of the gifts of the spirit among the community's members. Through its worship and instruction, the community prepares members to discern and respond to the spirit in their individual lives and to practice the gifts given by the spirit in the common life. Above all, the gift of prophecy is encouraged and respected rather than suppressed. Knowing that the spirit works through the voice of prophets from within the community, the church is willing to suffer the inevitable and often creative tension between the pull of ecclesial tradition on one side and the push of prophetic voices on the other.

In terms of the church's presence in the world, the spirit-directed community is aware that the living God is not restrained by the tradition of the church and often works outside the boundaries of the community. The church therefore does not only have a prophetic voice with which to address the world; the church is equally challenged by the "words of the prophets written on the subway walls" (Paul Simon) and must be willing to respond to the work of the spirit as it is revealed through "signs and wonders" outside its own control. The narrative of Acts suggests that a community truly led by the Holy Spirit will be led in new and surprising directions. The prospect is at once thrilling and frightening.

CHAPTER FIVE

The Prophetic Word

When prophecy is understood not as predicting the future but as speaking to other humans as God's spokesperson, it is necessary to ask about the content of the "word of God" the prophet declares. I have suggested that, in the broadest terms, the prophetic word can be considered as "God's vision for humanity," which more often than not, comes into conflict with humanity's own vision for itself. As with the understanding of the prophet as one led by the Holy Spirit, Luke's presentation of the prophetic message draws in general on two consistent themes of biblical prophecy.

First, the prophet calls Israel to repentance or conversion. The ancient Israelite prophets summoned the people to "turn from" their previous perceptions and practices that did not conform to God's will, and to "turn to" those that were pleasing to the one God (see Luke 10:13; 11:32). In Luke-Acts, the call to repentance is declared by John (Luke 3:3, 8; Acts 13:24; 19:4), by Jesus (Luke 5:32; 13:3, 5; 15:7, 10), and by the disciples (Luke 24:47; Acts 2:38; 3:19; 8:22), both to Jews and Gentiles (Acts 17:30; 20:21; 26:20). The prophet's demand that people convert, or change, implies that something in their present understanding and behavior is fundamentally wrong. The call to repentance serves as God's judgment on the present human construction of the world.

Second, conversion involves both the shift of religious loyalties — from the worship of foreign gods to the worship of the Lord alone as God — and a return to a life shaped by the terms of the covenant with the Lord God of Israel. The prophets consistently connected the worship of foreign gods with the betrayal of the covenant, above all with the covenant's demand for social justice. The return to Yahweh, then, demanded as well the observance of the laws concerning the care of the poor and doing justice in the land. It is in this sense that the prophetic vision represented a genuine "politics" within ancient Israel.

The fundamental prophetic message that runs throughout Luke-Acts — and poses the demand for repentance — concerns the *basileia tou theou* (see Luke 6:20; 7:28; 8:1; 9:2, 11; 10:9, 11; 12:31-32; 13:18-29; 14:15; 16:16; 17:20-21; 18:16-17; 19:11; 21:31; 22:16, 29-30; Acts 1:3; 8:12; 14:22; 19:8; 20:25; 28:23, 31). This "rule" or "kingdom" of God is, in Luke-Acts, in conflict with an opposing "rule" governed by Satan and demonic powers, which oppress humans (Luke 4:5, 11:17-20). The central prophetic message, then, concerns the "good news of God's rule," a proclamation that combines two elements: (1) that God has established his rule in the world (Luke 11:20; 12:32), and (2) that God requires of humans behavior consistent with God's rule. Conversion in Luke-Acts means, therefore, recognition and acceptance of the form of God's rule declared by Jesus and his disciples and a commitment to live in accordance with the prophetic vision of how God wants humans to live within God's rule.

Since Luke-Acts is a historylike narrative and makes meaning through the medium of story-telling, expectations concerning a complete statement of "God's rule" in propositional form should be kept low. Indeed, we will learn as much about the content of God's vision from our subsequent analysis of prophetic embodiment and enactment, precisely because Luke in this fashion "shows" the character of God's vision, more than he "tells" it. The contrast with Matthew is clear in this regard: Matthew's organization of Jesus' sayings into discrete discourses — all of which concern, in some fashion, "the kingdom of heaven" — invites an investigation of Jesus' "teaching" in a manner that Luke's narrative does not. Nevertheless, in a variety of ways, Luke does "tell" the reader what God's rule is and what it demands of humans.

To speak of a rule of God to which humans adhere through their behavior is clearly to speak of a form of politics, and the prophetic message of Luke-Acts does have a definite political dimension. It is important to note from the start, however, that Luke does not propose a form of "politics" in the obvious sense of that term — he does not call for, or describe, an alternative way of structuring the common life of Israel or an alternative social order for the people of the Mediterranean to the Roman Empire within which Judaism of the first century existed.

Certainly there are elements in Luke-Acts that can be read as a challenge to imperial pretensions. We note the juxtaposition of the angelic announcement of Jesus' birth as a savior who is both Christ and Lord to the imperial demand for universal taxation under Augustus (Luke 2:1-11) as well as the sardonic observation that Pilate and Herod became "friends" (that is, political allies) because of their collaboration in the trial of Jesus (23:12). But Luke has the risen Jesus deflect the question of the disciples concerning the restoration of the kingdom to Israel and responds in terms of the witness they are to bear to the ends of the world once they have been empowered by the spirit (Acts 1:7-8). And there are other elements that tend to confirm rather than challenge the Roman order. Jesus does not deny Caesar's right to levy taxes or have his image imprinted on coinage (Luke 20:20-26). Luke regards Paul's Roman citizenship — and his ability to appeal to the emperor — as a providential means of bringing him to the capital city of the empire (Acts 22:25-29; 25:11-12). Rather than expecting a "kingdom of God" that replaces the human political order with a theocratic state, Luke appears to envisage the shaping of a people who live by an alternative construction of reality — he presents, in the proper sense of the term, a "utopian politics," that is more possible to be realized by small intentional communities than by worldwide administrations.

Nor does Luke propose a way of organizing society in terms of economy. He neither calls for a return to the agricultural legislation of ancient Israel nor explicitly attacks the practice of absentee land management or financial investment — though his parables show him keenly aware of them (see Luke 19:11-27; 20:9-19). He does not have Jesus advocate the abolition of slavery, even though the practice of slavery was a huge part of the first-century economic system. And although Luke has Jesus drive out the sellers from the temple because, he says, "you have made it a den of thieves," this act does not represent a rejection of the temple economy so much as a restoration of the temple's role as "a house of prayer" (19:45-46), a role it fills as Jesus teaches and his followers worship there (19:47; see Acts 2:46; 3:1-7).

The prophetic character of Luke's politics has less to do with the specific arrangements of human society than it does with the deep derangement of human dispositions that make political and economic institutions oppressive and enslaving. Thus, the emphasis in Luke-Acts on "repentance for the forgiveness of sins" (Luke 1:77; 3:3; 5:20-24; 7:47-49; 11:4; 24:47; Acts 2:38; 3:19; 5:31; 10:43; 13:38; 22:16; 26:18) does not provide a social program, but a liberation from dispositions that corrupt all social programs and a demand for dispositions and actions that work for the transformation of all social practices in accordance with God's vision for humans. The forgiveness of sins in Luke-Acts is neither a program of institutional reform nor a matter of private piety: it is the reformation of human politics that begins in the human heart and is expressed above all in an intentional community filled with and led by the Holy Spirit.

The Infancy Account

The pronouncements and canticles of the infancy account provide the preliminary clues to the way Luke understands God's prophetic word. We realize at once that, in this opening section, the frame of reference is entirely Israel. Only bit-by-bit will the narrative open to show that God's vision of the people includes all of humanity. But Gabriel's announcement to Zechariah already alerts the reader to a particular understanding of God's people. After designating John as one full of the Holy Spirit, the angel describes his mission as one of "preparing a people fit for the Lord," a phrase that can also be translated as "preparing a people for the Lord that is fully equipped" (Luke 1:17). The point is that this "people" is defined in moral and not simply physical or ethnic terms. How is the people to be prepared? Gabriel declares that John "will turn many of the children of Israel to the Lord their God" (1:16): many but not all the children of Israel will "turn" or "convert" to become part of this people. Here, only two aspects of that turning are mentioned: the hearts of fathers will turn to their children, and the faithless or disobedient will turn "to the understanding of the righteous" (1:17). In short, the people that is prepared for the Lord is one that will change its moral dispositions and social relations.

The language of this opening announcement of God's vision echoes the language of the prophet Zephaniah, who sought to shape a "remnant people" within Israel that was defined in terms of its moral character, and that would survive destruction precisely because it sought the Lord rather than human power or prestige: "Seek the Lord, all you humble of the earth, who have observed his law; seek justice, seek humility; perhaps you may be sheltered in the day of the Lord's anger" (Zeph 2:3). Similarly, Zephaniah speaks of "the remnant of Israel" in this fashion:

> But I will leave as a remnant in your midst a people humble and lowly, who shall take refuge in the name of the LORD: the remnant of Israel. They shall do no wrong and speak no lies; nor shall there be found in their mouths a deceitful tongue; they shall pasture and couch their flocks with none to disturb them. (Zeph 3:12-13)

A similar echo of biblical prophecy is found in Mary's canticle (Luke 1:46-55), which resonates with the language of the Song of Hannah (1 Sam 2:1-10) in which Hannah dedicates her prophet-son Samuel to the Lord. The wondrous reversal of expectation that God accomplished in the birth of Samuel is seen as pointing to a much larger reality, namely that God's power trumps human arrogance, and that the God who "puts to death and gives life" (1 Sam 2:6) also can reverse every human perception of success based on social position or wealth. In like manner, Mary connects God's looking upon "the lowliness of his servant" (Luke 1:48) in her conception of the messiah Jesus to the mercy that he shows to "Israel his servant" by remembering the promise to Abraham (1:54-55). Mary also makes God's surprising remembrance of her and of Israel as exemplary of God's pattern of reversing human pretense by "the might of his arm" (1:51): God throws down the arrogant in mind and heart, casting the powerful from their thrones, while lifting up the lowly; God sends the rich away empty, while he fills the hungry with good things (1:51-53). The contrast Luke has Mary draw between God's power and human arrogance, as well as God's reversal of human status markers involving wealth and power, anticipates Luke's portrayal of Jesus' prophetic message.

In contrast to the sense of conflict and division expressed by Mary's song, the canticle of John's father, Zechariah, is entirely positive (1:67-79). Zechariah first states what God has done for "his people" in terms of redemption/salvation. God "brought redemption for his people" (1:68) by "raising up a horn for our salvation" within the house of David (1:69). Salvation is understood here first as a form of rescue. It is "salvation from the hands of our enemies and of all who hate us" (1:71) and rescue "from the hand of enemies" (1:74). But this salvation also has a positive result. It enables the people "to worship him in holiness and righteousness before him all our days" (1:74-75). John's role is spelled out in terms of giving the people "knowledge of salvation through the forgiveness of their sins" (1:77). The visitation of God's mercy will result in light for those in darkness and death's shadow and will guide their feet in the way of peace (1:79). Lacking in Zechariah's canticle is any sign of the violent reversals that God is accomplishing; salvation means safety for the people, and this safety is to allow righteous lives and true worship.

The themes of Mary's song are picked up more explicitly by the account of Jesus' ministry, but Zechariah's words do not lack importance. It is not by accident, for example, that "peace" *(eirēnē)* is mentioned so frequently in connection with Jesus' work (Luke 2:14, 29; 7:50; 8:48; 12:51;

19:38, 42; 24:36; Acts 10:36), and that of his followers (Luke 10:5-6; Acts 9:31; 15:33; 16:36), or that the restored Israel in Acts is described as a community that persevered in prayer and worship (Acts 2:42-47; 4:23-31). Finally, Zechariah agrees with Mary that the shaping of this people prepared for the Lord, its "lifting up," and its redemption/salvation are all the result of God's visitation, are all the work of God (1:46-50, 68-69), rather than the accomplishment of human cunning and will.

The Prophet John

Luke provides a much more rounded portrait of John the Baptist than do Mark or Matthew. Luke provides John with a distinctive prophetic ministry of his own. The depiction of John serves to show both the continuity between the cousin-prophets John and Jesus and their differences. The differences, it should be noted at once, do not have to do with the content of their message so much as the degree to which the Holy Spirit works through them. I have already discussed the portrayal of John as the one who moves in the power and spirit of Elijah, receives God's word (3:2), and proclaims good news to the people (3:18), as well as how John's distinction between his own water-baptism and baptism in the Holy Spirit (3:15-16) plays a thematic role in Luke-Acts (see pp. 55-56). Here, I focus on the content of John's message to the people.

First, consistent with his literary habit of having a subsequent narrative "fulfill" an earlier statement, Luke immediately identifies John as "son of Zechariah" and characterizes his message in the terms used by his father in 1:77: John preaches a "baptism of repentance for the forgiveness of sins" (3:3). Second, in the same manner that he will use Isaiah to interpret Jesus' prophetic ministry in 4:16-19, Luke (3:4-6) provides a citation from Isa 40:3-5. Mark 1:2-3 supplies here a mixed citation from Mal 3:1 and Isa 40:3; Matthew 3:3 eliminates the Malachi verse and cites only Isa 40:3. Only Luke supplies the full citation, with this effect: (a) the preparation of the way of the Lord is portrayed in terms of reversals, with valleys elevated and mountains lowered, with crooked paths made straight and rough ways made smooth; (b) the result of all this is that "all flesh shall see the salvation of God," a note that echoes Zechariah (Luke 1:69, 77) and anticipates Paul's final declaration concerning the Gentiles (Acts 28:28).

Third, as in Matt 3:7-12, Luke reports John as challenging the crowds who approach. The "brood of vipers" who assume that they are children of

Abraham because of descent are told that God can raise up children to Abraham from stones — it is necessary to "produce good works as evidence of repentance" in order to escape God's wrath. Indeed, God's ax is already laid to the root of every tree, and those not producing good fruit will be cut down and thrown into the fire (Luke 3:7-9). Similarly he warns them that the one coming after him will winnow out the wheat and chaff, with the chaff being burned "with unquenchable fire" (3:16-17). The prophetic word demands a change of life and the stakes are ultimate.

Fourth, and most revealing, Luke inserts between the two eschatological challenges in 3:7-9 and 3:16-17 a distinctive section in which John responds to the question "what then shall we do?" (3:10), a question that anticipates the one asked of Peter at Pentecost (Acts 2:37). John's teaching here identifies what Luke regards as the "fruits of repentance," and as we might expect from the hints provided by the infancy account, they focus on the use of possessions and power. To the crowds in general, John requires that those who have clothing or food share such possessions with those who do not have them (3:11). The response is more specific to the questions posed respectively by tax collectors and soldiers. It is already noteworthy that such people — ordinarily regarded as oppressors — should also seek the baptism of repentance; Luke will make special note of the tax collectors in this respect later in the narrative (7:29). Equally noteworthy, however, is what Luke does not have John tell them. He does not identify them as enemies or oppressors, does not demand that they leave their employment, does not enter into a condemnation of the economy or rule of the empire that they serve. Rather, John (Luke) demands of them the refusal to take advantage of the power they have over others for their own profit. The tax collectors should "stop collecting more than what is prescribed" and the soldiers are warned off the types of behavior that truly are oppressive: "do not practice extortion, do not falsely accuse anyone, and be satisfied with your wages" (3:13-14). The vice of acquisitiveness (not being satisfied with one's wages) drives the profit-making power plays of extortion and false accusation.

The Prophet Jesus

I have discussed earlier the significance of Luke's redaction and placement of Jesus' inaugural sermon and rejection at Nazareth (4:16-30) for his depiction of Jesus as the prophetic Messiah because of his anointing by the

Holy Spirit (see pp. 58-59). Jesus' citation of Isa 61:1-2; 58:6 in Luke 4:18-19 also serves as a programmatic statement of Jesus' prophetic word. First, the spirit-anointed prophet has been "commissioned" by the Lord to "proclaim" (the Greek verb *kēryssein* occurs twice; 4:18, 19). The word of the prophet takes the form first of all of a proclamation from God. Second, the proclamation concerns a "liberation" or "release" (the Greek term *aphesis* also appears twice). It is the same noun used in the phrase "forgiveness of sins," which therefore should be taken to mean a "release" from sins. Third, those receiving the proclamation of release — delivered by a delegate from an ancient "Lord," such a proclamation would be performative, that is, authorize and effect release — are the captives and the oppressed.

The proclamation of release, Isaiah declares, is equivalent to the proclamation of "an acceptable year of the Lord" (4:19). Although the term *dektos* ("acceptable") is not used by the Septuagint in this connection, the view of many readers is that both Isaiah and Luke have in mind here the proclamation of the "Jubilee Year" in ancient Israel. Leviticus 25:10 declares, "This fiftieth year you shall make sacred by proclaiming liberty in the land for all its inhabitants. It shall be a jubilee to you, when every one of you shall return to his own property, every one to his own family estate." Among the elements in this year of liberty was the release of debts and of slaves (Lev 25:40-55). Such release would also clearly constitute "good news to the poor" who had been enslaved by their debts (Lev 25:35-43).

It is difficult to say how literally Luke might have intended this proclamation of the Jubilee Year. The question concerns *Luke's* understanding and intention, rather than that of the historical Jesus, if he in fact had uttered such words. Three facts warn against a precipitous conclusion that Luke understood the Jubilee in literal terms. First, the words "sight to the blind" in Luke's version of the Isaiah citation — Isaiah had "heal the brokenhearted" — expand the good news of Jesus' enactment of the prophetic agenda that suggests a literal Jubilee — that is, beyond liberation from economic circumstances. Second, there is nothing in Luke's subsequent narrative that suggests an economic agenda; rather, Luke develops the theme of healing as the dominant expression of the good news. Third, Jesus' words following the citation, "Today this scripture passage is fulfilled in your hearing" (4:21), refer most obviously to the fact that Jesus was anointed by the spirit as prophetic messiah; and, we can note, the examples from Elijah and Elisha that Jesus proffers are acts of healing. It is appropriate, however, to understand Luke's use of the Isaiah passage as an announcement to all those who are in any way captive or oppressed (including those captive by poverty or sickness) that what is acceptable to God is that they receive "deliverance." In different words, the passage restates the proposition that God visits the people for their salvation.

The fullest formal expression of Jesus' prophetic message is found in his Sermon on the Plain in Luke 6:20-49, a discourse addressed explicitly to his "disciples" (6:20), though in the hearing of a large crowd that had gathered around him and experienced healing through his touch (6:17-19); the shift to "you who hear" in 6:27 appears to enlarge the audience even as Jesus moves from proclamation to teaching. As in Matthew's Sermon on the Plain, a much larger and far differently structured discourse (Matt 5:1-7:29), Luke begins Jesus' sermon with a set of beatitudes (6:20-23). The most obvious literary function served by Jesus' public words, "Blessed are you poor, for the kingdom of God is yours," is to fulfill the programmatic prophecy of 4:18. The prophetic messiah here proclaims to those who are poor the message that God entrusted to the one anointed by the Holy Spirit.

There are easily discerned differences between the version of the beatitudes found in Matthew and in Luke. Matthew has eight blessings in the form of general propositions, "Blessed are the poor in spirit, for theirs is the kingdom of heaven" (Matt 5:3), followed by the final blessing in the second person that elaborates the last, "blessed are you" (5:11-12). In Matthew, the beatitudes are connected to spiritual or moral dispositions, which serve as the premise for the blessed result: people will "see God" because they are "pure of heart" (5:8). In contrast, Luke's blessing are directed to the hearers, "blessed are you" and are connected to specific conditions, rather than dispositions: being poor, hungry, mourning, and persecuted (Luke 6:20-23) — these represent versions of four of Matthew's eight beatitudes. Luke adds to these four blessings a corresponding set of four "woes" connected to the opposite conditions of life: rich, replete, glad, and popular (6:24-26). The contrast of blessing and woe obviously makes Luke's version more closely resemble the offer of blessing or curse that Moses extends to Israel when presenting them with the law (Deut 30:15-20). The note of reversal also echoes the Song of Mary, which speaks of filling the hungry with good things and sending the rich away empty (Luke 1:53).

Luke's blessings and woes do not prescribe attitudes or behaviors of humans, but declare good news from God, which may not at first seem particularly like good news, namely that God is reversing human measures of success and failure, of blessedness and woe. Being wealthy, well-fed, happy, and enjoying the favor of others seems the perfect recipe for human success; poverty, hunger, mourning, and persecution, in contrast, are the measure of failure. The first of the blessings establishes a new measure: the rule of God. Poverty, rather than a reason for being excluded from God's power, is the premise for participation in it. This is the fundamental and present reversal that derives from God's visitation. The remaining three blessings declare a future reversal. Those hungry now "will be filled," those mourning now "will rejoice," and those rejected now will have a great reward in heaven (6:21-23).

The statement of future reversal, both with respect to blessing and woe, points the reader to understand that the "rule of God" is, for Luke, not one entirely realized on the plane of human history, but will be fully accomplished in God's future. Thus, while the majority of Luke's language about "heaven" can be understood vertically, as referring to God's realm or God's measure (Luke 10:20; 11:2, 13; 15:18, 21; 17:29; 19:38; 20:4-5; 21:11, 26, 33; 22:43; 24:51; Acts 1:10; 7:56; 10:11-16; 11:5-10), at times it has a future reference (Luke 6:23; 12:33; 15:7; 18:22). In this way, it corresponds to Luke's language about the kingdom of God: most references are present (Luke 4:43; 7:28; 8:1; 9:2, 11, 60; 10:9, 11; 11:20; 12:31-32; 13:18-20; 16:16; 17:21; 18:16-29; Acts 14:22), but some are future (9:27; 11:2; 13:28-29; 14:15; 19:11; 21:31; 22:30). Other language about future realization of God's rule includes Luke's speaking about "eternal dwellings" (16:9), future judgment (11:30-32; 13:25-30; 21:34), and the day of the Son of Man (17:22-35; 21:27-36).

In Jesus' later parable of Lazarus and the Rich Man (16:19-31) — a parable unique to his Gospel — Luke provides a narrative commentary on his version of the blessing and woes. The characters are simply types: "a certain rich man," and "a certain poor man." No moral actions or attributes are ascribed to either. The story straightforwardly relates a dramatic change in their fortunes, from this life to the next, as expressed in 16:25-26: the one who had "enjoyed good things" in his mortal life is now tormented, while the one who had "evil things" now has "a consolation" (compare 6:24: the rich "have received consolation" in the present life). The denouement of the parable, it is true, does imply a moral judgment on the rich man who had systematically ignored the poor man who lay every day at his door: he should indeed have "listened to Moses and the prophets" and shared his possessions with Lazarus (16:29-31). But in its bare bones, the parable expresses the "good news" for the poor that God wishes them to be consoled and the "woe" to the rich that their present consolation is all they get.

In Matthew's Sermon on the Mount, the logical connection between the beatitudes and woes is clear, because the moral dispositions required for blessings prepare for the moral exhortation to the disciples. Luke's much shorter version does not flow as smoothly from the blessings and woes. The connection can perhaps best be stated in these terms: God's reversal of human expectations and values is to be matched by a corresponding reversal in moral behavior among disciples. That this is the implied logic is suggested by the transition in 6:26-27: the last woe concludes with the way in which the false prophets were treated well in the past, in contrast to the way the true prophets were scorned and rejected (6:23); then Jesus says "to you who hear," that they are to love their enemies.

The command to love one's enemies is stated twice (6:27 and 6:35), and is given extensive elaboration. Luke has Jesus challenge the ancient (indeed, virtually universal) premise that one should love friends and hate enemies. For the disciples, the moral premise is not to do as others have done to us, or to do in order that it might be done to us, but rather to do to others as we would have others do to us (6:31). The examples Jesus sets out are powerful and paradoxical: the disciples are to do good to those who hate them, bless those who curse them, pray for those who mistreat them (6:28). When struck on one cheek, they must offer the other to be struck, rather than retaliate; when an outer garment of clothing is stolen, they must be ready to offer the thief their inner garment as well (6:29). They are to give to whoever asks and not seek to be repaid (6:30).

The challenge that such love puts to conventional cultural norms is spelled out in 6:32-34. Jesus asks three questions that echo the direct injunctions he has just issued. If they love, do good, and lend only to those who love them, do good to them, and can repay them, Jesus points out, they are living by a measure that is employed even by sinners. What credit is it to them to act by such a measure? The measure that Luke then has Jesus propose is the measure of how God acts (is acting) among humans. To love their enemies (6:35), to do good to others without expecting a return, is possible because the "credit" or "reward" comes to them from God (6:35), yes, but also because they are children of the Most High who can act toward others the way God acts toward them. God is kind to the ungrateful and wicked. Their moral measure, therefore, is not social convention but the good news itself: "be merciful just as also your Father is merciful."

The discourse then shifts to a disposition that is the opposite of mercy and love, namely judging. We note that the tenses used here require the translation "stop judging" and "stop condemning," suggesting that these are behaviors that are already being indulged. A few verses later, Luke has Jesus chastise those who seek to remove a speck from a brother's eye, when they have a wooden beam in their own eye: "You hypocrite! Remove the wooden beam from your eye first, then you will see clearly to remove the splinter in your brother's eye" (6:41-42). Their judgment is to turn inward toward their own integrity, not assume the "seeing of the heart" that belongs to God alone, and judge others — even if the others are enemies who have harmed them.

If, instead, they forgive their enemies, then they themselves will be forgiven (6:37-38). This command anticipates the statement in the Lord's Prayer, "forgive us our sins, for we forgive everyone in debt to us" (11:4), and makes the disciples' behavior consistent with the good news concerning the forgiveness of sins by God (Luke 1:77; 3:3; 24:47) and the model of forgiveness demonstrated by Jesus (23:34). In 6:38, Luke has Jesus introduce once more the vertical relationship with God rather than the horizontal relations among humans as determinative: "the measure by which you measure will in turn be measured out to you." This does not reintroduce the *quid pro quo* of human interaction, but instead places human judgment and forgiveness within the divine measure: the way humans "measure" their fellows is the measure God applies in turn to them. The model once more, therefore, is the divine beneficence: "Give and gifts will be given to you; a good measure, packed together, shaken down, and overflowing, will be poured into your lap" (6:38). The repentance to which this prophet calls the people is to a manner of life that is as extravagant in love and generous in giving as has been demonstrated by God toward them. The prophetic agenda is radical, not because it calls for the restructuring of human society, but because it demands the transformation of the human heart according to the measure of God.

The perfect parabolic expression of the prophetic message in this sermon is given by Jesus' parable of the Samaritan (10:29-37). This parable is told to illustrate how Jesus subverts the principle of Torah, "You shall love the Lord, your God, with all your heart, with all your being, with all your strength, and with all your mind, and your neighbor as yourself," by transposing the terms of conventional understanding. The Lawyer asks the question, "Who is my neighbor?" But Jesus' story shows how the Samaritan shows mercy toward the one who should have been his enemy and "was neighbor to the robber's victim."

Luke concludes the sermon with three wisdom tropes. Two of them (the house built on rock and the fruit-bearing tree) Luke shares with Matthew, but the first is unique to him and gives a distinctive emphasis to the other two. In a "parable," Jesus reminds his hearers that if the blind lead the blind, both fall into a pit (6:39). He then applies this to the teacher-student relationship: no disciple is superior to the teacher, but when the disciple is "fully trained up," then he will be like his teacher. Luke uses the image to suggest that moral reformation is not instantaneous, but a matter of training. Second, Jesus compares moral competence to a tree bearing good fruit, suggesting that moral training is a matter of character: "A good person out of the store of goodness in his heart produces good, but an evil person out of a store of evil produces evil, for out of the fullness of the heart the mouth speaks" (6:43-45). Finally, the image of a house built on rock rather than sand points to the fact that repentance is not a matter of verbal profession of belief — "Why do you call me 'Lord, Lord,' but not do what I command?" (6:46) — but a matter of action, not a matter of hearing but a matter of doing. The person who does what Jesus says is like someone building on rock, but the person who hears and does not do "is like a person who built a house on the ground without a foundation" (6:47-49).

These last notes of the sermon are picked up in the subsequent narrative. Luke's version of the interpretation of Jesus' parable of the Sower (8:5-8) speaks of the seed explicitly as "the word of God" (8:11) and of the seed that fell among thorns as "the ones who have heard, but as they go along, they are choked by the anxieties and riches and pleasures of life, and they fail to produce mature fruit" (8:14). Matthew and Mark also speak of riches as choking the seed, but given Luke's emphasis on possessions throughout his work, it is significant that wealth above all prevents "maturity." Luke's understanding of the seed that fell on rich soil is also distinctive: "They are the ones who, when they have heard the word, embrace it with a generous and good heart, and bear fruit through perseverance" (8:15). Repentance is not a once-for-all event, but a process of growth.

Finally, only four verses later, Luke places the account of Jesus' family unable to approach him because of the crowd, and his response, "My mother and brothers are those who hear the word of God and keep it" (8:21). This declaration, in turn, resembles Jesus' response to the voice that praised "the womb that carried you and the breasts at which you sucked," that "Rather, blessed are those who hear the word of God and keep it" (11:28). In Luke's Gospel, these declarations certainly include Jesus' human mother, who, when she heard the message of the shepherds, "kept all these things, reflecting on them in her heart" (2:19), and when she saw her son teach in the temple, "kept all these things in her heart" (2:51).

Opposition to the Prophetic Word

The positive response of faith in Luke's Gospel, we see, is not simply a matter of recognizing Jesus as a prophet — calling him "Lord" (6:46) — but is a matter of truly hearing and acting on the word of God that the prophet speaks. It means adopting a new measure for evaluating all relationships, and a new behavior with respect above all to power and possessions.

The same point is made by the way Luke characterizes those who oppose Jesus' prophetic activity and message. Luke's set of "woes" in 6:24-26 suggests that those who are rich, filled, glad, and enjoy good repute in human eyes do not recognize the challenge of the rule of God because they already have their "comfort" (6:24) and therefore are not open to the good news announced by God through the prophet. They profit from the present dispositions and arrangements and therefore resist the change that the prophet Jesus demands. Throughout the Gospel narrative, those who oppose Jesus also have dispositions and practices antithetical to the ones proposed by Jesus.

The climax of Luke's presentation of Jesus as a prophet occurs in chapter 7. After performing works of healing that mimic Elisha and Elijah, and being proclaimed by the crowd as "a great prophet" (7:1-16), Jesus responds to the query sent by John's messengers, whether Jesus was "the one who was to come" (7:20), by reciting all the powerful deeds he had been performing, culminating with "the poor having the good news proclaimed to them" (7:22). He then declares, "Blessed is the one who takes no offense at me" (7:23). Jesus then speaks of John as prophet, and Luke inserts into Jesus' praise this parenthetical comment: "All the people who listened, including the tax collectors, and who were baptized with the baptism of John, acknowledged the righteousness of God. But the Pharisees and scholars of the law, who were not baptized by him, rejected the plan of God for themselves" (7:29-30). Rejecting the prophet is to reject the prophetic program for the people, God's vision for humanity. In fact, as Jesus goes on to note, "the people of this generation" have rejected both John (too ascetical) and Jesus (too little ascetical and a "friend of tax collectors and sinners," 7:31-35).

That "the people of this generation" who reject the prophets are the Pharisees and Lawyers is shown by the following story. Jesus is welcomed by "the sinful woman in the city" and shows Jesus extravagant hospitality, receiving forgiveness of her sins (7:36-50). She belongs to the prophetic people because her "faith" (7:50) expresses itself in fruits worthy of repentance (3:8). In her, "wisdom is vindicated by her children" (7:35). In sharp contrast, Simon the Pharisee appears to practice hospitality to the prophet Jesus, but in fact he fails to show the tokens of true hospitality (7:44-46). In contrast to showing love as did the woman — according to the measure of the kingdom (6:27-36) — Simon displays the disposition of arrogance, revealed by his judgment or condemnation of both his guests — forbidden by the measure of the kingdom (6:37-42). With remarkable efficiency, he manages to express this judgmental attitude toward both guests in a single sentence: "If this man were a prophet, he would know who and what sort of woman this is who is touching him, that she is a sinner" (7:39).

Another Pharisee invites Jesus to dinner and is shocked that Jesus did not observe ritual ablutions (11:37-38). Jesus attacks their inner dispositions of "plunder and evil" and the way they "love the seat of honor in synagogues and greetings in marketplaces" (11:39, 43) — we remember that the false prophets of old were spoken well of (6:26). When the lawyers object that they are also being insulted by Jesus' attack, he accuses them both of laying burdens on people (not showing mercy) and of killing the prophets (11:46-54). The Pharisees who mock Jesus' teaching on the use of possessions in 16:8-13 are characterized as "lovers of money" (16:14). Jesus addresses the parable of the Pharisee and the Tax Collector "to those who were convinced of their own righteousness and despised everyone else," that is, to Pharisees — the character in the story judges the tax collector to be "dishonest and adulterous," whereas the tax collector identifies himself as a sinner and asks for mercy (18:9-14). The rich man who asks Jesus what he needs to do to become perfect and leaves desolate when told he had to sell his possessions and give them to the poor was not only "very rich" but also a "ruler" of the people (18:18-23).

Finally, in the parable that the scribes and chief priests recognized as being addressed to them (20:19) — the scribes are described as those who "devour the houses of widows" (20:47) — the tenant farmers resist paying the owner of a vineyard his share in the produce, beat, insult, and "send away empty" those delegates the master sent, and finally kill the owner's beloved son; they say, "This is the heir. Let us kill him, that the inheritance may become ours" (20:9-18). The allegorical character of the parable is clear: the story interprets the successive rejection of God's prophets (6:23; 11:49-51; 13:33-35), climaxing in the rejection of Jesus, the beloved son (19:41-44). Their violence, however, is driven by their greed and their desire for power, moral dispositions cleanly contrary to the vision for humanity enunciated by the prophet.

The Prophetic Word in Acts

We would not expect Acts to advance the prophetic word of Jesus as explicitly or with the same clarity as Jesus' own words in the Gospel, although enough is said to show that "the things concerning the kingdom of God" remain the topic of concern throughout the narrative (Acts 1:3; 8:12; 19:8; 20:25; 28:23, 31). The so-called missionary speeches in Acts serve to advance the claims being made for Jesus as the prophet whom God exalted through resurrection and how these claims fulfill the Scripture (2:14-36; 3:12-26; 10:36-43; 13:16-41; 17:22-31), and the cycle of speeches at the end of Acts serves to defend Paul's call and ministry in terms of the "hope of Israel" (22:1-21; 23:1-6; 24:10-21; 26:2-23). Beyond the ritual of baptism, there is no statement of what repentance requires.

Even more than in the case of the Gospel, then, the demonstration of Luke's understanding of the prophetic vision for humanity must await analysis of its embodiment and enactment by Jesus and his followers. Luke is consistently richer in narrative characterization than he is in didactic discourse. Two passages, however, show such consistency with Luke's perspective in the Gospel that we can assume Luke intends his readers to understand these "things of the kingdom of God" even when they are not explicitly stated.

At the end of Peter's Pentecost sermon, when he declares, "God has made him both Lord and Messiah, this Jesus whom you crucified" (Acts 2:36), his hearers respond with precisely the question that was put to John in Luke 3:10, "What are we to do?" (Acts 2:37). Peter says that they must repent and be baptized "in the name of Jesus Christ for the forgiveness of your sins; and you will receive the Holy Spirit" (2:38). The connection of repentance and forgiveness of sins is familiar from the Gospel (Luke 3:3), as is the connection of baptism and the Holy Spirit (Luke 3:16; Acts 1:5). These are now joined by the phrase "in the name of Jesus Christ," and while it is natural and customary to link "in the name" particularly to the ritual of baptism, it is equally legitimate to connect "in the name of Jesus Christ" to the act of repentance for the forgiveness of sins. The shape of repentance, in other words, is given by the prophetic program announced, embodied, and enacted by the prophet Jesus.

The suggestion is strengthened by Peter's next exhortation, "save yourselves from this corrupt generation" (Acts 2:40). The language echoes that of Luke's Gospel when it speaks of "saving one's soul" (Luke 9:24), and of the fewness of those who will be saved; in Luke 13:24-30, in response to a question whether only a few would be saved (13:23), Luke has Jesus report the harsh dismissal by the "master of the house" to those who seek entry by calling him "Lord" and appeal to the fact that "we ate and drank in your company and you taught in our streets": he says, "I do not know where you are from. Depart from me, all you evildoers." Peter's exhortation to the crowd to save themselves "from this corrupt generation" is also completely consistent with the words attributed to Jesus in the Gospel narrative concerning "this generation" (see Luke 7:31; 9:41; 11:29-51; 16:8; 17:25). Finally, the response of the crowd is to be baptized and then to live a life that conforms completely to the prophetic program announced by Jesus (Acts 2:42-47); from the embodiment described by Luke, the reader understands the vision on which it is based.

Luke provides only one example of a sermon addressed to an already-formed community, and even that has a special character, since Paul's audience is made up of the elders of the church at Ephesus, who come to meet Paul at Miletus (Acts 20:18-35). By the time Paul delivers this address, the reader is abundantly aware that he is as much a prophetic emissary of Jesus as were Peter and John: he is commissioned by the risen Lord (9:4-6; see also 22:6-10, 18-21; 23:11; 26:14-18) and by the spirit-filled prophetic church at Antioch (13:1-3). He himself is full of the Holy Spirit (13:9) and works signs and wonders among the people (14:3; 15:12). Indeed, immediately before this sermon, he raises a young boy to life (20:7-11).

In his discourse, Paul claims to have been led by the spirit (20:22-23) and to have proclaimed to them "the entire plan of God" (20:27). Strikingly, he speaks of his work as "a ministry that I received from the Lord Jesus to bear witness to the good news of God's grace" (20:24) and says that this involved for both Jews and Greeks "repentance before God and faith in our Lord Jesus" (20:21). He reminds them that he himself lived by the measure that Jesus established:

> I have never wanted anyone's silver or gold or clothing. You know well that these very hands have served my needs and my companions. In every way I have shown you that by hard work of that sort we must help the weak, and keep in mind the words of the Lord Jesus, who himself said, "it is more blessed to give than to receive." (20:33-35)

At least in Luke's own view, Paul's manner of life and prophetic message were based squarely on the "good news" proclaimed by Jesus and, indeed, the very words of Jesus. Although no written Gospel contains this saying, its tenor accords perfectly with the words of Jesus throughout Luke.

Challenge to the Contemporary Church

The process of ecclesial self-examination might begin with the realization that the frequently-used Christian term "Word of God" means for the most part something else than what it means in Luke-Acts. For many Christians, the "Word of God" means the incarnate Christ, the word made flesh (John 1:14); for many others, the term is instantly equated with Scripture, which both as a whole and in each of its parts can be designated "word of God." The "Good News," likewise, tends to be understood either as the literary work called a Gospel or the distinctive Christian proclamation of what God has accomplished in the death and resurrection of Jesus. The term does not, in common Christian parlance, refer to a prophetic message from God.

In Luke, however, the word of God does bear this meaning. The prophet announces "God's rule," meaning what God has done and is doing among humans for their salvation and what this demands of humans in response: repentance for the forgiveness of sins, living by a new measure of success and failure, doing the deeds that demonstrate repentance, growing into full maturity. The prophetic message of Luke's Sermon on the Plain in particular challenges conventional notions concerning power and possessions, status and success. Faith in the prophetic messiah means, in Luke-Acts, deciding to live by the measure of God that the prophet announces.

Churches today might take the reading of Luke-Acts as an opportunity to examine themselves with respect to the clarity and consistency of their "message" to the world. What do Christians really stand for? The difficulty in answering this question points to something more profound than a problem in communications — "we can't get our message out!" — it points to confusion among Christians themselves concerning the character and the entailments of claiming allegiance to the kingdom of God. The process of self-examination can begin by asking what each of the key elements in Luke's understanding of God's word means for churches today. I do not pose these questions to the actual practice of Christians (we consider that in the next chapters) but only to the clarity of Christian understanding.

Kingdom of God

The very term is problematic for many Christians, for what they regard as its triumphalistic and even militaristic overtones; notions of God's "rule" or "sovereignty" seem to associate the church with domination. In fact, the notion of God as "king" seems to some to be needlessly masculine. Some translations of the New Testament avoid all these terms in favor of what is considered to be a softer image, such as "domain" or "dominion." There are some silliness and excessive linguistic sensitivity in all this, but in fairness, the language of God's kingdom has been used in ways that have generated such reactions. Too often in Christian history, language about God's rule has served as camouflage for human tyranny.

Unfortunately, revulsion at past misappropriation and manipulation does not equal a corresponding positive appreciation for what the central scriptural metaphor of God's rule or kingdom might mean today. Christians who think in terms of this symbol are divided concerning its connection to empirical reality: is it totally an eschatological hope, something to be realized outside of history, or is it a hope that is already in process of being realized in the present? Is it accomplished solely through the cataclysmic intervention by God from without, or is it realized also through human effort?

Most of all, Christians differ concerning the location of God's rule. Some claim to find it solely within the heart of the individual believer — misreading the famous line from Luke, "the kingdom of God is among you" (Luke 17:21), as "the kingdom of God is within you." Others insist that God's kingdom demands a full social realization in a Christian state, that Constantine had the right idea all along, and that acquiescing in Christianity's present diaspora condition is a huge mistake. Those seeking the kingdom within their hearts find the notion of a Christian politics nonsensical, while the other extreme longs for Christendom to be restored.

Luke-Acts offers a vision of God's rule that cuts across all these options and provides the contemporary church a basis for renewal in its thinking on the subject. First, Luke clearly thinks in terms of an already and not yet of the kingdom. In successive sentences, Luke has Jesus tell his disciples, "seek his kingdom and these other things will be given you besides," and "do not be afraid any longer, little flock, for your father is pleased to give you the kingdom" (Luke 12:31-32). The rule of God, furthermore, is both intensely personal and political, for it demands of every individual a conversion to the prophetic message and a maturing in faith through perseverance, and at the same time places this personal commitment within the context of a people shaped by shared convictions and practices. It is precisely this combination which classically constitutes the nature of the church, but because being church in this full communitarian sense is a demanding and difficult thing, Christians have found it all too easy to slip toward a private piety or a public politics as options.

Repentance

Luke's Greek term *metanoia* is often translated as "repentance," and for some Christians today, the word has the same negative associations as kingdom, sacrifice, self-denial, and suffering. Repentance is for them associated with a mournful and joyless piety driven by sin-consciousness and guilt. For Christians tending to equate grace with "unconditional love" and faith with "self-esteem" or "self-acceptance," none of these associations has much appeal. Christianity must be about happiness or about nothing at all, and the church failing to provide enjoyment with its edification is in danger of losing members. Luke's term *metanoia* certainly does not mean repentance as so caricatured, but neither does it have anything to do with an "I'm OK, you're OK" version of Christianity. Repentance means, and demands, change.

The noun *metanoia* can also be translated as "conversion," but this term also has suffered its distortions, as when it is used primarily for the change of religious affiliation: "I was once a Muslim but I converted to Christianity"; sometimes even within the same faith: "I once was a Catholic, but I converted to Christianity." Such usage captures the sense of change, to be sure, but only at the formal, external level. Somewhat more adequate is the use of conversion from the turning from sin to faith; this use captures the biblical sense of "turning" (Hebrew *těshûbâ,* Greek *epistrephein*) in the prophetic call to convert to the living God and the observance of the covenant. But this use of conversion among Christians tends to stress the turn from more than the turn "toward" and tends as well to be thought of as a once-for-all turn.

The call of *metanoia* in Luke-Acts offers contemporary churches the chance to think through this important dimension of discipleship. In his narrative, it certainly does not mean a life of remorseful guilt; repentance is a matter of great joy (Luke 15:7-9, 23). Nor is it a change of formal religious affiliation: those who heed the prophet become part of remnant Israel, a remnant that includes the Gentiles who become part of "a people for his name" (Acts 15:14). Positively, Luke's Gospel in particular envisages *metanoia* not only as a commitment of faith but also a genuine "change of mind": it entails the acceptance of God's measure of reality as enunciated by the prophet Jesus, a commitment to live by the reversal of values and behaviors demanded by the good news of God's rule. Being part of the "people prepared for the Lord" (Luke 1:17) means the willingness to accept God's measure as the measure of success and failure and to make that measure the one by which we actually measure ourselves and others.

Luke's insistence on the formation of good character in order to display good deeds (the image of the tree and its fruit, Luke 6:43-45) and on the need to become mature in such character through perseverance — not letting the word be choked by anxieties and riches and pleasures of life (8:14-15) — reminds contemporary Christians that conversion is far from a once-for-all event, but is a slow process that demands attention throughout life. I note that Luke subtly modifies Jesus' demand that disciples take up the cross to follow him: "If anyone wishes to come after me, he must deny himself and take up his cross *daily* and come after me" (Luke 9:23). Both individual Christians and churches can enrich the meaning of conversion/repentance by contemplating, on one side, the values-reversing standards of Luke's Sermon on the Plain, and on the other side, the specific ways in which life's "entanglements" impede the process of continuous conversion.

Baptism

In Luke-Acts, repentance or conversion is signaled by the ritual of baptism, both in response to the prophet John (Luke 3:7; 7:29; Acts 1:5; 19:4) and the prophet whom God raised up, Jesus (Acts 2:41; 10:48; 19:5). In present-day Christianity, baptism continues to mark an individual's admission to the community and the commitment — even in the case of infants by proxy — to the standards by which the community lives. The renewal of baptismal vows practiced by some communities at the Easter Vigil retains some vestigial element of how serious a matter such a commitment was in earliest Christianity, when associating oneself with the crucified Messiah meant placing oneself in danger of the same rejection and persecution as that experienced by Jesus (see Luke 6:22-23; 21:12; Acts 5:41). Such renewal of vows taps into something ancient and profound when it asks Christians again to renounce Satan and to renounce all his wiles.

The element of baptism that is singularly lacking in today's churches, however, is the element of risk and danger. I must qualify this, to be sure. There are places in the world where persecution of Christians remains real and where baptism carries with it great risk. For most Christians, and certainly for the ones likely to read this book, such danger is remote. Baptism serves more as an accommodation to a lingering Christian culture than a rejection of Satan and his pomp. Is the lack of risk associated with baptism logically connected to the lack of genuine challenge to the ways of the world by the Christian community? Perhaps churches can give at least some attention to the gap between the practice of baptism as cultural initiation and baptism as sign of a radical and divisive prophetic program, as it is stated by Jesus in Luke 12:49-53:

> I have come to set the earth on fire, and how I wish it were already blazing! There is a baptism with which I must be baptized, and how great is my anguish until it is accomplished! Do you think that I have come to establish peace on the earth? No, I tell you, but rather division. From now on, a household of five will be divided, three against two and two against three; a father will be divided against his son and his son against his father, a mother against her daughter and a daughter against her mother, a mother-in-law against her daughter-in-law and her daughter-in-law against her mother-in-law.

Forgiveness of Sins

Christians today gladly celebrate the forgiveness of sins as a benefit they receive from God. For them, "baptism for the forgiveness of sins" means that the ritual of entry into the community relieves them of the burden of their past behavior and its consequences. This is undoubtedly a correct understanding: an essential dimension of the prophet's mission is the liberation of the oppressed (Luke 4:18), and, as we shall see, Luke shows Jesus enacting this mission through "healing all who were oppressed by the devil" (Acts 10:38).

Less well-developed among contemporary Christians is an appreciation for baptism as a commitment to practice forgiveness of the sins of others against us. Yet such forgiveness is clearly the demand of the good news as expounded by Jesus in the Sermon on the Plain. I noted in that passage how striking was the transition from suffering persecution to having love for one's enemies (Luke 6:27). The first important point here is that the Christian ethos is not about being friends with everyone; such a state of agreement with all people means simply that one does not stand for anything definite. Enemies are real. Enemies are those who do not wish us well, who actively seek our harm. How can an individual or a church "love" those who are actively persecuting them? They must somehow will the good for those who do not will the good for them. But this demands "forgiveness," namely the refusal to define the other simply and totally as enemy, and the desire to will the good for the other that is not defined solely by enmity toward me or us. Such forgiveness and love is antithetical to the disposition of judging and condemning (Luke 6:37-38), which is based on the premise that the other is defined in terms of how they are toward us, rather than the other and us being defined by our relation to God, who is merciful, and is the measure for our relations to each other.

The ethic of love and forgiveness is far from sentimental. It is a serious and stringent effort to live by the measure God has shown us in the mercy and forgiveness shown us in the good news. Churches today can well reflect on how pervasive this ethic is in their common life and how it might be possible for the community to pray with "everyone in debt to us" (Luke 11:4). The demand is not simply to forgive obvious enemies from outside the community. It applies as well to the sins committed against us within the community: "If your brother sins, rebuke him, and if he repents, forgive him. And if he wrongs you seven times in one day and returns to you seven times, saying, 'I am sorry,' you should forgive him" (Luke 17:3-4).

Power and Possessions

To a disconcerting extent, contemporary Christian discourse about the kingdom involves issues of sexuality. Language about oppression and liberation, forgiveness of sins, judgment and mercy is much more frequently attached to the ways humans act sexually than to the ways they make use of possessions or deploy power. If an earlier era of the church might fairly be called sex-repressed, the contemporary age could be called sex-obsessed. Such interest is understandable simply because the sins of the flesh are so obvious and easily isolated. But the contemporary concentration on sex is far distant from the prophetic concerns of Luke-Acts. In the Gospel narrative, the topic of sex occurs only twice. In Luke 16:18, the prophet Jesus forbids divorce: "Everyone who divorces his wife and marries another commits adultery, and the one who marries a woman divorced from her husband commits adultery." Marriage on earth is to be permanent. But it does not exist in heaven: in response to the trick question of the Saddu-cees, Jesus declares, "The children of this age marry and remarry; but those who are deemed worthy to attain the coming age and to the resurrection of the dead neither marry nor are given in marriage" (20:34-35). The sins of the "sinful woman of the city" in Luke 7:36-50 are sexual only through the fantasies of Simon the Pharisee and the reader; that the prodigal son spent his living on prostitutes likewise derives from the imagination of the older son.

In sharp contrast, Luke portrays the prophetic vision in terms of the reversal of human norms, above all with respect to wealth and power: the poor are blessed and the hungry are filled; the rich receive woes and the full will be hungry; the powerful will be cast down from their thrones. Whether in the mouth of Mary, of John, of Jesus, or of the apostles (see Acts 1:18-20; 5:1-11; 8:18-23), the kinds of oppression and sin that God most opposes have to do with the abuse of possessions and power. I will elabo-rate this theme in greater detail in the next chapter, when I consider pro-phetic embodiment. But even on the basis of what has already been shown to be the prophetic focus, churches today should be moved to ask certain questions.

Why, for example, are Christians' conceptions of sin so concentrated on the weaknesses of the flesh rather than on the willful and predatory practices of economic and political oppression of the weak? Does the church have a prophetic vision with respect to power and possessions that can challenge a world in which both economics and politics are so disor-dered? Or is the church too often coopted by the world's vision rather than the prophet's in these areas? How can the church challenge the world's use of power when its own structures of authority exhibit the same patterns of self-seeking and exclusion? How can churches today profess to be Chris-tian when their "prosperity gospel" has no connection with the prophetic vision and so obviously mimics the worst of an acquisitive society that measures worth by wealth? How can the practice of tithing be taken as the mark of the serious evangelical Christian when there is no trace of this practice in the New Testament? At the communal level, it is clear that most churches today would measure "success" in terms of membership and wealth more than in terms of good deeds, would find Luke's ideal of "blessedness" in poverty and persecution to be less persuasive than to be prosperous and popular.

CHAPTER SIX

Prophetic Embodiment

In the tradition of biblical prophecy, as we have seen, the word of God was not only announced verbally by the prophet but was embodied through physical gesture. The prophet's body served as the medium of revelation in speech, yes, but also in symbolic actions, as transparent as marrying a prostitute (Hosea) or as arcane as burying a soiled loincloth (Jeremiah). The conviction that truth was expressed not simply in words but above all in personal behavior — in character — was also widely shared among Greco-Roman philosophers; parodies of false philosophers, such as those deliciously developed by Lucian of Samosata (see, e.g., *Timon*), focused particularly on the gap between a philosopher's fine spoken sentiments and the sordidness of his personal life. How then does Luke's narrative portray the character of Jesus and his disciples? Is this depiction consistent or inconsistent with his understanding of the good news of God's kingdom?

Luke does not show Jesus proceeding in ways that, at least hypothetically, might have been available to someone with a prophetic call in first-century Palestine. He does not gather money from the wealthy or the support of the religious elite; he does not organize his followers into units of economic production or cadres of economic reform; he does not manipulate the obvious mechanisms of political or economic power; he does not — as present-day academics and politicians might — establish a center for messianic studies in the city of Jerusalem.

Instead, Jesus' prophetic challenge is embodied in four interlocking dimensions of his ministry. The focus here is not on what Jesus did; we study that under the rubric of prophetic enactment. Here we look at Luke's depiction of Jesus' prophetic character in terms of poverty, itinerancy, prayer, and servant leadership. I examine each of these characteristics in turn, looking first at the Gospel narrative for what it says about Jesus and what Jesus demands of the disciples. Then, I look at Acts to see how the actual behavior of the disciples conforms to the pattern established by Jesus.

Prophetic Embodiment in the Gospel

Poverty and the Sharing of Possessions

The good news announced by the prophet Jesus is that the kingdom of God belongs to the poor (see 1:52; 6:20; 7:22; 16:19-31). This announcement is not delivered from on high by a member of the privileged population, but by one who is himself among the poor. Jesus speaks to the poor as one of them. Luke shows him embodying poverty even as he announces God's rule to the poor. This depiction begins in Luke's infancy account. I noted earlier how Luke uses narrative midrash to suggest to the reader that the characters who hear and receive God's word are among the "poor of the land" who are to form Israel's remnant.

The circumstances of Jesus' birth, however, point to a degree of actual poverty as well as spiritual receptivity. Luke does not mention any means of economic support for Jesus' family. He omits the identification by the townspeople of Nazareth of Jesus (Mark 6:3) or his father (Matthew 13:55) as a *tektōn*, a wood-craftsman. Luke's lack of interest in Joseph — whose son Jesus was "thought to be" (Luke 3:23) — is striking when compared to Matthew's infancy account, in which Joseph plays the leading role (Matt 1:16, 18, 19, 20, 24; 2:13, 19). Luke's concentration on Mary, a young virgin who becomes pregnant out of wedlock, means as well a focus on the "lowliness" of Jesus' origin (Luke 1:48).

John's birth is announced to a member of the priestly class in the midst of public worship and creates a public commotion (1:8-19, 21-22); Jesus' birth is announced in private to a young woman with no special status (1:26-27). Luke deliberately contrasts the social marginality of this "servant of the Lord" and her exaltation because of "God's favor" (1:30, 38). A similar double contrast is found in Luke's account of the births of John and Jesus. While John's birth to Elizabeth takes place in the rejoicing presence of friends and neighbors and the new-found speech of his father causes fear and excitement throughout the hill country of Judea (1:57-66), Jesus' birth is celebrated by an angelic host praising God (2:13-14). The cosmic celebration, however, makes even starker the actual physical circumstances attending the Messiah's birth: the young parents are far from home; they find no place among other pilgrims; the baby is placed in a feeding bin; and those delivering the angels' message are shepherds, socially and religiously among the most despised occupations held by Jews.

When Jesus announces, "Blessed are you poor" (6:20), then, the reader understands that this man who had spent forty days wandering in the wilderness, filled and led by the Holy Spirit (4:1), is among them as himself a poor man. Jesus' radical poverty is demonstrated by his resistance to the testing of the devil: he spurns the offer of magical food, rule over empires, and guaranteed protection by God, clinging to the words of Scripture that demand absolute obedience to God alone (4:3-12). His marginal social status at birth, when there was no room for him in the inn, is confirmed when he proclaims this good news to the poor in his hometown of Nazareth, where his neighbors rise up, drive him out of the town, and seek to kill him (4:28-29). From this point in the narrative forward, Jesus has no fixed abode, no place of security. He tells those who would follow him, "Foxes have dens and birds of the sky have nests, but the Son of Man has nowhere to rest his head" (9:58). Luke shows Jesus supported by the women who have accepted his message and move with him toward Jerusalem: they "provided for them out of their resources" (8:3). He is dependent as well on the hospitality offered him by others (see 10:38-42; 19:1-10).

Luke's narrative indicates that Jesus' earliest disciples "left everything and followed him," whether it was their livelihood as fishermen (5:11) or as a tax collector (5:28). Peter later states to Jesus, "We have given up our possessions and followed you" (18:28), and is promised that there are none "who have given up house or wife or brothers or parents or children for the sake of the kingdom of God who will not receive an overabundance in this present age and eternal life in the age to come" (18:29-30). He says to his disciples, "Every one of you who does not renounce all his possessions cannot be my disciple" (14:33). When Jesus sends out the Twelve, he tells them, "Take nothing for the journey, neither walking stick, nor sack, nor food, nor money, and let no one take a second tunic. Whatever house you enter, stay there and leave from there" (9:3-4). And he tells the Seventy-two, "Carry no money bag, no sack, no sandals, and greet no one along the way . . . stay in the same house and eat and drink what is offered to you" (10:4, 7). In a word, to be a disciple is to live poor in the same way as Jesus.

Those who fail in their discipleship are those who prefer familial relations and filial responsibility over a commitment to the prophet (9:60-

61): Jesus tells such a one, "no one who puts his hand to the plow and looks to what was left behind is fit for the kingdom of God" (9:62). Paradigmatically, the wealthy ruler who professes the fulfillment of all the commandments, cannot follow Jesus when he is told, "Sell all that you have and distribute it to the poor" because he was "very rich" (18:21-23), leading Jesus to declare, "How hard it is for those who have wealth to enter the kingdom of God" (18:24).

In tension with the demand of radical dispossession is another mode of disposing possessions, namely, through almsgiving. The Sermon on the Plain advocates giving to all who ask without demanding repayment (6:30). Jesus tells the Pharisees to give alms, "and behold, everything will be clean for you" (11:41). He tells his followers, "Sell your belongings and give alms. Provide money bags for yourselves that do not wear out, an inexhaustible treasure in heaven that no thief can reach nor moth destroy" (12:33). He draws the lesson from his parable of the Dishonest Steward (16:1-8) with similar imagery: "I tell you, make friends with yourselves with dishonest wealth, so that when it fails, you will be welcomed into eternal dwellings" (16:9). Zacchaeus the chief tax collector receives Jesus into his house, declaring, "Behold, half my possessions, Lord, I give to the poor, and if I have extorted anything from anyone I shall repay it four times over" (19:8), and Jesus says in reply, "Today salvation has come to this house" (19:9). Finally, in contrast to the Scribes, who are condemned for devouring the houses of widows (20:47), Jesus praises the poor widow who, by donating two small coins into the temple treasury for the poor, "put in more than all the rest; for those others have all made offerings from their surplus wealth, but she, from her poverty, has offered her whole livelihood" (21:2-4).

There is considerable complexity in Luke's specific directives concerning the use of possessions. It is not easy to reconcile radical abandonment of possessions with the ideal of almsgiving. If "giving all to the poor" is a once-for-all gesture, to be sure, then the two can go together. But logically, one is required to have funds in order to share them, and once one has "left everything" it is impossible to fulfill the command of almsgiving. We shall see below how this tension is resolved in Luke's portrayal of the first community in Acts. What is consistent within this complexity, however, is Luke's complete avoidance of wealth and acquisition as the expression of God's kingdom. There is here no prosperity gospel, no identification of fruitfulness with worldly success. The kingdom belongs to the poor and to those whose sharing of possessions with others includes them among the poor.

Itinerancy

Closely related to Jesus' poverty is his itinerancy. He does not have a fixed abode. He does not occupy a cult center. Instead, Luke shows him constantly on the move. Such restlessness or rootlessness most resembles ancient prophets like Elijah and Elisha and Greco-Roman philosophers in the Cynic tradition. After Jesus' forty-day sojourn in the wilderness (4:1-13), Jesus makes the circuit of Galilee (4:14-15) before preaching in his hometown of Nazareth (4:16-30), then moving on to Capernaum (4:31), where in rapid sequence he appears in the synagogue (4:31-37), in Simon's house (4:38-41), and in a deserted region (4:42), before setting out to preach in the synagogues of Judea (4:44). He passes by the Lake of Gennesaret (5:1) and enters another town (5:12). He passes through fields on the Sabbath (6:1), enters a synagogue (6:6), ascends a mountain (6:12), and then descends to a plain (6:17-19) where he delivers a lengthy sermon.

After the sermon, Luke locates Jesus back in Capernaum (7:1) and then immediately in the town of Nain (7:11). In a summary passage unique to his narrative, Luke describes Jesus: "He journeyed from one town and village to another, preaching and proclaiming the good news of the kingdom of God" (8:1). The evangelist draws explicit attention to the peripatetic character of Jesus' ministry. In 8:22, Luke has Jesus set sail, arriving in the "territory of the Gerasenes, which is opposite Galilee" (8:26). He returns to Galilee after healing the man with demons (8:40). All of this movement occurs even prior to Jesus' turn to Jerusalem and long journey there.

As I stated in Chapter One above, Luke is entirely responsible for the construction of the long journey narrative that brings Jesus to Jerusalem and the destiny that awaits God's prophets there. From one perspective, this expansion of his story enables Luke to include a wealth of sayings material that otherwise he would have difficulty fitting into his fast-moving story — since he has chosen to avoid Matthew's practice of inserting long discourses. From another perspective, the journey enables Luke to make a specific point about the character of prophetic embodiment as itinerant. The journey has a formal opening in 9:51: "When the days for his being taken up were fulfilled, he resolutely determined to journey to Jerusalem." The translation "resolutely determined" is correct as to meaning, but it fails to capture the scriptural allusion Luke created by the Greek phrase meaning "he hardened his face," which echoes the language used by the LXX for the prophet Ezekiel, when he is told to "set his face against Jerusalem" and "prophesy against the land of Israel" (Ezek 21:7-8[Eng. vv. 2-3]).

From that point forward, Luke reminds the reader constantly that Jesus is journeying (Luke 9:56; 9:57; 10:1; 10:38). Luke notes in 13:22, "he passed through towns and villages, teaching as he went and making his way to Jerusalem," and in 17:11, "As he continued his journey to Jerusalem, he travelled through Samaria and Galilee." Luke has Jesus approach Jericho (18:35) and then pass through it (19:1) as he drew near to Jerusalem (19:11). He approached Jerusalem (19:28), and as he drew near to it (19:41), he wept over Jerusalem because it did not recognize the time of its visitation (19:44). Because the prophet is always on the move, he has "nowhere to lay his head" (9:58), making this journey narrative a particularly apt means of expressing the importance of hospitality and inhospitality as modes of response to the prophet and his message. Jesus is shown hospitality by Martha and Mary (10:38-42) and by Zacchaeus (19:1-10). He is refused hospitality by the hostile Samaritans (9:51-55). And although he is invited to table by Pharisees and Lawyers, their hostility shows them to be inhospitable to the prophet — their invitations serve as an occasion for testing Jesus (11:37-53; 14:1-6). The supreme inhospitality, to be sure, is shown by the leaders of the people in Jerusalem, who actively seek his death even as the common people throng to hear him teach (19:47-48).

The themes of itinerancy and hospitality are found as well in the commands given to the disciples whom Jesus commissions to expand his prophetic ministry. Luke shares the account of the sending of the Twelve (Luke 9:1-6) with Matt 10:1, 5-15 and Mark 6:7-13: they are to proclaim the kingdom of God and to heal, taking nothing for the journey (9:3), staying in houses that welcome them (9:4), and if not welcomed, shaking the dust from their feet (an apotropaic gesture) as they leave that town. Luke reports that the Twelve "went from village to village" (9:6). When Jesus sets his face to travel to Jerusalem, Luke notes that "he sent messengers ahead of him," who were refused by the Samaritans because they were headed to Jerusalem (9:52-53).

Distinctive to Luke's narrative is the sending of the Seventy-two (10:1-12). Commentators have always puzzled over this apparent duplication in an author who dislikes doublets: what purpose does this sending serve? Does it symbolically anticipate the mission to the Gentiles in Acts? Answers are complicated by the text-critical problem. It is not clear whether Luke intended to write seventy or seventy-two. If the correct reading is seventy, then Luke must intend an allusion to the appointment of seventy elders by the prophet Moses to share in his work with the people (Num 11:16-17), who also have a share in the spirit of prophecy (Num

11:25). In either case, those sent out by Jesus share in the same mission as the Twelve, namely to proclaim the kingdom of God and to heal (10:9); they are to "go on [their] way . . . greet no one along the way" (10:3-4); they are to stay in one house where they are welcomed (10:7); if rejected, they are to move on (10:10-11).

In sum, Luke clearly understands the "Jesus movement" to be precisely that, a mode of God's visitation that is constantly on the move. Prophecy does not find a single center or a secure home. It moves as the Holy Spirit directs, moves lightly and with as little encumbrance as possible. Itinerancy is another way of speaking about prophetic poverty.

Prayer

That prayer is of special interest to Luke has been noted by many readers. Less frequently observed is the way in which Luke's attention to the prayer of Jesus and his disciples is a form of prophetic embodiment. The prophet is led by the spirit not least because the prophet is one who is attentive to the workings of the spirit in prayer. Moses was the Lord's intimate friend because of his prayer (Exod 33:12-17); he "knew the Lord face to face" (Deut 34:10). Elijah was powerful in prayer when he raised the widow's son (1 Kgs 17:20-22) and when he called down fire on the sacrifice prepared for the Lord and then rain for the drought-stricken land (1 Kgs 18:36-45). Isaiah is in prayer in the temple when he sees the Lord, "seated on a high and lofty throne," and receives from the Lord his prophetic commission (Isa 6:1-13). So Luke shows Jesus to be a prophet whose ministry is defined not by a set program but by the practice of prayer.

Every significant moment in Jesus' ministry is marked by prayer. Luke alone among the Gospels portrays Jesus as praying after his baptism at the moment that the Holy Spirit descends on him bodily (Luke 3:21). The effect on the reader is to establish the connection between the activity of prayer and the bestowal of the spirit. And as Jesus is led by the spirit into the wilderness to be tested by Satan, the reader knows that he is able to persevere through this testing because he is a man of prayer. Before he chooses the Twelve, "he departed to the mountain to pray, and he spent the night in prayer to God" (6:12). The choice of his prophetic successor, we are to understand, itself requires the direction of the spirit, and the channel for that discernment is prayer (22:32).

Similarly, Luke shows Jesus "praying in solitude" before asking his disciples concerning his identity (9:18). In his version of the transfiguration (9:28-36), Luke alone attributes to Jesus the express intention for ascending the mountain with his disciples: he "went up the mountain to pray" (9:28). It was, in fact, "while he was praying" that his appearance changes and Moses and Elijah appear with him in glory, speaking of the exodus that Jesus was to accomplish in Jerusalem (9:29-31). Jesus' true identity, spoken to him privately while in prayer at his baptism — "You are my beloved son, with you I am well pleased" (3:22) — is here declared to his closest followers: "This is my chosen son; listen to him" (9:35). And the disciples who reported popular opinions concerning Jesus, that he was one of the ancient prophets or Elijah, here see Jesus' prophetic mission confirmed, as Moses and Elijah discourse with him concerning his destiny in Jerusalem. All this through the experience of prayer; true identity is revealed in the presence of God.

At the Last Supper, Jesus speaks of his prayer in behalf of Peter: "I have prayed that your own faith may not fail, and once you have turned back, you must strengthen your brothers" (22:32). In the garden, before his arrest, Luke describes Jesus kneeling and praying, "Father, if you are willing, take this cup away from me; still not my will but yours be done," and continues, "He was in such agony and he prayed so fervently that his sweat became like drops of blood falling on the ground" (22:41-44). With this prayer, Luke shows how totally Jesus embodies the poverty of those who live by God's rule, the poverty of utter obedience. As his mother has said before him, "Behold the servant of the Lord, be it done to me according to your word" (Luke 1:38), so does Jesus define himself totally by God's will rather than his own.

At the crucifixion, Luke further shows Jesus embodying the prophetic message when he prays for those who have shown themselves his enemies. In his Sermon on the Plain, Jesus told his disciples, "Bless those who curse you; pray for those who mistreat you" (6:28). Now, as the leaders of the people mock him, Jesus prays, "Father, forgive them; they know not what they do" (23:34). The response of total submission to God's will is once again expressed at the moment of Jesus' death, when Jesus prays with the words of Psalm 31:5: "Father, into your hands I commend my spirit" (23:46).

Like Matthew, Luke has Jesus provide his disciples with a sample of prayer. The placement of instruction in each Gospel reminds us of the evangelists' respective methods. Matthew includes the Lord's Prayer in a section of the Sermon on the Mount devoted to modes of piety (Matt 6:1-

18). Luke places the instruction within the context of Jesus' own practice. Luke observes that, while on his journey to Jerusalem, he was praying "in a certain place," and when he had finished, one of his disciples said to him, "Lord, teach us to pray just as John taught his disciples" (11:1). The prayer Jesus teaches them, then, is based in his own practice, and part of Jesus' program of forming his disciples. Luke's version of the prayer is notably shorter and less liturgically shaped than its parallel in Matthew 6:9-13:

> Father, hallowed be your name. Your kingdom come, Give us each day our daily bread and forgive us our sins for we ourselves forgive everyone in debt to us, and do not subject us to the final test. (11:2-4)

With its emphasis on the coming of God's kingdom and on the forgiveness of sins, this prayer sounds much like an epitome of Jesus' prophetic word in the Sermon on the Plain. The further instructions on prayer Jesus gives his disciples in 11:5-13, however, provide a turn on his command to give without expecting a return. In relationship with God, it appears, constant demand is not out of place: the client is expected to be persistent in making requests of the patron. The parable of the "Friend at Midnight" concludes with the lesson, "He will get up to give him whatever he needs because of his persistence" (11:8). Likewise, the command to ask, seek, and knock in the expectation of receiving, finding, and entering is based on the conviction that God as a loving father will give what the children need. Luke's fascinating version of the conclusion, moreover, draws once more the connection between prayer and the Holy Spirit: "How much more will the Father in heaven give the Holy Spirit to those who ask him?" (11:9-13). The same point about persistence in prayer is the subject of another journey parable, this one about the persistent widow who demands of an unjust judge what is her due; Jesus tells this parable to his disciples, Luke tells the reader "about the necessity for them to pray always without becoming weary" (18:1-8).

The final plea of the Lord's Prayer was "Do not subject us to the final test." The Greek term *peirasmos* is, literally, "testing." After his baptism, Luke showed us the man of prayer Jesus, full of the Holy Spirit, being led by the spirit into the wilderness, where he was "tested" by the devil (4:1-2). Having failed to turn the prophet Jesus from his obedience to God, when the devil had finished all this test, he left him for a time (4:13). The time of Jesus' arrest, trial, and death is now another time of testing by Satan, who enters into Judas (22:3) and is sifting the disciples like wheat (22:31). Jesus, we have already seen, prays for Peter that he can later strengthen his fellows (22:32). And when Jesus enters the garden to pray, he tells his disciples both before and after his agony, "Pray that you may not undergo the test" (22:40, 46).

Perseverence in prayer is required not only in times of crisis but also in order to remain faithful to the commitment of faith. In Jesus' exhortation to his disciples concerning the future, he declares in words that clearly echo the interpretation of the parable of the Sower (8:14):

> Beware that your hearts do not become drowsy from carousing and drunkenness and the anxieties of daily life, and that day catch you by surprise like a trap. For that day will assault everyone on the face of the earth. Be vigilant at all times and pray that you have the strength to escape the tribulations that are imminent and to stand before the Son of Man. (21:34-36)

Servant Leadership

The people the prophet gathers around himself as the remnant of Israel is constituted by faith. After establishing Jesus in chapters 3–7 as the prophet who brings God's visitation to the people, Luke devotes chapter 8 in particular to the forming of this people. It is here we learn that as the prophet sows the word of God (8:11), "those who hear the word of God and keep it" (8:19-21) are the ones who make up the people. Throughout this section of his narrative, Luke stresses the response of faith (7:50; 8:25, 48, 50) as that which "saves," that is, restores those in need to full participation in the people.

Luke makes no discrimination among those who have the faith that saves — there is equality among the members of this prophetic community. Luke provides an initial glimpse of the people forming around Jesus in Galilee: the Twelve and some women who had been cured of evil spirits and infirmities — these provide support out of their resources. As Jesus moves toward Jerusalem and his death, Luke shows him gathering disciples around him and instructing them in prayer, the use of possessions, and perseverance. When Jesus enters the city, Luke has him greeted "by a whole multitude of his disciples" (19:37).

Because the Twelve are to follow the prophet Jesus as leaders over Israel (22:30) — the implication of Luke's parable of the Pounds in its narrative context (see 19:11-27) — Luke is particularly concerned to connect his mode of leadership and theirs. It is a mode that challenges the conventional understanding of power and patronage in the ancient world. The Twelve are to share in Jesus' ministry of proclaiming God's rule and enacting that rule through healing (9:2); like Jesus, they are to receive support by way of hospitality (9:4). But Luke is also concerned that the Twelve be schooled in a mode of leadership like his own.

The first such lesson occurs when Jesus feeds the five thousand, immediately upon the return and report by the Twelve of what they had accomplished (9:10-17). Luke draws a close connection between their delegated mission and his when he has Jesus receive the crowd that gathers and speak to them about the kingdom of God, and heal those who needed to be cured (9:11). When the Twelve urge Jesus to allow the crowd to find provisions, he tells them, "Give them some food yourselves" (9:13). Then Jesus blesses the loaves and fishes, "and gave them to the disciples to set before the crowd" (9:16). Luke here connects prophetic leadership with the service of others and establishes the symbol of table service as the marker of genuine leadership.

The second lesson in countercultural leadership occurs on the journey to Jerusalem, immediately after Jesus' second prediction of his passion, and it has two aspects. The disciples fall into a dispute over who was the greatest among them. Jesus puts a child in their midst and declares that receiving such a child in Jesus' name is to receive Jesus himself (9:46-48). He then states, "For the one who is least among all of you is the one who is the greatest" (9:48). The measure for "greatness" must change within the rule of God: becoming great means becoming little. As Luke has Jesus say twice in his narrative, "Everyone who exalts himself will be humbled, and everyone who humbles himself will be exalted" (14:11; 18:14). Such humility is reinforced by the next incident: the disciples want to prevent someone casting out demons in Jesus' name "because he does not follow in our company" (9:49). Jesus reminds them that the point of leadership is not membership in an exclusive club, but advancing the kingdom of God: "Do not prevent him, for whoever is not against you is for you" (9:50).

The third lesson is embedded in a set of parables Jesus tells his disciples during the journey to Jerusalem. The first compares the sort of vigilance and alertness they should have in awaiting the Son of Man to the eager expectation of servants awaiting their master's return from a wedding: they should be ready at all times, "for at an hour you do not expect, the Son of Man will come" (12:35-40). Intriguingly, Luke has Peter interject a question at this point, "Lord, is this parable meant for us, or for everyone?"

(12:41). Jesus responds with another parable, concerning the "faithful and prudent steward whom the master will put in charge of his servants to distribute the food allowance at the proper time" (12:42). The effect of Peter's question is to shift attention from all servants to those put in charge of servants; we therefore understand his question — "is it meant for us?" — to refer to the Twelve. We note that they are set over other servants and that they are to "serve" them by allotting the food they require; we see again the symbolism of table service for leadership. The parable makes clear that an abuse of leadership is to treat those under them badly while seeking their own pleasure and that all authority is answerable to the master, who will punish those who use their authority wrongly: "Much will be required of the person entrusted with much, and still more will be required of the person entrusted with more" (12:42-48).

The fourth and final lesson is given at the Last Supper. Immediately after Jesus shares with them the bread and cup that signify "my body which will be given for you" and "my blood which will be shed for you" (22:19-20) — in gestures that vividly recall his feeding of the five thousand — and after Jesus predicts that one of them will betray him (22:21-22), the disciples fall into an argument, first over who might betray Jesus (22:23) and then "which of them should be regarded as the greatest" (22:24). It is difficult to conceive a more poignant juxtaposition of prophetic embodiment and the mind-set of the world, here expressed by those chosen to be the prophet's representatives. Luke has Jesus respond in a manner that makes clear both that the Twelve are to hold positions of leadership over Israel (22:29-30) and that the manner of that leadership must be in accord with the prophetic reversal of values expressed in the Sermon on the Plain.

In contrast to the "kings and those in authority" among the nations, whose leadership is expressed through power ("lord it over them") and who receive the honor of being called "benefactors," authority in God's people is to be measured by the status of those who are youngest — remember the child in 9:47-48 — and the leader is to be a servant (using the Greek verb *diakonein* in 22:26, with specific reference to table service). Luke then has Jesus develop the table service image of leadership: "Who is greater, the one who sits at table or the one who serves? Is it not the one who is seated at table?" The observation contains the same realistic appreciation of conventional social status that is reflected as well in Jesus' statements concerning seating positions at a banquet in 14:7-10. This is the way the world is: the people who sit and are served are greater than those who serve them; Luke has Jesus make the same point in 17:7-10. The point, then, is not to place the Twelve in the position of being served, but rather in the position of those serving: leadership is not benefaction at the whim of the patron, it is service to the needs of others. Luke startlingly connects this understanding of leadership by the Twelve to Jesus' own authority among them. He has just served them at table, with his own body and blood! So Luke has Jesus say, with utter simplicity, "I am among you as the one who serves" (22:27). As Jesus embodies the countercultural prophetic vision through his own leadership, so are the disciples to embody the same manner of leadership within the messianic and prophetic community.

With impressive consistency, Luke has characterized Jesus and the disciples in a manner consistent with the word of God announced by the prophet. Jesus embodies the prophetic message in his manner of life and instructs his disciples in the same dispositions. The themes of prayer, poverty, itinerancy, and service leadership, we see, are not random, but are internally consistent and interrelated aspects of that faith which "hears the word of God and does it." The disposition of prayer places one in attendance on God and in receptivity to God's Holy Spirit, rather than with reference to human rulers or conventional social expectations. Poverty indicates a complete reliance on the God who gives graciously and in abundant measure to those who ask in prayer, freeing the one who has "been given the kingdom" to share possessions with others rather than cling to them as a means of security. Similarly, itinerancy declares that the one who attends to God's spirit has nothing to lose and is free to move as the spirit directs. Since security is not sought in place, family, friends, or wealth, faith can move into spaces that might otherwise be frightening, expecting a hospitable reception among those of good heart. Servant leadership, finally, makes the most powerful statement — because most public, visible, and contrastive — that the measure of the kingdom is not the measure of the world and that the function of power within the prophetic people is to empower others.

Prophetic Embodiment in Acts

In order to appreciate the way in which Luke continues to show Jesus' disciples as embodying the prophetic word in Acts, we need to shift the question from the individual to the community and ask about the extent to which Luke shows the reader a church that has a radical character. The answer to this question is of the greatest importance for interpreting Acts. I suggested earlier how some readers understand the powerful spirit at work in the apostles through signs and wonders as a form of theology of glory: the institution of the church in Acts, therefore, must necessarily be triumphalistic. Such a reading misses the point of Luke's prophetic characterization. He has shown in the Gospel how the power working signs and wonders is God's, and how the authority of the prophet is expressed through servant leadership. If Luke continues to show prophetic embodiment in the new community formed by the Holy Spirit in Acts, this means that, in his view, the Jesus movement reached its full expression in the earliest church and was at least as radical in its character as was the one through whose spirit it exists.

The question of prophetic embodiment in the church of Acts is also of first importance for self-examination by the present-day church. Christians today might be tempted to dismiss the radical characterization of Jesus: he acts the way he does because he is son of God, or he has special prophetic gifts that are unique to him. If such is the case, then the contemporary church can admire but need not worry about emulating Jesus' radical manner of life. But if the church in Acts — clearly a community and institution that exists over generations and spans nations — is portrayed in equally radical terms, then the church today is more directly challenged. There is no real reason why the prophetic spirit that expressed itself in radical terms among the apostles might not also find such embodiment today.

The place to start the analysis is clearly the two descriptions of the first community's life in 2:41-47 and 4:32-37. These passages have long been recognized as distinctively Lukan summaries, which he uses to expand and generalize on the few specific stories available to him. By means of such summaries, Luke gives amplitude to an account that otherwise might seem overly spare. Readers have also perceived how Luke's language in these passages concerning unity and the sharing of possessions echoes that of foundation stories occurring in Hellenistic philosophers, with the strongest resemblances to the accounts in Iamblichus and Porphyry of the founding of the Pythagorean school. The nature of these passages suggests that Luke had maximum freedom for expressing his understanding of the community that was shaped by the prophetic spirit poured out on them by Jesus (Acts 1:8; 2:4, 17-18, 33, 38).

In 2:41-47, Luke describes the internal community life of the three thousand who were added by baptism to the initial 120 who had gathered before Pentecost to await the Holy Spirit (1:15). Concerning the apostles,

Luke notes that the community was "devoted to" their teaching (2:42) and that "signs and wonders were done through the apostles" (2:43). The two items correspond to Jesus' command to the Twelve in Luke 9:1-6 to proclaim the kingdom of God (teach) and heal (signs and wonders). No further attention is given to the authority of the Twelve in this description. In addition to their devotion to the apostles' teaching, Luke focuses on three activities of the first believers. First, they prayed and gave praise to God (Acts 2:42, 47). Second, they practiced fellowship *(koinōnia)*. Luke seems to have in mind two discrete practices in this respect: they "broke bread" in their houses and ate together (2:46); and they shared their possessions. Luke gives particular attention to this:

> All who believed were together and had all things in common; they would sell their property and possessions and divide them among all according to each one's need. (2:44-45)

Third, they met together every day in the temple area (2:46). This practice prepares for the next sequence of stories that take place in the temple precincts — especially the very next story, in which Peter's healing in the name of Jesus restores to a lame man participation in the temple worship (3:1-7) — and it also continues the careful exposition concerning the temple that Luke had woven into the Gospel narrative. We remember that when he drove merchants out of the temple, Jesus had declared, "It is written, 'My house shall be a house of prayer, but you have made it a den of thieves'" (Luke 19:46). After that prophetic act of cleansing (echoing Isa 56:7 and Jer 7:11), Jesus in effect occupies the temple area as the place for his daily public teaching (Luke 19:47; 20:1; 21:1; 22:53), and it is actually within the temple area that he predicts its destruction (21:5-6). Showing the prophetic community at prayer and praise in the temple indicates that this is the authentic Israel that fulfills the intended role of the temple as a "house of prayer."

Finally, Luke describes the internal dispositions of the believers and the response of outsiders. The believers take their food with "exaltation and simplicity of heart" (Acts 2:46). The first term echoes the language of the infancy account for the birth of John, Elizabeth's recognition of Mary as the mother of her Lord, and Mary's song of praise (Luke 1:14, 44, 47). It is the same Greek term used by Luke for Jesus' exaltation "in the Holy Spirit" when he praised God for revealing not to the wise and learned but to the childlike (Luke 10:21). The term "simplicity of heart" recalls the dispositions advocated by the Sermon on the Plain and exemplified by those who hear the word of God and "embrace it with a generous and good heart" (Luke 8:15). In the first description, Luke portrays the response of ordinary people to be entirely positive: "fear" or "awe" comes on them all (Acts 2:43), and the entire people shows favor *(charis)* toward the believers. As a result, "every day the Lord added to their number those who were being saved" (2:47).

Luke had considerable leeway in depicting the first believers. The points of emphasis in his description indicate the two major impressions he wanted to make on his reader. The impression that best serves his overall narrative purposes is the portrayal of the church as the restored Israel according to the spirit. By emphasizing the positive response of the people, the gathering of the people in the temple area, their life of prayer and praise, and their eschatological exaltation, Luke shows how "God's visitation" through the prophet whom God raised up created a people, in Zechariah's words, "that, rescued from the hand of enemies, without fear . . . might worship him in holiness and righteousness before him all our days" (Luke 1:74-75).

But by emphasizing their attention to the apostles' teaching, the working of signs and wonders, the sharing of possessions, the practice of prayer, and their simplicity of heart, Luke also indicates that this is a people formed according to the prophetic vision first enunciated by Jesus. They have "save[d] [themselves] from this corrupt generation" and committed themselves to the countercultural mode of life demanded by the prophet as the works that demonstrate repentance. It is perhaps worth noting that the notes of servant leadership and itinerancy are not struck in this first passage. Both will appear later in the narrative. By placing the first community in the environs of the temple, however, Luke indirectly asserts something about the first community as diasporic in character. It does not build its own place, establish its own center. The believers break bread in their houses and gather in the temple for prayer. But this is only a temporary place. Even before the temple is destroyed, the people are able and willing to move elsewhere according to the direction of the Holy Spirit.

Luke provides a second description of community life in Acts 4:32-37, again following a powerful outpouring of the Holy Spirit in response to prayer (4:23-31). In this summary, we find two elements listed also in 2:42-47: the apostles bear witness to the resurrection of the Lord Jesus "with great power" and the community enjoyed great favor — it is not clear whether this is from the populace, as in 2:47, or from God (4:33). Otherwise, the passage focuses completely on the sharing of possessions. The believers were "of one heart and mind," virtually a definition for friendship in antiquity; and "no one called anything his own." The axiom for friendship was "friends hold all things in common," and Luke states that among the believers, "all things were common" (4:32).

Two aspects of this sharing are stressed. By observing that "there was no needy person among them," Luke makes clear allusion to Deut 15:4, which promises that when Israel keeps all the commandments concerning the land, there would be no poor among them. The first believers' sharing of possessions signals, once more, the realization of the authentic Israel restored through the spirit of prophecy. Luke also places the apostles at the heart of the practice of sharing possessions. Now, those who owned property or houses would sell them, bringing the proceeds of the sale and lay them at the feet of the apostles, who would, in turn, "distribute to each one according to need" (4:35). The specific example is Barnabas, who sold a field and "brought the money and put it at the feet of the apostles" (4:37) — foreshadowing the future narrative role of this "son of consolation" (see Acts 9:27; 11:22-24, 30; 12:25).

Placing the apostles at the heart of the sharing of possessions — having the goods put at their feet and then having them distribute to others — represents the biggest difference between the first and second descriptions of community life and serves an important narrative function within Luke's overall story. Immediately after the first description and Peter's speech following the healing of the lame man in the temple precincts, the apostles are hauled before the Sanhedrin and warned not to speak in Jesus' name (4:1-22). The narrative question is whether they or the Jewish court truly "rules Israel." Following this first arrest, the apostles are powerfully filled with the Holy Spirit (4:23-31) and are shown to hold unquestioned authority within the community — they receive possessions from the faithful, and they strike dead those who falsify this sharing (5:1-11); when they travel in the street, "signs and wonders" are done even by the casting of their shadow (5:12-16). When the Sanhedrin tries to arrest them a second time, they are not able to keep them in prison and are reduced to feeble resistance (5:17-42).

Luke has thus shown the Twelve to "sit on thrones judging the twelve tribes of Israel" (Luke 22:30). They are the true authorities within the restored prophetic people. At the same time, having the apostles not only receive the goods placed at their feet but also distributing to each one according to need, Luke continues to develop the theme of servant leadership. In imitation of the Jesus who declared, "I am among you as the one who serves" (Luke 22:27), they serve at the table by distributing goods to others. Finally, Luke's two descriptions show the distinctive way in which a community can fulfill the radical demands of the prophet in a manner that no individual can. We saw in the Gospel that there was a tension between the command to leave all one's possessions to follow Jesus, and the command to give alms. But a community can do both, for by sharing everything, they both "call nothing their own" and "give to each one as needed."

By placing these two descriptions of community life immediately after bestowals of the prophetic spirit, and by putting them at the very beginning of Acts, Luke indicates to his readers his understanding of the church as the embodiment of the prophetic word. In the history of Christianity, it is worth noting, these passages have served to inspire radical forms of communal discipleship. It was hearing Jesus' command to the rich man to sell all his possessions and follow him that impelled Antony to leave all he owned to his sister and plunge into a life of prayer in the wilderness. But for the founders of the coenobite (communal) form of monasticism — Augustine, Basil, John Cassian, Benedict of Nursia — these passages in Acts described the nature of the "apostolic" Christianity they sought to emulate. The radical Anabaptist reformation likewise found precedent for their poor and countercultural form of discipleship in Luke's description of the primitive church, and appeal to that example continues in Mennonite and Hutterite communities. Present-day Christian communities based in liberation theology similarly find in these passages an inspiration for their vision of the church as one in which all things are shared alike.

The Christians through the ages who have based their own radical forms of discipleship precisely on the apostolic church in Acts stand opposed to the scholarly habit — based, to be sure, in a distinctively Protestant reading of Paul — of regarding Acts as advocating institutional and theological triumphalism. In my view, those who see Luke as portraying ideal Christianity in terms of a prophetic embodiment that is radical and countercultural, rather than accommodating and comfortable, read him more rightly than do the academics who fail to grasp either Luke's literary methods or religious vision. But there is still more evidence to consider. We have yet to look at the rest of the Acts narrative, to see whether the four marks of prophetic embodiment — poverty, itinerancy, prayer, and servant leadership — are consistently ascribed to the church of the apostles.

Poverty/Possessions

Following the description of the community sharing of possessions in 2:42-47 and 4:32-37 — as well as the "falsification of the spirit" represented by the conspiracy to withhold possessions by Ananias and Sapphira (5:1-11) — Luke provides another glimpse of the Jerusalem community's practice of sharing possessions in his account of the dispute that arose over the feeding of the Hebrew and Hellenist widows (6:1-6), a conflict that necessitated a decision to expand ministry within the community. Since the feeding of orphans, widows, and sojourners was a common obligation taken on by Jewish synagogues, attested also among the early Christians in 1 Timothy 5:3-16, Luke once more shapes his portrait of the church as the restored Israel that observes all the commandments of Torah ensuring there be "no needy person among them" (Deut 15:4). By showing the community devoting its resources to those totally unable to reciprocate, furthermore, Luke indicates that it embodies the prophetic mandate of giving to others without expecting a return (Luke 6:30-35).

Consistent with the Gospel narrative, Luke uses a character's disposition of possessions as a character indicator. In Joppa lived a disciple named Tabitha who was "completely occupied with good deeds and almsgiving" (Acts 9:36) and who appears to live at the center of a community of poor widows (9:39). Like the Gentile centurion in Luke's Gospel, of whom Jesus is told, "he loves our nation and he built the synagogue for us" (Luke 7:5), the Gentile centurion Cornelius in Caesarea is identified as one who was "devout and God-fearing along with his whole household, who used to give alms generously to the Jewish people and pray to God constantly" (Acts 10:2). Cornelius is told by the angel that "your prayers and almsgiving have ascended as a memorial offering before God" (10:4). By focusing on his prayer and sharing of possessions, Luke identifies Cornelius as one who lives by the prophetic program even before hearing the good news. He is, as Peter subsequently states, among the righteous: "In every nation whoever fears him and acts uprightly is acceptable to him" (10:35). In the case of both Tabitha and Cornelius, furthermore, the household hospitality shown Peter further demonstrates openness to the prophetic visitation (9:38-41; 10:24-33).

In three ways, Luke shows Paul embodying the prophetic word through the use of possessions. As noted earlier, when Paul addresses the elders of the church of Ephesus he describes his personal practice as based in the words of Jesus:

I have never wanted anyone's silver or gold or clothing. You know very well that these very hands have served my needs and my companions. In every way I have shown you that by hard work of that sort we must help the weak, and keep in mind the words of the Lord Jesus who himself said, "It is more blessed to give than to receive." (Acts 20:33-35)

Although Luke — undoubtedly for reasons of his own — does not explicitly state that Paul gathered a collection for the church in Jerusalem from among his Gentile communities, something that, according to the letters, occupied much of Paul's time and effort (Gal 2:10; 1 Cor 16:1-4; 2 Cor 8–9, Rom 15:25-29), he does have Paul state in his defense before Felix, "After many years I came to bring alms for my nation and offerings" (Acts 24:17), leading the prefect to anticipate receiving a bribe from him (24:26). Finally, Luke shows Paul as intimately involved in the collection for the Jerusalem church taken up by the church in Antioch. Because the great famine threatened the church in Jerusalem, "the disciples determined that, according to ability, each should send relief to the brothers who lived in Judea. This they did, sending it to the presbyters in care of Barnabas and Saul" (11:29-30). Just before the two are commissioned for their itinerant mission in 13:1-4, Luke takes care in 12:25 to note that they had completed "their relief mission" *(diakonia)*.

With respect to the use of possessions, then, Luke shows the church to be thoroughly in line with the prophetic word announced by Jesus. There is no trace of ecclesiastical wealth or the desire for wealth. Indeed, when Simon Magus offers money to acquire the power to bestow the spirit (8:18-19), he is told by Peter, "May your money perish with you, because you thought you could buy the gift of God with money. You have no share or lot in this matter, for your heart is not upright before God. Repent of this wickedness of yours and pray to the Lord, that, if possible, your intention may be forgiven" (8:20-22). The translation "share or lot in this matter" does not quite capture the Greek phrase, which suggests a sharing in the prophetic word from which Simon's self-aggrandizement excludes him. The mark of true discipleship in Acts is the sharing of possessions, especially with those most needy. The greatest difference in this part of Luke's narrative is that such sharing is embodied by the practice not only of individuals (Peter, Barnabas, Tabitha, Cornelius, Paul), but by the community of disciples as such.

Itinerancy

I suggested that in the Gospel narrative the Jesus movement truly was a "movement" because Jesus and the disciples were constantly in motion. I also suggested that itinerancy is a dimension of poverty: lack of a proper location and the willingness to move anywhere in response to the promptings of the spirit demand a complete dependence on God and on the willingness of others to provide hospitality. Itinerancy in this sense is another name for homelessness.

The first impression one gets of the church in Jerusalem is that it is settled in that place. But I suggested above that Luke already points to a certain marginality with respect to place when he describes the first believers as gathering in the temple precincts while they are selling field and house to provide for the needs of others. But immediately after the death of Stephen, Luke suggests that only the apostles stay in Jerusalem, while other disciples are "scattered" through Judea and Samaria. This small notice sets the pattern for the remainder of the narrative, which shows the prophetic message spreading across the Mediterranean world and its proclaimers constantly on the move. As I observed earlier, Luke makes the continuation of the gospel mission unmistakable by having the disciples travel two by two (in fulfillment of Jesus' command in Luke 10:1) and shake the dust off their feet when they are rejected (Acts 13:51; see Luke 9:5; 10:11).

Peter and John visit the church in Samaria (8:14) before returning to Jerusalem (8:25). Peter travels on his own to Lydda (9:32), Joppa (9:36), Caesarea (10:24), and back to Jerusalem (11:2), before leaving "for another place" (12:17) after his escape from prison. Luke brings him back to Jerusalem for the council deciding the inclusion of the Gentiles in 15:7. Philip, another one filled with the prophetic spirit, travels to Samaria (8:5) and then to Gaza (8:26) before being snatched by the spirit and ending in Azotus and other towns on the way to Caesarea (8:39-40). Hellenists travel from Jerusalem to Antioch where they proclaim the good news to the Greeks (11:19-20). Barnabas travels from Jerusalem to the church in Antioch (11:22), then to Tarsus to pick up Paul (11:25) and bring him to Antioch (11:26), and from there delivers (with Paul) the collection for the church in Jerusalem (11:30).

Paul travels from Damascus, where he was instructed in the faith and baptized (9:18), to Jerusalem (9:26) to join the community there. He is sent on to Tarsus (9:30) and then brought by Barnabas to Antioch (11:26). After completing the delivery of the collection to Jerusalem (11:30; 12:25), Paul and Barnabas together are commissioned by the church in Antioch (13:2) and travel to Cyprus (13:4), Antioch of Pisidia (13:14), Iconium (14:1), Lystra and Derbe (14:6, 8, 20), and then circle back through the same communities (14:21). They then make their way through Pisidia to Pamphylia (14:24), to Perga and Attalia (14:25), before arriving back at Antioch (14:26), and then, in response to controversy, to the council in Jerusalem (15:2). After the dispute with Barnabas, Paul travels with Silas (and Timothy) through Syria and Cilicia (15:41) to Lystra (16:1) and the Phrygian and Galatian territory (16:6). He moves from Troas (16:8) to Neapolis and Philippi (16:11-12), then to Thessalonica (17:1), Beroea (17:10), Athens (17:15), and Corinth (18:1). After some time, he travels to Ephesus (18:19), Caesarea (18:22), Antioch (18:22), Galatia and Phrygia (18:23), and back to Ephesus (19:1). Again after some time, he travels to Macedonia (20:1), Greece (20:2), back to Philippi (20:6), then to Troas (20:6), Miletus (20:14-15), Tyre (21:1-6), Ptolemaeus, and Caesarea (21:8), and finally to Jerusalem (21:17). As a prisoner, he moves from Jerusalem to Caesarea (23:23), and then is taken on a lengthy and dangerous sea voyage that ends in shipwreck (27:1-44). He moves from Malta (28:1-10) by stages to Rome (28:16).

The impressive journeys of Peter, Philip, Paul, Barnabas, and Silas are coordinated with the movements of minor characters: the prophets who come to Antioch from Jerusalem (11:27) or who deliver the apostolic letter from Jerusalem to the churches of Antioch, Syria, and Cilicia (15:22-23, 30-32) before being sent back to Jerusalem (15:33); Silas and Timothy, who travel from Thessalonica to meet Paul in Corinth (18:5); Priscilla and Aquila, who come from Rome to Corinth (18:2) and then travel from Corinth to Ephesus (18:26-27); Apollos, who comes from Alexandria to Ephesus and is sent by the disciples to Corinth (18:24-27). This constant movement and mission depicts a church that responds to the promptings of the spirit and is not defined in terms of place; the church emphatically continues the prophetic style of itinerancy practiced and commanded by the prophet Jesus.

Prayer

The Gospel emphasized the prayer of the prophet Jesus as the practice that enabled the communication of the Holy Spirit and the discernment of God's will in the concrete circumstances of his life; the Gospel also showed Jesus teaching his disciples how to pray, above all with perseverance. The narrative of Acts is rich in its display of this form of prophetic embodiment among the disciples. Even before Pentecost, those who had come from Galilee and gathered around the Eleven "devoted themselves with one accord to prayer" (Acts 1:14). The assembly likewise prayed to be shown who was to replace Judas among the Twelve (1:24). The community thus shows itself, just as Jesus did at his baptism, prepared for the outpouring of the prophetic spirit (2:1-4).

The community that responded to Peter's proclamation by being baptized also received the Holy Spirit (2:38) and "devoted themselves . . . to the prayers" (2:42), as shown by the intense petition expressed "with one accord" by the gathered associates of the Twelve after the first harassment by the Sanhedrin (4:23-30). The connection between prayer and the spirit is shown vividly by Luke's description of the outcome: "As they prayed, the place where they were gathered shook, and they were all filled with the Holy Spirit and continued to speak the word of God with boldness" (4:31). As in the Pentecost story, it is the community as such and not simply an individual that receives the spirit and speaks God's word. Luke shows the Jerusalem community gathered again in prayer when Peter is imprisoned (12:12) and the church at Antioch at worship when the Holy Spirit commissions Barnabas and Paul for their ministry (13:2-3)

Luke also shows individual prophetic characters in acts engaged in prayer. In imitation of Jesus at his death, Stephen cries out as he is being stoned, "Lord Jesus, receive my spirit" (Acts 7:59; see Luke 23:46), and, embodying both the command of Jesus' concerning forgiveness (Luke 6:35) and the example of Jesus at his death (Luke 23:34), he asks forgiveness for his enemies: "Lord, do not hold this sin against them" (Acts 7:60). Peter prays before raising Tabitha from the dead (9:40). Both Peter and Cornelius are at prayer when they experience the visions that set in motion a new stage of God's visitation (10:2, 9, 30; 11:5).

Paul in particular is a man of constant prayer. He remains in prayer after his encounter with the risen Lord (9:11). In his later defense speech before the Jerusalem Jews, Paul reports that while praying in the temple he experienced a vision of Jesus (22:17-18). Paul and Barnabas appoint elders in local churches "with prayer and fasting" (14:23). It is when they are seeking "a place for prayer" that Paul meets Lydia and exorcizes the slave girl with an oracular spirit (16:13, 16), and while in the Philippi jail, Paul and Barnabas "were praying and singing hymns to God as the prisoners listened," when an earthquake frees them from their captivity (16:25). On his way to Jerusalem and his final arrest, Paul prays together with the Ephesian elders at Miletus (20:36); in the same fashion, he kneels on the beach to pray with all the believers at Caesarea (21:5). When Paul declares his determination to continue to Jerusalem despite prophecies of his death, the community responds, "The Lord's will be done" (21:14). When he and his shipmates were in deadly peril because of the storm at sea, Paul "gave thanks to God in front of them all, broke [bread], and began to eat. They were all encouraged and took some food themselves" (27:35-36). Finally, when landed on Malta, Paul prays before laying hands on the father of Publius and healing him (28:8).

In sum, the narrative of Acts displays the consistent embodiment of the prophetic word with respect to prayer, consistent both with the command and practice of Jesus. The prophetic leaders and the community as a whole engage in prayer, not as a matter of formal ritual — although Luke never suggests that such formal prayer is problematic — but as a matter of prophetic consciousness: prayer is the place above all where empowerment by the Holy Spirit can happen.

Servant Leadership

This aspect of prophetic embodiment is particularly important for properly assessing Luke's understanding of the church in Acts. The very first thing that should be stated is that, as soon as one speaks about a community rather than an individual, issues of boundary and authority necessarily come into play. It is a sociological fantasy to conceive of a "charismatic community" with no structure and no decision-making apparatus. There are necessarily going to be elements in Luke's depiction of the church, therefore, that are lacking in his portrayal of Jesus and the disciples on the road. The real question is the extent to which his portrayal of institution and authority has a character consistent with the prophet's vision of a countercultural people.

Several aspects of Luke's depiction of leadership in Acts are immediately striking when compared, for example, to a contemporary Jewish sectarian movement. At Qumran, there is a distinct hierarchical authority structure that imitates the biblical legislation for the temple cult: leadership is conceived in terms of priests and Levites. Such leadership is theologically legitimated, furthermore, by the ideological conviction that the Dead Sea community is the authentic temple where the spiritual sacrifices of study and prayer are offered to God — in contrast to the corrupt worship and leadership in the Jerusalem temple. Luke lacks either a hierarchical structure of leadership or an elaborate theological legitimation for leadership. He treats respectively the charismatic leadership of the Twelve and others who are "filled with the spirit" as apostles and witnesses, and whose ministry, as we have seen, is almost entirely itinerant, and the local leadership over specific communities exercised by "elders."

Although Luke wants to show the Twelve as "ruling over the tribes of Israel" (Luke 22:30) and, as I have shown, emphasizes the authority of Peter and John particularly over the people, in contrast to the decreasing ability of the Sanhedrin to stop the prophetic movement, it is equally the case that he conceives of their authority in terms of the servant leadership mandated and exemplified by the prophet Jesus. Thus, although the placing of possessions at the feet of the apostles (Acts 4:34-35, 37; 5:2) symbolizes the recognition of their authority within the community, Luke's description of the same apostles as distributing the goods to each one according to need also continues the theme of leadership as table service established by the Gospel (Luke 9:10-16; 12:35-48; 22:25-30).

The same symbolism is employed in Luke's account of the choice of the Seven in Acts 6:1-6. Readers have often puzzled over the fact that the proposed solution to the crisis of the neglect of Hellenist widows made little practical sense. The withdrawal of the Twelve is inadequately compensated by the addition of the Seven. And in fact, the Seven do not wait on tables in the literal sense. Stephen and Philip are described as prophets and exercise the "ministry of the word" in the same manner as the Twelve, leaving — if we are to be rigorously logical — no one to feed the widows! The best explanation for the anomalies is that the story was really about the transmission of authority from the Twelve to others, and that a prophetic authority — using the imagery of "waiting on tables" to signify that this authority, like that of the Twelve — must conform to the pattern of service taught and practiced by Jesus.

Luke's perception that apostolic authority should be for the service of others rather than the glory of the minister is made clear as well by the instances in which both Peter and Paul deflect efforts to honor them as more than human. When Peter enters Cornelius's house, the centurion "falling at his feet, paid him homage," and Peter responds, "Get up, I myself am also a human being" (10:25-26). Even more dramatically, when Paul heals a lame man in Lystra, the native population sought to honor him as Hermes and Barnabas as Zeus, saying, "The gods have come among us in human form" (14:11). Paul and Barnabas tear their garments in response, and Paul declares, "Men, why are you doing this? We are of the same nature as you, human beings. We proclaim to you good news that you should turn from these idols to the living God who made heaven and earth and sea and all that is in them" (14:15).

Even more remarkable, Luke shows the prophetic leaders as eschewing an authoritarian mode in favor of collaborative discernment and decision-making. In the account of the election of Matthias (1:15-26), for example, Peter identifies the issue for the gathered assembly and interprets it through the citation of Scripture, but it is the assembly that puts forward two candidates over whom the community then prays for God's choice of who would replace Judas in the circle of the Twelve. Similarly, in the crisis over the need for an expanded ministry (6:1-6), the Twelve identify the problem and ask the community to nominate from among their number seven men; the apostles then pray and lay hands on those chosen. When the church in Jerusalem is presented with the challenge of a former enemy (Saul) seeking a place in its fellowship, Barnabas sponsors Paul, presenting the story of his conversion and prior ministry to the apostles; they accept him, and he practices his ministry in their midst (9:26-29). But when the Hellenists seek to kill Paul, it is "the brothers" who secure his safety by taking him to Caesarea and sending him on to Tarsus (9:30).

The most impressive example of servant leadership is displayed in Luke's long narrative about the beginning of the Gentile mission, first with Peter's baptism of Cornelius's household (10:44-48), then with anonymous Hellenists preaching directly to Greeks (11:19-21), then with an expanded mission through Paul and Barnabas (13:1–14:28). At each stage, Luke shows the interplay of experience, narrative, and the discernment of God's plan, carried out by all the leaders involved (see 11:1-18). The climactic council in Jerusalem brings all these factors together, as Peter, Barnabas, and Paul all testify to the work that God had done among the Gentiles, and after debate and discussion, James and the other Jerusalem leaders concur that Gentiles need not be circumcised or observe Torah, beyond the minimum required to maintain communion between Jewish and Gentile believers (15:1-21). The declaration, "It is the decision of the Holy Spirit and of us" (15:28) — which at first blush may sound like an arrogant usurpation of divine authority — is actually the humble recognition that the church needed to catch up with what the Spirit was doing in the world. The tone of the letter sent to the troubled churches is likewise humble and conciliatory, with apologies for the commotion caused by "some of our number" (15:24); the letter, moreover, is delivered to those churches by personal delegates who strengthened and exhorted the believers (15:32).

In addition to the itinerant, charismatic leadership of the Twelve and other apostolic witnesses, Luke notes the presence of elders in specific communities, especially Jerusalem (11:30; 21:18); in the council deciding the question of Gentile admission, Luke consistently pairs "apostles and elders" in Jerusalem (15:2, 4, 6, 22; 16:4). Paul and Barnabas appoint elders in the churches they had founded (14:23), and Paul gives his farewell address to the elders of the church of Ephesus (20:17). Only two things need be said about these elders. The first is that such boards of elders were the standard form of organization in both Greco-Roman and Jewish associations and synagogues, and for the most part they served straightforward administrative rather than cultic functions. The second is that Paul's farewell discourse to the Ephesian elders, in which he places himself explicitly as a model of leadership, emphasizes service over dominance.

Paul reminds them of his own "service of the Lord" (using the Greek term for slavery) that was carried out with "lowly-mindedness" and tears and testings (20:19). All these terms echo Jesus' words in the Sermon on the Plain. Paul taught them both in public and in their houses "what was for their benefit" (20:20), as he proclaimed repentance to both Jews and Gentiles (20:21). Paul knows through the spirit that imprisonment and hardship await him, but he regards this as "finishing the ministry" (Greek *diakonia*) he received from the Lord (20:24). At the end of the sermon, as we saw above, Paul speaks of his own practice of working to share possessions with the weak as obedience to the words of Jesus (20:34-35). There is nothing in Paul's mode of leadership that suggests anything but an embodiment of the prophetic word.

What, then, about those elders in Ephesus whom "the Holy Spirit has appointed as overseers (Greek *episkopoi*) to shepherd the flock that is the church of God" (20:28)? In this context, the Greek term has no cultic or hierarchical connotations. The translations "overseer" or "superintendent" or "supervisor," are all more accurate than "bishop." Paul tells them to "keep watch over yourselves and over the whole flock" (20:28): the stress is not on their position or honor but on their personal integrity and the well-being of the community. The church, furthermore, does not belong to them, but is one that God acquired "through his own blood." Their task, then, is to stay steady even when false teachers ("wolves") seek to savage the flock (20:29-31). If the local leader can be called the shepherd of a flock whose task is to protect against wolves, then leadership is not about glory but about selfless service to God and to the people.

Challenge to the Contemporary Church

Luke's portrayal of Jesus and his disciples as embodying God's counter-cultural vision for "a people prepared for the Lord" is consistent throughout the narrative of both the Gospel and Acts. We do well to remember that it is an idealized picture: Luke constructs the character of Jesus and the early church in accord with what he understood Jesus' prophetic message to have been. I do not mean to suggest that there was no basis in reality for his portrait, only that his portrait isolates and develops those traits that form an embodiment of the prophetic word. His is, as I have suggested, a utopian vision for the church.

It is, therefore, slightly unfair to use his depiction as a rigid measuring stick for the contemporary church. In every age, finding the failures to match the prophetic vision would be easy work, simply because the church is human and humans are frail. They have been gifted by the Holy Spirit, we are convinced, but however willing the spirit is, the flesh is always weak, and the church always has been and always will be but an imperfect instrument for expressing God's word and showing forth the good news. If failure and sin are the constant companions of individuals, they are even more persistently and publicly the bane of institutions, whose natural tendency is toward corruption.

Even when this has been recognized, however, it remains important for the contemporary church (in every age) to regard Luke's characterization as a measure for its life, not because the church lives up to it, but because without attention to such a utopian vision the church will fall even more disastrously short of its best identity. At stake, after all, is the credibility of the message that the church proclaims. If the church proclaims as good news God's reversal of conventional norms, and teaches as the requirement of repentance that believers live according to the measure of the prophetic word, its proclamation and teaching reveal itself as empty, even hypocritical, when the church itself lacks convincing signs of living by, embodying, the values it espouses. What can it mean to be "saved from this generation" if nothing in the actual behavior of the church distinguishes it from this generation? A serious engagement with the prophetic challenge of Luke-Acts means, then, that every community calling itself church must include in its examination of conscience a consideration of the four marks of prophetic embodiment.

Prayer

The form of prophetic embodiment to which the church has been most faithful through the centuries has undoubtedly been prayer. Whether with the formal cadences of the *Book of Common Prayer,* or the blessings in the *Rituale Romanum,* or the ecstatic utterance in Pentecostal assemblies, or the free-style conversations with God practiced by many Evangelicals, the steady commitment to prayer by Christians is obvious. The most precious examples of Christian literature, from Augustine's *Confessions* to the *Journals* of Thomas Merton, are shot through with prayer. And virtually every act of Christian worship has included the prayer taught by Jesus to his disciples, so that, from the time of the apostles to the present, believers have prayed that God's kingdom be realized (Luke 11:2).

The church can rightly examine itself, however, concerning the prophetic character of its prayer. The prayer of believers today tends to take the form either of public worship (the prayer of praise) or of individual request (the prayer of petition). These are both legitimate expressions of prayer, found in the mouth of Jesus and of the apostles. But still, it is appropriate to ask if the prayer found in worship is more often ritual expression than heartfelt commitment. It is not unseemly to ask whether the prayers uttered in private are exercises in self-interest, more often pleas that what we will be done rather than what God wills.

More pertinent to the issue of prophetic embodiment, though, is the question whether Christians appreciate and practice their communal prayer as an expression of the politics of God's kingdom. The single greatest countercultural act Christians perform is to worship together and proclaim that Jesus is Lord. To cease from the constant round of commerce and consumption, to resist the manipulation of media that insists that working and possessing defines worth, and to proclaim with the body language of communal gathering that Jesus, not any other power, is Lord is to enact the politics of God's kingdom and to embody the prayer "your kingdom come." Yet, that community prayer has this prophetic dimension is seldom even part of Christian consciousness.

Similarly, the prayer of individuals can be a form of prophetic embodiment when it is not a matter of petition but of silent attentiveness. Whether taking the form of set times of silence before the Lord — again, a gesture of withdrawal from and resistance to the claim of the world that worth is measured by effort and acquisition — or taking the form of constant attentiveness to the presence of God and of God's word within and behind the surfaces of the world's self-presentation, such prayer serves for believers today, as it did for Jesus and the apostles, as a means of prophetic discernment and readiness. The recovery of contemplative prayer and mysticism in the church today is part of the recovery of prophetic consciousness.

Poverty/Sharing Possessions

As with the practice of prayer, we must acknowledge at once the many ways in which churches have through the ages shared possessions, especially with the most needy. Christians have built and managed hospitals and orphanages and shelters for the homeless; they have donated money and good for the needy of lands far away; they have participated in efforts to make better the lot of the diseased and depressed. Missionaries have worked tirelessly to improve the conditions of the world's destitute. The "doing of good works" has always included the practice of almsgiving, and continues to do so today.

It must also be acknowledged that many Christians both in the past and the present have pursued a more radical ideal with respect to possessions, embracing an evangelical poverty either as a sign of identification with Christ or the little ones with whom Christ identified himself; joining in communities that practiced a sharing of possessions in imitation of the apostolic church in which nothing is claimed as one's own and everything is shared equally; adopting a mendicant manner of life dependent on the generosity and hospitality of others; living among the poorest of the poor in city slum and rural village.

Over against all these admirable expressions of obedience to the prophetic vision, however, stands the unassailable fact that the church, as institution, has far more often through the centuries been a sign of wealth rather than of poverty and has aligned itself with the rich and powerful on earth more than the weak and lowly. The favor shown the Catholic church by wealthy patrons made of medieval monasteries treasure-troves of gold and jewel-encrusted vessels, fabulous vestments, and priceless libraries; made of Renaissance churches showplaces of architecture and art. The astounding material wealth accrued by the Catholic church, symbolized by the glittering grandeur of the Vatican, makes it difficult to make the case that the church stands as a prophetic challenge to the acquisitive instincts of the world or its measurement of worth through possessions.

The notorious wealth of the Vatican makes an easy — and legitimate

— target for prophetic criticism. But the wealth of Roman Catholicism is not the only example of Christianity's failure to realize an institutional witness to the prophetic word. The various Crystal Cathedrals and Towers of Power and suburban megachurches that stand as witness to the spirit of entrepreneurship more than to the spirit of evangelical poverty, which exemplify the modes of rationalization and investment and advertising that precisely mimic the corporate culture of the First World, are no less scandalous as the settings within which the beatitudes of the prophet Jesus are read from gilded pulpits. When the word proclaimed in such settings by preachers in fine garments or splendid haberdashery is "the Gospel of Prosperity," to be sure, there is at least a consistency between message and embodiment. But both message and embodiment are far from the good news announced and personified by the prophet Jesus.

The spirit of competition and commodification characterize contemporary churches in subtler ways, whenever they think of success in terms of swelling membership or expanded staff or elaborate programs or new buildings or expanded reputation, rather than in terms of fruitfulness of life, faithful discipleship, and constant conversion. Even when such modes of success lead to programs that "share possessions" with others, they tend to resemble the patterns of patronage rejected by Jesus (Luke 22:26) rather than the "giving of one's very life" that he praised in the case of the poor widow (Luke 21:4). We remember that when Jesus announced that the poor were blessed because theirs was the kingdom of God, he did so not as a wealthy benefactor but as one who shared the state of the poor. Somehow, the church needs to think through the question of how, as an institution, it might at least approximate such embodiment.

Itinerancy

In Luke-Acts, itinerancy is as much a mark of prophetic embodiment as poverty and prayer. Indeed, it can be seen as an aspect of those other two marks: moving from place to place in response to the Holy Spirit demands travelling light, being unencumbered by relationships and possessions; and such freedom of movement demands in turn an openness to the Spirit's direction, available through constant prayer. It is safe to say that it is an ideal that has been realized or even attempted only sporadically in the history of Christianity, simply because when movements become institutions they become less mobile, and the larger and more complex they become as institutions, the more their tropism is toward stability. The more stable and complex the organization, in turn, the more of its energy is expended in upkeep and maintenance and the less of its attention is given to the ever-changing needs of those it serves.

Itinerancy has been tried. Certainly the many missionaries who from the earliest centuries left home and family (or took them along) in order to travel to strange locales and engage alien culture with the good news practiced itinerancy, at least in the early stages of their mission. Once the church has been established in a place or culture, however, the itinerant dimension of its mission has often been lost. Similarly, the rise of mendicant orders of religious in the Middle Ages represented this specific dimension of prophetic embodiment. The Franciscans and Dominicans cultivated itinerancy as a form of poverty above all in order to free them to serve without encumbrance the needs of the poor and neglected. But these religious orders also lost true itinerancy to the degree that they became complex and centralized organizations. Most recently, Methodism arose as a reform movement within the Church of England with a commitment to the radical discipleship of the apostolic church. John Wesley practiced itinerancy to a remarkable degree and demanded it of all preachers within the movement. Itinerancy of a sort is still a feature of Methodist polity, but it is only a shadow of the movement's early ideal and practice.

If the corollary of itinerancy is responsiveness to the movement of the Holy Spirit, the corollary of stability is concern for institutional preservation, which leads in turn to centralized and hierarchical authority structure. Once more, the Vatican as the seat of all authority within Roman Catholicism is the obvious and extreme example. There is movement among ministers and missionaries in this system. It is not, however, movement impelled by the Holy Spirit, but movement controlled by central planning. Such central planning may display admirably clear lines of command, but it is slow and clumsy in its response to specific needs. The sexual-abuse crisis within Catholicism in recent decades has startlingly revealed the self-protective reflexes of an ungainly organization whose supposed leaders are driven by fear of administrative failure more than a pastoral instinct that is flexible and responsive to human distress. Roman Catholicism is scarcely alone in its push toward centralization and complex organizational systems. The World Council of Churches, the Southern Baptist Convention, the transnational convocations of virtually every denomination within the Christian family — all tend to privilege the values of uniformity and institutional control over the values of living by the prophetic spirit.

Precisely because Acts shows us the disciples — as a community — continuing to embody the ideal of itinerancy in imitation of Jesus, it poses a particularly sharp question to the church today. Like the other prophetic values (prayer, poverty, servant leadership), itinerancy requires translation to changing circumstances. Such translation, after all, is an example of the responsiveness and flexible freedom that itinerancy symbolizes. Churches today are not likely to abandon all things and hit the road as did the Twelve and the Seventy and Paul and Barnabas. But they need to ask themselves about the cost of abandoning this form of prophetic abandonment entirely. And they can begin by examining the ways in which their organizational structures actually hamper rather than facilitate obedience to the Holy Spirit.

Servant Leadership

The church's failures to embody the prophetic ideals of poverty and itinerancy are connected to its failure to exercise servant leadership in the manner taught and exemplified by Jesus and the apostles. Perhaps the most obvious example is found among the seriously self-aggrandizing televangelists whose manner of life and style of leadership resemble much more those of the scribes who "love places of honor at banquets and devour the houses of widows" (Luke 20:46) rather than serve at tables as did Jesus who declared, "I am among you as the one who serves" (Luke 22:27). The cult of personality encouraged by some such preachers leads them to invite rather than repel inappropriate homage, quite unlike Peter, who deflected the honor shown him by Cornelius, "Get up. I myself am also a human being" (Acts 10:26). The problem of servant leadership, however, goes far beyond personal style or even personal disposition. It arises also from institutional structures.

The greater the wealth of the church, the more centralized and elaborate its authority structures, the more ministry within the church becomes a matter of career advancement and privilege rather than of simple service to the needs of people. The hierarchy becomes a caste that exhibits the same instincts for self-preservation and mutual protection against outsiders — other believers! — found among members of other castes. The leaders at the very top, the leaders at the very center are concerned mainly with what happens at the top and at the center; they grow ever more remote from the discernment of what God is doing at the margins — the place, we shall see in the next chapter, where God's spirit most characteristically acts for creative change.

Such remoteness, in turn, breeds attitudes of entitlement and privilege: leadership appears to those who exercise it as an endowment rather than a mandate; position is held for the sake of honor more than for sacrificial devotion to others; authority easily becomes domination; direction quickly becomes control, and dissent regarded as an apostasy that requires first discipline and then exclusion. The words of Jesus to the disciples at the Last Supper as they fought over "which of them should be regarded as the greatest" ought to haunt such leaders and ought to generate prophetic critique among the people of God: "The kings of the Gentiles lord it over them and those in authority over them are addressed as benefactors; but among you it shall not be so" (Luke 22:25-26).

The four marks of the prophetic character or prophetic embodiment in Luke-Acts are, as I have shown, interconnected. Poverty and the sharing of possessions, prayer, itinerancy, and servant leadership form an internally coherent set of dispositions and practices that give real expression to God's vision for humanity. For the church to seek such embodiment, it must first repent, that is, undergo a real conversion in the way it thinks about things and assigns value. But in addition to a change of dispositions, the church must also practice those actions that demonstrate repentance, and this means the church must undergo the painful and slow process of actual institutional change.

CHAPTER SEVEN

Prophetic Enactment

The prophet is led by the Holy Spirit not only to announce God's word —
that is, God's vision for humanity — but also to embody that word in the
prophet's own manner of life, and to seek to realize that word through action in the world. I have shown already that Luke shows the prophet Jesus
announcing as the good news of God's rule the reversal of human values
and standards, so that the poor receive blessing and the rich woe. I have
shown as well that Jesus embodies this reversal by a manner of life marked
by poverty and the sharing of possessions, by itinerancy, by prayer, and by
servant leadership. Luke similarly shows the church of the apostles to be
led by the Holy Spirit, to proclaim as good news how God has initiated his
rule through the dramatic reversal of exalting a crucified messiah, and to
embody the prophetic challenge of Jesus in its life of prayer, sharing possessions, itinerancy, and servant leadership. I turn now to the way Luke
shows Jesus (and the church) enacting the prophetic vision through a remarkable ministry of embracing those whom the world excludes: God's vision for humanity is put into action by Jesus' mission to the outcast.

The prophetic mission in Luke-Acts can properly be called remarkable because it stands in such stark contrast both to the standard *modus
operandi* of the world and competing prophetic agendas. The conventional
standards of ancient culture — indeed, of virtually every culture then and
now — privilege the male over the female, the free over the slave, the rich
over the poor, the powerful over the weak, the healthy over the sick. Indeed, societies can and do marginalize and even exclude those whose
weakness, illness, and poverty stand in too great a contrast to the standards
of acceptability. Above all, cultures define their identity on the basis of

similarity rather than difference; they seek association with those with the same color of skin and of the same social background, with the like-minded and the similarly-situated rather than with those of different views and life situations.

The same logic of self-definition was operative in the cult of ancient Israel, which carefully distinguished between the clean and the unclean, between the holy and the profane, between those who were fit for participation and those who were not. One of the important functions of the priesthood was determining precisely what things fit into one category or another; the case of "leprosy" in all its forms is the classic example (Lev 13:1–14:57): the "strangeness" of appearance in skin or in clothes or in houses presented a threat to the "sameness" of what was assumed to be normal. It was therefore necessary to exclude from the common life whatever presented with any form of "leprosy" until the disappearance of the growth, tested by priestly oversight, enabled reentry, step-by-step, into the life of the people.

Israel was to be holy as the Lord was holy (Lev 11:44); in practice, this meant being different from those around them. The worship and the moral standards of Israel were constantly contrasted to the surrounding nations; "Everyone who does any of these abominations shall be cut off from among his people. Take my charge, then, not to defile yourselves by observing the abominable customs that have been observed before you. I, the Lord, am your God" (Lev 18:29-30).

The prophetic call for a return to the covenant in ancient Israel similarly emphasized the particularity of God's elect people by means of contrast to the nations, above all the hated Canaanites among whom Israelites lived. The postexilic prophet Malachi, for example, attacks all the usual ways of breaking the covenantal moral code (Mal 3:5), but puts special emphasis on the failure to offer appropriate animals in sacrifice (Mal 1:7-14) and on profaning the temple by divorcing an Israelite wife (2:14) and marrying "an idolatrous woman" (2:11). The prophet declares, "May the Lord cut off from the man who does this both witness and advocate out of the tents of Jacob and anyone to offer sacrifice to the Lord of hosts" (2:12). The price of embracing the outsider is to become an outsider.

Luke's description of Jesus' mission of embrace stands in starkest contrast to what might be considered two alternate prophetic programs within contemporary Judaism, each of which sought to secure a holy people, a restored people, on the basis of a strict observance of Torah and a sharp distinction between insiders and outsiders. The Essene community was the most radical expression of purification through separation. Led by the Teacher of Righteousness and his interpretation of Torah, the sectarians physically withdrew from other Jews and lived communally in the Judean desert. Their observance of purity regulations was strict; indeed, their community of possessions served to symbolize and reinforce the "pure community" that had no contact with outsiders — even Jews who did not belong to the community and continued to associate with the profane. Those who made such contact were cut off from the "pure meal" of fellowship celebrated by the community. The Essenes can be viewed as a prophetic movement precisely because of their emphasis on a people bound by covenant and their demand for "works of repentance" according to the severest standards of separation.

Less dramatic but no less serious was the prophetic program of the Pharisees. Their withdrawal was more moderate but was driven by the same desire for holiness. It is likely that the very name Pharisee derives from the Hebrew verb *parash,* meaning "to separate." The Pharisees did not, however, advocate complete physical withdrawal from others. Even though they made sharp distinctions between the "righteous" and the "sinners" on the basis of the observance of the law, their use of scribal expertise in the interpretation of Torah enabled them to practice purity in a more flexible fashion, through ritual washings after coming into contact with the profane. The Pharisees also placed great emphasis on table fellowship: the fellowship shared meals that symbolized their shared commitment to the strictest observance of Torah possible while remaining in the world.

Luke reveals no knowledge of the Essenes. But he is keenly aware of the Pharisees and their understanding of holiness. Throughout Luke-Acts, in fact, the Pharisees (and to a lesser extent, the scribes/lawyers) represent a powerful foil to the prophetic program announced, embodied, and enacted by Jesus and his followers. In order properly to appreciate their role as foil — revealed most consistently in disputes concerning table fellowship — it is important for present-day readers to recognize that it is not their vision of holiness that is odd or idiosyncratic; it is the vision that Luke ascribes to Jesus that is out-of-step with tradition. The Essenes and Pharisees are fully consistent with the logic of holiness that was enunciated by Torah and reinforced by the earlier prophets. The truly remarkable character of Luke's presentation of Jesus as enacting a mission of the embrace of outsiders is possible only when placed in contrast to these powerful contemporary prophetic movements that proclaimed and enacted a holiness through exclusion.

Healing as Restoration of the People

The two programmatic statements that Luke uses to announce the prophetic word, we have seen, appear in Jesus' inaugural sermon at Nazareth (Luke 4:16-30) and in his Sermon on the Plain (6:20-49). At Nazareth, the prophetic Messiah anointed by the spirit declares that he has been sent to proclaim good news to the poor, the blind, the captive, and the oppressed. Jesus then claims as prophetic precedent the healings that Elijah and Elisha perform outside the boundaries of Israel. This is the statement that arouses the hostility of the crowd and leads it to seek his death. In his Sermon on the Plain, Jesus then declares as blessed the poor (theirs is the rule of God), the hungry, the grieving, and the despised, while he pronounces a woe on the rich, the full, the joyful, and the popular.

In his narrative, Luke shows Jesus enacting this program through "the signs and wonders" that he works among the people. His actions flow from his character and serve the cause of making the rule of God present and effective. Precisely in the healing ministry of Jesus Luke legitimates his response to the Pharisees in 17:21, "the rule of God is among you."

Liberating the Captives: Exorcisms

The power that most obviously oppresses the people and holds them captive is that of Satan. In Luke-Acts, the figure of Satan represents a powerful counterkingdom that fights and seeks to destroy the rule of God among humans. Satan (or the devil) works through spiritual instruments, namely "demons" and "unclean spirits," who oppress humans and hold them captive, thereby preventing their full and free participation in God's people. Luke shows Jesus entering into combat with this counterkingdom in his account of the temptations (4:1-12). Of particular significance is the second test, when the devil shows Jesus "all the kingdoms of the world in a single instant" and promises, if Jesus worships him, that he will give him "all this power and their glory" (4:5-7), for, he says, "It has been handed over to me, and I may give it to whomever I wish" (4:6). Jesus refuses and emerges victorious over the devil as he returns "in the power of the spirit" to Galilee and his ministry (4:14). But Luke notes, "When the devil had finished every temptation, he departed from him for a time" (4:13); he will return to test Jesus and the disciples in the passion narrative (22:3, 31).

As they do also in Mark's Gospel, exorcisms play a critical role in

Luke's portrayal of Jesus' ministry, as a sign of God's rule breaking into human experience. When Peter recounts Jesus' activity in his speech to Cornelius's household, he characterizes it this way: "God anointed Jesus with the Holy Spirit and power. He went about doing good, and healing all those oppressed by the devil, for God was with him" (Acts 10:38). Exorcisms, we understand, are a form of healing in which the power of the devil is the overt enemy. Because such afflicted persons are "oppressed" — the Greek term in Acts 10:38 has the sense of violent suppression — they are alienated from others, because they present themselves as strange and out of control, and they are alienated as well from themselves, since they are "inhabited" or "possessed" by spiritual forces (Luke 11:24-26).

The very first action Jesus performs after his announcement of good news to the oppressed is an exorcism of a man with an "unclean demon" in the synagogue at Capernaum, which leads the people there to respond, "What is there about his word? For with authority and power he commands the unclean spirits and they come out" (4:31-37). Luke combined the healing of diseases and the exorcizing of demons in his summary of the first part of Jesus' ministry (4:40-41). Immediately before the Sermon on the Plain, which reiterates the declaration of good news to the poor (6:20), Luke notes that people sought him "to hear him and to be cured of their diseases; and even those who were tormented by unclean spirits were cured . . . because power came forth from him and healed them all" (6:18-19). Among those following Jesus on the road were "some women who had been cured of evil spirits and infirmities," including "Mary, called Magdalene, from whom seven demons had gone out" (8:2).

Possession by multiple demons is found also in the violent man of the Gerasenes, who must be kept bound among the tombs yet whose impulses drove him repeatedly to "break his bonds and be driven by the demon into deserted places" (8:29). When Jesus releases the demons into the swine (8:32), they come out of the man (8:35). He is "saved" (8:36), which means that he has been restored to his proper identity — he was clothed and in his right mind and sitting at the feet of Jesus (8:35) — and that he was restored to community: when the man seeks to follow Jesus, he is told "return home and recount what God has done for you," and he proclaims throughout the whole town "what Jesus had done for him" (8:38-39). Liberation as restoration to community is a feature as well of the story about the boy whose demon is so violent that it causes seizures and foaming at the mouth; his father begs Jesus to cast it out, and when he does, he "returned him to his father" (9:37-43).

The final exorcism reported in Luke's narrative is that of a demon that was mute, "and when the demon had gone out, the mute person spoke and the crowds were amazed" (11:14). This act of liberation gives rise to the controversy concerning the power by which Jesus casts out demons: is it, as some declare, "by the power of Beelzebul, the prince of demons" that he does this (11:15)? Jesus responds by speaking of "a kingdom divided against itself," thereby identifying his ministry specifically as that of God's kingdom in battle with the rule that Satan exercises over humans: "If it is by the finger of God that I drive out demons, then the kingdom of God has come upon you" (11:20). God's rule is established by liberating humans from "the strong one" who holds them captive and oppresses them:

> When a strong man fully armed guards his palace, his possessions are safe. But when one stronger than he attacks and overcomes him, he takes away the armor on which he relied, and distributes the spoils. (11:21-22)

Healing the Sick: Restoring the People

Driving out demons is a form of healing, since those possessed are liberated from their captivity and are restored both to themselves and others. Other illnesses likewise prevent people from full participation in the life of the people; in the Gospel narrative, Luke pays particular attention to the afflictions that stigmatize and separate the sick, and the way in which Jesus' healing word and touch restores them to community. The first story of healing, cure of Peter's mother-in-law (Luke 4:38-39), follows immediately the first exorcism story and reveals the continuity between the two forms of liberation and restoration: Peter's mother-in law is afflicted with a severe fever (4:38), a condition in which psychological dissociation is a common symptom. Jesus "rebukes" the fever; Luke uses the same Greek term as for Jesus' rebuke of demons during exorcisms (4:35, 41; 9:42). The result of the release is that Peter's mother-in-law gets up and "waited on them," being restored to her normal household place (4:39).

The other illnesses from which Jesus liberates people are of the sort that separated them from full participation in the cultic life of the people. Thus, he tells two stories of Jesus purifying from leprosy (5:12-14 and 17:11-19) and accounts of a healing of paralysis (5:17-26), dropsy (14:1-5), a withered hand (6:6-11), a hemorrhage (8:40-48), and blindness (18:35-43). He shows Jesus raising the dead to life (7:11-16; 8:49-56) and saving from near death (7:1-10). A story unique to Luke (13:10-17) shows the link between healings and exorcisms as well as the end point of healing being restoration to the people. It concerns a woman who for eighteen years had been "crippled by a spirit," incapable of standing erect (13:11), whom Jesus sees as he is teaching in a synagogue. When Jesus heals her, he speaks of her being "set free of [her] infirmity" (13:12). Most revealing is Jesus' response to his opponents who object to his healing on the Sabbath: "This daughter of Abraham, whom Satan has bound for eighteen years now, ought she not to have been set free on the Sabbath day from this bondage?" (13:16). Jesus restores the woman to a place in the synagogal gathering as a "daughter of Abraham."

That Luke understands these exorcisms and healings as enacting the "good news to the poor" that Jesus announced at the beginning of his ministry is indicated by the response he gives to the emissaries from John the Baptist, who ask whether he is the one who is to come (7:20). Before reporting Jesus' response, Luke tells the reader, "At that time, he cured many of their diseases, sufferings, and evil spirits; he also granted sight to many who were blind" (7:21). Then he has Jesus say: "Go and tell John what you have seen and heard: the blind regain their sight, the lame walk, lepers are cleansed, the deaf hear, the dead are raised, the poor have the good news proclaimed to them" (7:22).

Luke's use of the language of healing/saving — the same Greek term, *sōzein,* can be translated both ways — is connected to the restoration of the people around God's prophet. Thus, when he tells the sinful woman whom he forgives, "Your faith has saved you. Go in peace" (7:50), it refers not only to her individual condition but also to becoming part of the "saved/healed" people. In this way, "faith" is both the cause of being healed and also the condition of membership in the people that lives by the word of the prophet (see also 8:12, 36, 48, 50; 9:56; 13:23; 17:19; 18:26, 42; 19:10).

Indeed, Jesus' healing ministry continues to the end; at his arrest, when one of his disciples cuts off the ear of the high priest's servant, Jesus "touched the servant's ear and healed him" (22:51). At the beginning of his work, Jesus puts in the mouth of his opponents, as a sign of their rejection of him as prophet, the proverb, "Physician, cure yourself" (4:23). As he hangs on the cross, the rulers pass by and taunt him, "He saved (or 'healed') others; let him save himself if he is the chosen one, the Messiah of God" (23:35). And one of the criminals executed with him also says, "Are you not the Messiah? Save yourself, and us" (23:39). Both charges are ironic, for the point of Jesus' power has never been to serve himself but to liberate others. Thus, at the point of his death, when the other criminal asks him to "remember me when you enter into your kingdom," Jesus responds that he would be with him that day in paradise (23:42-43).

Finally, Luke makes the mission of the disciples continuous with that of their teacher. Thus, when Jesus sends out the Twelve, it is to "proclaim the kingdom of God and to heal" (9:2), and they "set out and went from village to village proclaiming the good news and curing diseases everywhere" (9:6). As noted earlier, Luke deliberately links their activity to Jesus' own: the Twelve return and report to Jesus all that they had done, and since the crowds gather to Jesus, "he received them and spoke to them about the kingdom of God and he healed those who needed to be cured" (9:11). That healing is the specific enactment of God's rule is indicated as well by the sending of the Seventy-two: Jesus tells them, "Whatever town you enter and they welcome you, eat what is set before you, cure the sick in it, and say to them, 'The kingdom of God is at hand for you'" (10:8-9). When these emissaries return from their mission, they declare to Jesus, "Lord, even the demons are subject to us because of your name," and he responds:

> I have observed Satan fall like lightning from the sky. Behold, I have given you the power to tread upon serpents and scorpions and upon the full force of the enemy and nothing will harm you. Nevertheless, do not rejoice because the spirits are subject to you, but rejoice because your names are written in heaven. (10:17-20)

Good News to the Poor: Embrace of the Marginal

The prophetic word reverses the ordinary human measures of success and acceptability. The way in which the casting out of demons and the healing of illness that stigmatize people is a reversal of such human measures is clear: those who are possessed by alien spirits are not welcome in polite company, and society works hard to keep the visibly ill and afflicted out of sight. Jesus' ministry of healing brings them into the people and in the process also "heals" the people by removing the stigma of mental and physical distress.

Luke also shows Jesus reversing conventional standards in the way he pays attention to and invites into fellowship those who, in the ancient world, were regarded as little deserving of attention and of little worth on the scale of social prestige. It is well known that Greco-Roman and Jewish cultures were both male-dominated and male-defined. Women are of importance primarily in terms of property and progeny, and little attention is given to them as persons. The positive portrayal of female capacities in the philosopher Musonius Rufus is remarkable mainly for its rarity in a largely sexist Hellenistic culture. And the progressive silencing of women as agents in the Hebrew Bible — see above all 1 and 2 Chronicles, Ezra, and Nehemiah — is continued in the earliest protorabbinic writings, in which women appear mainly as distractions from the male work of studying Torah.

Against this backdrop, Luke's portrayal of Mary, Elizabeth, and Anna as prophetic figures in the infancy account are particularly impressive. They are women with no official cultic status, but they are instruments through which the Holy Spirit speaks. Women are similarly prominent among those whom Jesus heals and exorcizes: Peter's mother-in-law (4:38-39), the mother whose son Jesus restores from the dead (7:11-16), the bent woman in the synagogue (13:10-17), the women from whom Jesus expelled demons, especially Mary Magdalene (8:2). The two stories that Luke took over from Mark 5:21-43 already intertwined are especially impressive illustrations of Jesus' willingness to cross social boundaries in order to touch and be touched by women in states of cultic impurity: the woman with the hemorrhage (8:43-48) and the daughter of Jairus whom Jesus raised from a state of death (8:40-42, 49-56).

Not only are women the recipients of healing, they become members of the prophet's movement. The close juxtaposition of the stories of the sinful woman who is saved by faith (7:36-50) and that of the women who accompanied and supported Jesus and the Twelve as they "preached and proclaimed the kingdom of God" (8:1-3) places women at the heart of the group that moves with Jesus from Galilee to Jerusalem. Martha and Mary are sisters whose reception of Jesus on that journey illustrates the positive response of the prophet (10:38-42). Jesus tells the story of the female homemaker whose loss and then recovery of a coin is parabolic for the rejoicing over a sinner who repents (15:8-10), and his story of the importunate widow who gains a just decision from an unrighteous judge because of her bold persistence is parabolic for faithful persistence in prayer (18:1-8). Jesus praises the poor widow who, in contrast to the wealthy who donate alms out of their abundance, "offers her whole livelihood" (21:1-4).

Luke portrays women as mourning and lamenting Jesus on the way to his crucifixion (23:27). At his death, "all of his acquaintants stood at a distance, including the women who had followed him from Galilee and saw these events" (23:49). These same women from Galilee follow the body of Jesus to the place of his burial (23:55). They are the ones, including Mary Magdalene, who came to the tomb with prepared spice to anoint his body (24:1) and encounter the two men who announce that the living one is not among the dead (24:2-7). They remember Jesus' words and announce the news of his resurrection to the Eleven — and are not believed (24:9-11). But their story enters the community narrative of Jesus' resurrection and is confirmed by the experience of others (24:22-24). They will be with the Twelve and Mary the Mother of Jesus in prayer before Pentecost (Acts 1:14) and will be among the "daughters" and "women slaves" upon whom the spirit is outpoured (Acts 2:17-18).

The attention that Jesus pays to children in Luke's narrative is, if anything, even more extraordinary by ancient standards. Women were regarded by dominant males as incomplete humans and therefore not to be taken seriously; children were even less significant when measured by male adults. They were weak, ignorant, and needy. In every respect, literally and figuratively, they represented "the poor" that dragged down the wealthy, powerful, and sophisticated. It is difficult to find an example in ancient biographical literature in which a "great man" would even take notice of a child.

Luke's portrayal of the birth and childhood of John and Jesus reveals his own conviction that child-parent relations and youthful experience are significant. The story of the twelve-year-old Jesus in the temple (Luke 2:41-52), found in the midst of the teachers, asking them questions and providing them answers that astound (2:46-47), indicates something of how special Jesus is, already as a youth finding it imperative to "be involved in the things of [his] Father" (2:49). But it also reveals Luke's understanding of the prophetic call: God's spirit can and does work among the young, the poor, the villagers, the powerless — as in the family of Jesus.

Luke's account of Jesus' healing of children pays particular attention to the way Jesus notices and respects the place children hold in families. When Jesus sees the widow in Nain following her son's bier and weeping, he is filled with pity and says to her, "Do not weep," before raising her son from the dead and "giving him to his mother" (7:11-15). It is in response to the poignant father's plea — "Teacher, I beg you, look at my son; he is my only child" (9:38) — that Jesus rebukes the demon and frees the epileptic boy from his oppression. He "healed the boy, and returned him to his father" (9:42). Similarly, Jesus responds to Jairus's plea — his only daughter was dying at twelve years old (8:41-42) — by going to his house and raising his child from her deathbed: he took her by the hand and called to her, "Child, arise!" (8:54). When she rose, to the astonishment of her parents (8:56), Jesus directed that she be given food to eat (8:55).

In two remarkable passages, Luke has Jesus propose children as the measure to be used within God's rule. We have already looked at the first, when tracing the theme of servant leadership. After Jesus makes his second passion prediction (9:43-45), the disciples fall into a dispute over "which of them was the greatest" (9:46). Jesus knows their intentions and takes a child and places the child at his side. He says to them: "Whoever receives this child in my name receives me and whoever receives me receives the one who sent me. For the one who is least among all of you is the one who is the greatest" (9:48). Two remarkable propositions are embedded in this statement. The first is that the way a child is received is the measure of receiving the prophet and his word — there can be no better test of living by the reversal of ordinary values than to accept as though receiving Jesus himself those who are always among the world's poor, because they are always needy, always dependent, always weak, and never able to repay (6:30-36). The second is that Jesus links authority, not to the status of the minister, but to the power of the sender. He here applies to children precisely what he states of the Seventy-two whom he sends out in 10:16: "Whoever listens to you listens to me. Whoever rejects you rejects me. And whoever rejects me rejects the one who sent me."

In the second child-as-measure passage (18:15-17), Luke follows Mark's version (Mark 10:13-16; see also Matt 19:13-15) closely. People bring even infants for Jesus to touch. The disciples rebuke them, but Jesus summons them, and declares, "Let the children come to me and do not prevent them. For the kingdom of God belongs to such as these. Amen, I say to you, whoever does not accept the kingdom of God as a child will not enter it" (18:16-17). The structure of the story suggests how the final statement is to be understood. Jesus is not calling here for people to "become like children in receiving the kingdom" — that is the point of another Matthean passage with which this one is sometimes conflated (see Matt 18:2-5). Rather, the way one receives a child is the measure of the way in which one receives God's rule (compare Luke 9:48). Luke's phrasing makes clear that children here embody "the poor": just as the poor are told "Yours is the kingdom of God" (6:20), so does Jesus say of the children, "The kingdom of God belongs to such as these."

A dominant characteristic of the programs for holiness in Israel was xenophobia, or fear of strangers. Israel's holiness was a matter of separateness, and, as I have shown, distinction from foreign nations was a fundamental element in separateness. In this regard as well, Luke's portrayal of Jesus reverses the conventional understanding and practice. He sets the stage for Jesus' embrace of those outside a narrow construal of Israel by having him appeal, in his Nazareth speech, to the precedents of Elijah and Elisha, whose healing work extended outside of Israel — despite the great need for healing within the boundaries of the people (4:25-27).

The centurion who asks Jesus to heal his slave is a Gentile soldier, who sends Jewish elders to witness that "he loves our nation and he built the synagogue for us" (7:5). He declares himself unworthy of having Jesus enter his house and trusts in the power of Jesus' word to heal even at a distance (7:6-7). Jesus praises the Gentile who foreshadows the centurion Cornelius in Acts: "I tell you, not even in Israel have I found such faith" (7:9). Jesus makes a similar comparison in 10:13-15 between the Galilean cities in which he has centered his work and cities outside historical Israel: "Woe to you, Chorazin! Woe to you Bethsaida! For if the mighty deeds done in your midst had been done in Tyre and Sidon, they would long ago have repented, sitting in sackcloth and ashes. But it will be more tolerable for Tyre and Sidon at the judgment than for you. And as for you, Capernaum, will you be exalted to heaven? You will go down into the underworld."

Luke's depiction of Jesus' openness to foreigners is shown also by the positive treatment of Samaritans in the Gospel narrative. He refuses to call fire down on the Samaritan villagers that do not receive him as he journeys toward Jerusalem, despite the pleas of his disciples (9:53-56). He tells a parable showing how a Samaritan proved himself to be more a neighbor to an injured man than did a priest and Levite (10:29-36) and exhorts his Jewish listeners, "Go and do likewise" (10:37). In a story unique to his Gospel, Luke has Jesus heal ten lepers outside a village as he passes "through Samaria and Galilee" (17:11-19). Only one of the ten returns to thank Jesus, leading the prophet to ask, "Ten were cleansed, where are the other nine? Has none but this foreigner returned to give thanks to God?" (17:17-18), and telling the Samaritan, "Stand up and go; your faith has saved you" (17:19).

The Call of Sinners

Perhaps the most startling example of Jesus' outreach to the marginal in Luke's Gospel is his embrace of sinners. The historical meaning of the designation "sinner" (Greek *hamartōlos*) in the Gospels is not entirely clear, but whether the term refers mainly to those who are morally flawed or are ritually incompetent (as were the *'am hā'āreṣ*, "the people of the land" in contrast to the Pharisaic brotherhoods), as a class the sinners were excluded from prophetic programs of reform that stressed holiness within Israel. Some occupations were "sinful" in and of themselves; thus, if "the sinful woman of the city" in Luke 7:37 was in fact a prostitute, the designation "this woman is a sinner" would be accurate when spoken by a Pharisee like Simon (7:39). Other trades placed people in a constant state either of impurity or temptation to immorality: tax collectors (see 3:12), soldiers (3:14), shepherds (2:8), tanners of hides (Acts 9:43). In any case, a sure sign of being a "sinner" was promiscuity of association in contrast to the maintenance of strict boundaries. For the Essenes and Pharisees, those who wanted to claim the name of Jew yet failed to observe the practices of "holiness" posed a fundamental threat to the entire project of prophetic reform.

As Luke portrays Jesus' prophetic ministry, in contrast, the outreach to sinners is consistent and deliberate. Simon Peter responds to the miraculous catch of fishes by declaring, "Depart from me, Lord, for I am a sinful man" (5:8), yet Jesus tells him, "Do not be afraid; from now on you will be catching men" (5:10). Jesus calls the tax collector Levi from his customs post, engendering the protest of the Pharisees and their scribes, "Why do you eat and drink with tax collectors and sinners?" (5:30). We remember in this connection the importance of table fellowship for all ancient fellowship: to eat and drink with "sinners and tax collectors" meant that one shared their indifference or defiance of the codes of holiness. Immediately after Luke notes that the tax collectors had responded to the prophet John by receiving his baptism, while the Pharisees and lawyers did not (7:29-30), he has Jesus quote the charge against him:

> John the Baptist came neither eating food nor drinking wine, and you said, "He is possessed by a demon." The Son of Man came eating and drinking, and you said, "Look, he is a glutton and a drunkard, a friend of tax collectors and sinners." (7:33-34)

Jesus does not deny the charge; in fact, Luke shows him fulfilling it by allowing the "sinful woman" to enter the meal he was sharing with Simon the Pharisee and display extravagant devotion to him (7:36-50). Luke notes again in 15:1 that "the tax collectors and sinners were all drawing near to listen to him," prompting the complaint from the Pharisees and scribes that "this man welcomes sinners and eats with them" (15:2). Finally, when Jesus goes to the house of the chief tax collector Zacchaeus, some in the crowd murmur, "He has gone to stay at the house of a sinner" (19:7).

The call of sinners is essential to the prophetic program of forgiving sins and thereby restoring the people (see 1:77; 3:3). The healing of the paralytic who is presented to Jesus in the presence of the Pharisees and lawyers takes the form of forgiveness: "As for you, your sins are forgiven" (5:20); when challenged, Jesus declares, "But that you may know that the Son of Man has authority on earth to forgive sins . . . I say to you, pick up your stretcher and go home" (5:24). Jesus responds to the question why he eats with tax collectors and sinners with this programmatic statement: "Those who are healthy do not need a physician, but the sick do. I have come not to call the righteous to repentance but sinners" (5:31-32).

Sinners are called, therefore, to repentance. They need to change in order to be part of the prophetic people. It is the sinner who repents that causes rejoicing in heaven (15:7, 10). Of the sinful woman who anointed his feet, Jesus declares, "Her many sins have been forgiven; hence, she has shown great love. But the one to whom little is forgiven loves little" (7:47). He tells her, "Your sins are forgiven" (7:48), and, "Your faith has saved you; go in peace" (7:50). Those who repent begin with hearing the word of the prophet (8:12-13) and having faith (5:20; 7:9, 50; 8:25, 48; 17:6, 19; 18:42), but they express that faithful hearing by doing the deeds of repentance (3:8), above all, living by the standards pronounced by the prophets John (3:10-14) and Jesus (6:20-49). The story of Zacchaeus is emblematic: although he is a wealthy chief tax collector, he expresses his faith by his intense desire to see Jesus (19:4) and his receiving Jesus into his house "with joy" (19:6). Zacchaeus responds to the charge that Jesus associates with sinful people by declaring to Jesus, "Behold, half of my possessions, Lord, I shall give to the poor, and if I have extorted anything from anyone, I shall repay it four times over" (19:8). Zacchaeus's repentance is marked by his adherence to the prophetic vision with respect to the use of possessions. Jesus therefore declares to him, "Today salvation has come to this house because this man too is a son of Abraham. For the Son of Man has come to seek and to save what was lost" (19:9-10).

Jesus' parable of the Pharisee and the Tax Collector gives perfect expression of the prophetic understanding of righteousness in Luke's Gospel. Luke notes that Jesus told this parable "to those who were convinced of their own righteousness and despised everyone else" (18:9), and we know from Jesus' description in 16:15 — "You justify yourselves in the sight of others, but God knows your hearts; for what is of human esteem is an abomination in the sight of God" — that he means by this that Jesus told the parable to Pharisees (see 16:14). The Pharisee in the parable thanks God for not being like others who are greedy, dishonest, and adulterous — "or even like this tax collector" (!) — while he fasts and pays tithes. This parabolic Pharisee defines "being righteous" by the standards of conventional holiness and "judging others." The judging of others, we recall, is precisely forbidden by the prophet's Sermon on the Plain (see 6:37-38). The tax collector, in contrast, declares himself to be a sinner and asks God's mercy; he departs as truly "righteous," for, as Jesus concludes, "Everyone who exalts himself will be humbled, and everyone who humbles himself will be exalted" (18:14).

Luke highlights the character of Jesus' prophetic enactment also by the way in which he shows the Pharisees and lawyers (scribes) opposing his embrace of the outcast of Israel. This narrative opposition reminds the reader that genuinely alternative visions of a restored people coexisted in first-century Palestine, just as they do in the narrative world constructed by Luke. The scribes and Pharisees object to Jesus' forgiveness of the paralytic's sins, thinking, "Who is this that speaks blasphemies? Who but God alone can forgive sins?" (5:21). They criticize Jesus' eating with Levi and other tax collectors: "Why do you eat and drink with tax collectors and sinners?" (5:30). When Jesus plucks grain from a field on a Sabbath with his disciples, some Pharisees say, "Why are you doing what is unlawful on the Sabbath?' (6:2).

The hostility shown Jesus escalates quickly to active opposition. When Jesus is confronted in a synagogue with a man with a withered hand, "The scribes and the Pharisees watched him closely to see if he would cure on the Sabbath so that they might discover a reason to accuse him" (6:7). After Jesus challenges his opponents' understanding of God's vision — "I ask you, is it lawful to do good on the Sabbath rather than to do evil, to save life rather than to destroy it?" — and heals the man (6:9-10), they do not change their mind, but "became enraged and discussed together what they might do to Jesus" (6:11). When Jesus welcomes the sinful woman, Simon the Pharisee thinks that he could not be a prophet, because he does not see that she is sinful (7:39). The Pharisee who invites Jesus to eat is shocked when Jesus does not observe the prescribed washing before a meal (11:38), and when Jesus engages in a sustained attack on the Pharisees and the lawyers, their hostility increases even further: "When he left, the scribes and Pharisees began to act with hostility toward him and to interrogate him about many things, for they were plotting to catch him at something he might say" (11:53-54). In return, Jesus warns his followers to "beware of the leaven — that is, the hypocrisy — of the Pharisees" (12:1). Such hypocrisy is revealed when Pharisees seek to turn Jesus from his prophetic destiny, under the guise of saving him from Herod (13:31-33).

This conflict with the scribes and Pharisees runs through the remainder of Jesus' journey to Jerusalem (13:17; 14:1, 6; 16:14) and, in the Jerusalem narrative, is assumed by the members of the Sanhedrin, the chief priests and scribes (20:1, 19, 20, 27; 22:2, 52, 66), who in the end, hand Jesus over to Pilate on the charge of political insurrection (23:2-4). As we have seen earlier, Luke characterizes the opposition of the Pharisees and lawyers with particular harshness: they are lovers of money (16:14), they devour the houses of widows while reciting long prayers (20:47), they justify themselves (18:11), they are hypocrites (12:1), and they approve of the killing of the prophets (11:47-51).

Beneath the polemic, however, it is possible to see a genuine conflict between two understandings of God's vision for humanity. The Pharisees represent the conventional approach of prophetic reform through a stricter observance of the law and the strengthening of the boundaries between insider and outsider, the clean and the unclean, the righteous and the sinner. Thus, they object to Jesus' assuming the authority to heal through the forgiveness of sins, because that is, they would argue, God's prerogative, while demarcating who is a sinner and who not is the human task (5:21). They question why Jesus does not show the marks of a prophet like John in prayer and fasting (5:33). They object to his eating promiscuously on the Sabbath (6:2) and, above all, healing on the Sabbath (6:7; 13:14; 14:3), for these are forms of "work." They are shocked at his failure to observe ritual cleansing (11:38). Above all, they criticize his willingness, even eagerness, to associate with sinners and tax collectors and choosing some of his disciples from their number (5:30; 7:34, 36-50; 15:1-2). Jesus' ministry of embrace should in fact shock, since it so clearly flies in the face of all precedent for reform within Israel and the prophetic tradition.

Luke shows his keen grasp of this conflict — as well as his impressive literary skill and psychological insight — in his distinctive shaping of chapter 15. He has one parable of repentance from the tradition: the parable of the Lost Sheep (15:4-7) is found also in Matthew 18:12-14, so probably was found in the hypothetical source Q. The image of God as the shepherd who seeks the sheep would also have been familiar from Ezekiel 34:11-12, 16. Although Luke shares with Matthew the bare bones of the story, he greatly increases the story's human dimension and makes clearer that this is a story about repentance by adding the explicit coda, "I tell you, in the same way there will be more joy in heaven over one sinner who repents than over ninety-nine righteous people who have no need of repentance" (Luke 15:7). Luke adds to this parable another involving a women who found a lost coin, and adds a virtually identical coda (15:8-10).

Luke then has Jesus tell the parable of the Lost Son (15:11-32), a story that is rightly treasured for its insight into the human drama of repentance and above all for its depiction of a father who is ready to forgive and embrace his lost child even before the child is ready to return. The story could satisfactorily have ended in 15:24, when the father declares a celebration, "because this son of mine was dead, and has come to life again; he was lost, and has been found." The celebration that begins with these words matches perfectly the "joy in heaven over one who repents" in the first two parables of the lost.

But Luke adds an extended coda in 15:25-32 that changes the story of the lost son who is found into the story as well of another son who is lost even though he has not left his father (has no need of repentance). The elder son who resents not only the reception of his erring brother but even more his own lack of recognition, even though "not once did I disobey your orders," perfectly represents the position of those who object to Jesus' mission that embraces the outcast and calls sinners. Even though the father assures him, "My son, you are here with me always; everything I have is yours" (15:31), he resists entering the place of celebration and refuses to acknowledge the younger son as his brother ("but when your son returns . . ." 15:30). The point of adding this coda is clear when we remember that Luke has positioned all three of these parables of the lost as Jesus' response to the criticism of the Pharisees and scribes concerning the tax collectors and sinners who drew near to him: "This man welcomes sinners and eats with them" (15:1-2).

Prophetic Enactment in Acts

The analysis in this section is particularly important to my argument that Acts continues and even intensifies the prophetic character of Luke's Gospel. I have already shown that although it is not as specific with respect to the prophetic word — partly because of the nature of the claims being made by the first preachers concerning Jesus as the prophet whom God raised up — Acts speaks constantly about the church in terms of the Holy Spirit and shows the church embodying the same prophetic qualities as taught and exemplified by Jesus: poverty and the sharing of possessions, itinerancy, prayer, and servant leadership.

We will not be surprised to find that the church in Acts continues the healing ministry of Jesus. But we intuitively suspect that the church will pull back from Jesus' embrace of the marginal and outcast. It is, after all, natural to communities as institutions to draw boundaries. Even communities of reform or restoration, once established, quickly lose the urge to reach out to the outcast. As the "new elect people," it appears natural to establish sharp lines between insiders and outsiders. If the "Israel of God" (Gal 6:16) is to be "holy," then it would appear necessary to divide between "us" and "them." We see such distinction already in Paul's letters to his churches, composed between 50 and 65 A.D. Paul sharply differentiates "the holy ones/saints" and "the world" in 1 Corinthians 6:1-3, as he does also between "those who believe" (1 Cor 1:21; 14:22) and the "faithless" (1 Cor 6:6; 14:22).

For Paul, the church needs to be holy (1 Thess 4:3), and Paul understands holiness as moral rather than in ritual terms. Believers are required to turn from every form of "unrighteousness" to a condition of righteousness and sanctification (1 Cor 6:10-11). Those in the community must separate themselves from the immoral (2 Cor 6:14) and expel members who do not meet the community standards (1 Cor 5:1-13). I point out the ways in which Paul's letters show the drawing of such boundaries, not to Paul's discredit, but only to reinforce the point that such is the instinct of all community formation. It also makes all the more impressive the complete absence of any such instinct in Luke's depiction of the church in the Acts of the Apostles. Instead, the church appears as extending and deepening Jesus' own embrace of the marginal. Only four of the fifty-five uses of the term "holy" *(hagios)* in Acts are applied to believers (9:13, 32, 41; 26:10), whereas forty-two instances apply to "the Holy Spirit."

Healing and Exorcism

In the Gospel narrative, Jesus' announcement of the good news of God's rule was enacted through exorcisms and healings. If he cast out demons by the finger of God, then, Jesus declared, "the kingdom of God has come upon you" (Luke 11:20). Jesus was able to heal those oppressed by the devil,

Peter asserts, because "God was with him" (Acts 10:38). The Acts narrative shows the followers of Jesus performing exorcisms and healings among the people "in the name of Jesus" (Acts 3:6; 4:10), showing that the power of the crucified and exalted Messiah is also "with them" and the rule of God continues to be enacted through the prophetic spirit working through them. Such healings and exorcisms are the preeminent "signs and wonders" that demonstrate the presence of the Holy Spirit. So the apostles pray after their first arrest and release, "Enable your servants to speak your word with all boldness as you stretch forth your hand to heal, and signs and wonders are done through the name of your holy servant Jesus" (Acts 4:29-30).

According to his literary habit, Luke makes the first such healing in Acts 3:1-10 the longest and most elaborate, using it — together with Peter's discourse in 3:11-26 and his defense before the Sanhedrin in 4:7-22 — to develop all the implications of this "sign and wonder" for the reader, in the process making clear the connection between the work of Jesus and the ministry of the apostles. The picture of the man who is crippled and begs every day for alms recalls Jesus' parable of Lazarus at the rich man's gate (Luke 16:19-31); as that poor man was not fed, so this one lacks access to the temple worship because of his condition and therefore full participation in the life of the people. We learn in Acts 4:22 that he had been at the gate forty years — a lifetime of poverty and exclusion.

Peter's declaration that he has neither silver nor gold (3:6) seems odd, until we realize that Luke has not yet placed the Twelve at the center of the community of possessions; indeed, that Peter is unable to give alms counts as evidence that a community of possessions and almsgiving are not entirely logically compatible. Peter heals the man "in the name of Jesus the Nazorean" and, imitating Jesus in gesture (see Luke 8:54), raises the lame man to his feet (Acts 3:7). The healed man enters the temple with them, "walking and jumping and praising God" (3:8). He is restored to the full life of the people. When the crowd responds with amazement, Peter assures them that he and John did not make the man walk "by our own power or piety," but it was rather the resurrected Jesus whose "name has made strong, and the faith that comes through it has given him this perfect health, in the presence of all of you" (3:16). This healing is, in fact, a symbol of the "times of refreshment" before the universal restoration that will come on them all if they repent and have their sins wiped away (3:20-21). It is, as Luke notes in 4:22, a "sign of healing," meaning this healing that serves as a sign of the restoration of the people.

The power of the resurrected one works through the apostles in healings and exorcisms that are even more spectacular than those done by Jesus during his ministry. "Many signs and wonders were done among the people at the hands of the apostles," Luke notes, "[people] even carried the sick out into the streets and laid them on cots and mats so that, when Peter came by, at least his shadow might fall on one or another of them," and great crowds came to Jerusalem from surrounding towns, "bringing the sick and those disturbed by unclean spirits, and they were all cured" (Acts 5:12-16). A reader of the Gospel narrative does not need reminding that precisely these deeds demonstrate and enact "the rule of God" in accord with the command (Luke 9:1-6) and by the power of Jesus. The Seven appointed by the Twelve after nomination by the community did not, as we have seen, wait on tables; they continued the same ministry of preaching and healing as that carried out by the apostles. Philip, for example, "preached the Messiah" to the people in Samaria, and they paid attention "when they heard it and saw the signs he was doing. For unclean spirits, crying out in a loud voice, came out of many possessed people, and many paralyzed and crippled people were cured" (Acts 8:6-7).

Luke also takes pains to tell of specific healings carried out by Peter and Paul, which extend help to those on the margins of the people and extend the ministry of restoration begun by Jesus. Peter's confrontation with the magician Simon in Samaria resembles a kind of exorcism: Peter rejects Simon's offer of money and tells him to repent, for "I see that you are filled with bitter gall and are in the bonds of iniquity' (8:22-23). Peter heals Aeneas, who had been paralyzed for eight years. The language that Luke ascribes to Peter — "get up and make your bed" (9:34) — reminds the reader of the command that Jesus gave to the healed paralytic in Luke 5:24 and helps establish continuity between the ministry of Jesus and his apostle, whose command comes not from himself but from the one whose spirit works in him: "Aeneas, Jesus Christ heals you" (Acts 9:34). Similarly, the raising of the widow Tabitha from the dead (9:36-42) not only recalls the precedent work of Elijah and Elisha for widows (1 Kgs 17:17-24; 2 Kgs 4:32-37; see Luke 4:25-27), but in its specific language ("taking her hand and raising her up," "Tabitha, rise up") echoes the healing words of Jesus in Luke's Gospel narrative (Luke 8:49-56).

Paul's healings likewise continue to demonstrate the power of God's kingdom that breaks in through the preaching of the apostles. His encounter with the magician Elymas on the island of Cyprus takes the form of an exorcism: "You son of the devil, you enemy of all that is right, full of every deceit and fraud . . . even now the hand of the Lord is upon you. You will be blind and unable to see the sun for a time" (Acts 13:10-11). He also exorcizes the girl with the oracular spirit in Philippi, saying, "I command you in the name of Jesus Christ to come out of her" (16:18). Paul's healing of the lame man in Lystra bears a strong resemblance to Peter's healing of the crippled man at the gate of the temple; when Paul sees that he has the faith to be healed and orders him, "Stand up straight on your feet!" the man "jumped up and began to walk about" (14:9-10; compare 3:4-8).

When Paul is in Ephesus, the divine power radiates from him in the manner Luke ascribed to the apostles in Jerusalem: "So extraordinary were the mighty deeds God accomplished at the hands of Paul that when face cloths or aprons that touched his skin were applied to the sick, their diseases left them and the evil spirits came out of them" (19:11-12; compare 5:12-16). As Peter raised Tabitha to life, and as Jesus raised up a little girl, so does the young man Eutyches receive healing from Paul when his fall appears to result in his death: "Paul went down, threw himself upon him, and said as he embraced him, 'Don't be alarmed; there is life in him'" (20:10). Finally, Paul's healing of Publius's father on Malta echoes Jesus' very first healing, of Peter's mother-in-law of fever (Luke 4:38-39): the father "was sick with a fever and dysentery. Paul visited him and, after praying, laid his hands on him and healed him" (Acts 28:8). That first healing by Jesus led to many others (Luke 4:40-41); Paul's healing of the man with fever and dysentery had a similar consequence: "The rest of the sick on the island came to Paul and were cured" (Acts 28:9).

The Embrace of the Marginal

In Luke's narrative, the first community at Pentecost already was made up of the marginal whom Jesus called into fellowship: the women who had followed him from Galilee, in whose number were some who had been exorcized, as well as the tax collectors and sinners who made up some of the Twelve. These were the "male slaves" and "female slaves" on whom the Holy Spirit fell and empowered as prophets (Acts 2:18). Among the three thousand who heard Peter's speech at Pentecost and joined the fellowship through baptism, moreover, were "devout Jews from every nation in heaven staying in Jerusalem" (2:5), each of whom heard Peter's discourse in his own language (2:6). Peter tells them all that "the promise is made to you and to your children, and to all those far off, whomever the Lord our

God will call" (2:39). Although the first community was entirely made up of Jews, it encompassed a wide range of the people. From the start, Luke tells the reader, Jews from the diaspora such as Barnabas played a leading role (4:36-37), and the number of Hellenist widows needing to be fed presented the community with its first crisis in leadership (6:1-2).

The apostles continue to enact the prophetic program of the embrace of the marginal by bringing the good news to those ethnically marginal to the people of God. The mission to Samaria (Acts 8:4-25) is more than a matter of geographical expansion: it is an embrace of the marginal. The Samaritans are not Gentiles, but rival claimants to the heritage of Israel, with their own temple, their own version of Torah, their own expectation of a "prophet like Moses." Far from considering themselves a corrupt version of Judaism, their self-designation of "the keepers" (*ha Shomrim*) indicates their conviction that they represented the authentic tradition of Israel better than their Judean rivals. Luke's Gospel narrative suggested the ancestral hostility between the Jews and Samaritans, as well as Jesus' own positive perception of them (see Luke 9:51-52; 10:30-37; 17:11-19) — although even Jesus refers to a Samaritan slightingly as "this foreigner" (17:18).

Luke's description of the mission in Samaria is an epitome of the prophetic ministry. Philip proclaims Jesus as Messiah (Acts 8:5), and the people hear it because he proclaims "the good news about the kingdom of God" (8:12) and because of the signs he performs: Philip works healings on the paralyzed and crippled and drives unclean spirits out of possessed persons (8:7). In short, Philip does precisely as Jesus commanded the disciples (Luke 9:1-6). Luke connects Philip's initiative to the Jerusalem community by having the apostles in that city send Peter and John when they heard that Samaria had "accepted the word of God" (Acts 8:14). Peter and John prayed that they might receive the Holy Spirit, then lay hands on them, and they received the Holy Spirit (8:15-17). After Peter's rebuke of Simon Magus (8:18-24), Luke indicates that the Samaritan mission was not a one-time effort by having the apostles "preach the good news to many Samaritan villages" (8:25).

The embrace of the marginal is also shown by Philip's encounter with the Ethiopian eunuch (8:26-40). We do not know, historically, whether the man from Ethiopia was a Gentile God-fearer or a Jew. In Luke's view, he must have been either a Jew or a proselyte (convert; see 2:10), because he would not have made so much of the conversion of Cornelius if he thought the Ethiopian had actually been the start of the

Gentile mission. From the perspective of Luke's literary intentions, there-fore, it is best to consider the Ethiopian as one of the marginal among the people of Israel. He is so because, despite his wealth and exalted social po-sition (in charge of the royal treasury), he is a eunuch. According to Deu-teronomy 23:1, a condition of sexual mutilation precluded full participa-tion in the life of the people, and this restriction was certainly practiced by the covenanters at Qumran as well. Luke may have had in mind concern-ing this official from Ethiopia prophetic texts that spoke of the inclusion of Ethiopia in God's blessings (Isa 11:11; Zeph 3:9-10) or of the honored place to be found among the people of eunuchs who keep God's covenant (Isa 56:3-5). In any case, by indicating that the eunuch had "come to Jerusalem to worship and was returning home" (Acts 8:27-28), Luke portrays him as a righteous man who affirmed the covenant of God with Israel — a fact con-firmed by his sedulous reading of the prophet Isaiah as he rode in his char-iot (8:28).

Luke has Philip respond to the eunuch's request for an interpretation of Isa 53:7-8 and then baptize him. When the Holy Spirit whisks Philip away, to continue preaching the good news from Azotus to Caesarea, the newly baptized official "continued on his way rejoicing" (8:39). In these two short stories involving the prophetic spirit's work through Philip, Luke has demonstrated how the movement begun by Jesus continues to em-brace those who are ethnically and ritually marginal within the people. These stories prepare the reader for the most dramatic extension of Jesus' mission of embrace, namely the inclusion of the Gentiles.

The Gentile Mission as Embrace of the Marginal

Because the vast majority of Christians today are Gentile, and have only known a Gentile-dominated Christianity, they take it for granted that God intended the Gentiles to hear the good news and become part of God's people. It is easy for them to miss the shocking, even outrageous, character of the initiative that dominates the entire second half of Luke's second vol-ume. The amount of narrative attention that Luke gives to the Gentile mis-sion shows, however, that at least he was fully aware of the difficulty and danger of this most radical realization of Jesus' mission of outreach, and how necessary it was for him to show, at every stage, how it was God's Holy Spirit that moved ahead of mere human agency in ensuring that "a people for [God's] name" (Acts 15:14) would be taken from among the Gentiles.

The impact of Luke's narrative can best be experienced if some historical imagination is exercised by present-day readers — an act of imagination not required of Luke's original readers, who would have been acutely aware of the radical implications of the story he told — to recover some sense of the scandal involved. For those claiming the heritage of Israel, after all, Gentiles were the ultimate "others," the ones by whom the holiness of the people was to be measured by means of contrast (see Lev 18:24-30). The nations were unclean by nature and filthy in their deeds: the association in Torah between idolatry and fornication is constant. The entire point of being a Jew — that is, to be a holy people set apart — was not to be a Gentile. The entire purpose of the laws concerning purity and diet was to ensure that Jews only ate with other Jews in a "pure meal" in contrast to Gentiles, who by definition would worship any god and eat with anyone. The choice was either to be particular or to be promiscuous. The pious Pharisee could praise God that he was made a male, not a female, a free man and not a slave, and a Jew, not a Gentile.

Luke's narrative must also be read against the historical backdrop of the decision made in earliest Christianity to include Gentiles without requiring of them circumcision and the observance of Torah. It was the most fundamental and important decision made in the entire history of Christianity, for it changed the movement from a Jewish sect into potentially a world-embracing religion, something truly new in the world. It is in Paul's letters that we gain an appreciation for the theological implications of the Gentile mission (in which Paul was such an important figure): Jesus is more than a Jewish messiah; as exalted Lord, he shares God's rule over all creation. In Christ, Paul declares, there is a "new creation" (2 Cor 5:17), and believers are to conceive of themselves as a "new humanity" (Col 3:11); Jesus is, for Paul, not a new Moses, but rather a new Adam (Rom 5:12-21), the "last Adam" who has become "life-giving spirit" (1 Cor 15:45).

Paul's letters to Gentile churches (above all Galatians and Romans) disclose both the historical reality of this decision, and the difficulty of its accomplishment. In Galatians 1:13–2:14, Paul traces some of the stages of the struggle from the perspective of his own participation: his independent mission after his encounter with the risen Lord (Gal 1:16-17), his first journey to Jerusalem to consult with Peter and James (1:18-24), his subsequent journey (after fourteen years) to Jerusalem with Barnabas and Titus that caused a commotion and opposition (2:1-5), the meeting in Jerusalem involving Paul, Barnabas, Peter, James, and John that decided the legitimacy of the Gentile mission (2:6-10), and a conflict over eating with Gentile believers in Antioch involving men from James, Peter, Barnabas, and Paul (2:11-14).

Luke's account diverges from Paul's firsthand — though not entirely disinterested — report in several ways, above all in the sequence of events: Luke has the Jerusalem council follow the Antioch dispute, whereas Paul has the dispute follow the council. But there is substantial agreement between the two sources on the essential points: (a) in the first generation of the Christian movement, the inclusion of Gentiles presented a crisis of self-definition; (b) not all believers were in agreement with the fact or the conditions of such inclusion, and there were disputes over these issues; (c) a meeting was held in Jerusalem involving the most important leaders; (d) a decision was made in principle that God willed the Gentiles to be included; (e) the issue of how Jewish and Gentile believers were to eat together was more difficult to resolve. The agreement on these points is far more significant than the disagreements and serves to secure both the historical fact as well as the importance of this early decision.

Luke's narrative version has three emphases: first, the Gentile mission was impelled from beginning to end by God's Holy Spirit: God moved ahead of human decision; second, this mission was continuous with, yet even more radical than, Jesus' embrace of the marginal in the Gospel; third, the human agents in the story only slowly and with difficulty came to realize the full implications of God's work.

Luke's Gospel provides hints of a vision for God's people that would extend beyond historic Israel, but they are only hints, and can be understood as a mission to the Gentiles only in hindsight. The songs of praise uttered by Zechariah (Luke 1:68-79) and Mary (1:46-55), for example, focus entirely on God's visitation to Israel in accord with the promises made to Abraham. Simeon's recognition of Jesus as "a light of revelation to the Gentiles and glory for your people Israel" (2:32) can similarly be read in accord with Isaiah 42:6 and 49:6 as indicating only the sight of Israel's glory by Gentiles. The same could be said of the citation of Isaiah 40:5 in Luke 3:6: "All flesh shall see the salvation of God." The tracing of Jesus' genealogy back to Adam rather than back to Abraham (3:23-38) is certainly suggestive, but has significance for the Gentile mission only in hindsight. The same applies to Jesus' statement in 13:29 to the question whether only a few would be saved: "People will come from the east and the west and from the north and the south and will recline at table in the kingdom of God" — this could apply as much to Jews of the Diaspora as to Gentiles. So could Jesus' commission of the disciples at the end of the Gospel: "Repentance for the forgiveness of sins would be preached in his name to all the nations, beginning from Jerusalem" (Luke 24:47). In light of later developments, it seems obvious that the Gentile mission was intended by God all along; but without Luke's later narrative development, such statements would not necessarily have had that meaning.

Even in the first part of the Acts narrative, the human characters do not seem to have understood the deeper implications of Jesus' prophecy that they would bear witness to the "ends of the earth" (Acts 1:8). The election of Matthias is carried out precisely to fill out the number of the Twelve to symbolize that the gift of the Holy Spirit is the restoration of Israel (1:15-26). Those who witness Pentecost are Jews and proselytes from every nation (2:9-11). When Peter declares that "the promise is made to you and to your children and to all those far off," this also could be understood to refer to Diaspora Jews (2:39). The depiction of the believing community in 2:41-47 and 4:32-37, as we have seen, evokes the picture of an Israel that enjoys the "times of refreshment" given by the Holy Spirit. The outreach to the Samaritans and the Ethiopian eunuch appears as an outreach to the ethnically and ritually marginal within Israel. Even Paul — who has been chosen, Ananias is told by the Lord, "to carry my name before Gentiles, kings, and Israelites" (9:15) — begins by proclaiming Jesus as Son of God in Jewish synagogues, first in Damascus (9:20-22) and then in Jerusalem to Hellenist Jews (9:29).

Luke takes particular pains to show that such a momentous step as embracing the Gentiles as part of God's people ("a people for his name from among the Gentiles," Acts 15:14) is impelled throughout by God's Holy Spirit, to which the church responds, sometimes fitfully, but ultimately faithfully. Thus, the story begins with the simultaneous but discrete religious experiences of the God-fearing centurion Cornelius and the Apostle Peter and moves through the mutual interpretation of these experiences as mediated by narrative, to the proclamation by Peter of the good news to the household of Cornelius, the outpouring of the Holy Spirit on the Gentiles, and the decision to baptize them since they had received the same gift that the Jewish believers had received in the beginning (10:1-48). By emphasizing continuity in the gift of the Spirit, Luke accords greater authority to the experience of God than to human custom — as Peter indicates, "It is not lawful for a Jewish man to associate with, or visit, a Gentile, but God has shown me that I should not call any person profane or unclean" (10:28).

It cannot be by accident, either, that in Peter's speech to Cornelius's household he gives such attention to the prophetic ministry of Jesus — a feature lacking in the other speeches of Acts — and above all, Jesus' liberating and healing outreach: "How God anointed Jesus of Nazareth with the Holy Spirit and power. He went about doing good and healing all those oppressed by the devil, for God was with him" (10:38). By so highlighting Jesus' ministry of healing, Peter (and Luke) draws an implicit connection between Jesus' embrace of the marginal and the church's inclusion of the Gentiles. The same implicit connection to the prophetic vision of Jesus is made when Peter defends his actions before the elders in Jerusalem who questioned his eating with the uncircumcised (11:3), by retelling the story, in sequence (11:4). In this iteration, however, Peter notes that when the Holy Spirit "came upon them as it had upon us in the beginning" (11:15), "I remembered the word of the Lord, how he had said, 'John baptized with water, but you will be baptized with the Holy Spirit'" (11:16). The experience of the Spirit's gift to the Gentiles not only connects to the Jewish believers' own experience of the prophetic spirit "when we came to believe in the Lord Jesus Christ" (11:17), but also gives deeper insight (and extension) to the meaning of Jesus' prophecy concerning baptism in the spirit.

Luke further shows the reader that the Gentile mission is God's work rather than the idiosyncratic fancy of a single leader by having the next stage carried out by spirit-filled but anonymous Hellenist Jews from Cyrene and Cyprus who had been scattered after the death of Stephen and who, in contrast to those who were "preaching to no one but Jews," began proclaiming the good news directly to "the Greeks" in Antioch; Luke notes, "The hand of the Lord was with them" (11:19-21). The Jerusalem leaders once more affirm the legitimacy of the mission through the embassy of Barnabas, who "saw the grace of God" and "rejoiced and encouraged them to remain faithful to the Lord in firmness of heart" (11:23). Luke reminds the reader at this point that Barnabas, too, shared the prophetic spirit: "For he was a good man, full of the Holy Spirit and faith" (11:24).

This church in Antioch was then directed by the Holy Spirit to send out Barnabas and Paul "for the work to which I have called them" (13:1-3), namely the proclamation of the good news to the Gentiles (see 9:15). First with Barnabas as his companion and then Silas, Paul tries repeatedly to proclaim the good news in the synagogue, and only when rejected there would turn to the Gentiles (see 13:38-45); he announces such a turn solemnly in 13:46: "It was necessary that the word of God be spoken to you first, but since you reject it and deem yourselves unworthy of eternal life, we turn now to the Gentiles" (13:46). The result of their efforts enables them to report back to the church of Antioch "what God had done with them and how he had opened a door of faith to the Gentiles" (14:27). It is worth noting here that Luke has "faith" be the same positive response to the prophetic word that marks repentance in Acts as in the Gospel.

Paul makes a second such announcement in Corinth, when he tries unsuccessfully to convince the Jews that Jesus was the Messiah: "Your blood be upon your heads! I am clear of responsibility. From now on I will go to the Gentiles" (18:6). Luke's narrative recognizes the edge of tragedy that accompanies the outreach to the Gentiles. God takes a great risk by pushing the community in this direction. The double edge of Paul's ministry is indicated when he is arrested in Jerusalem and seeks to defend himself before the Jews in Jerusalem (22:1-21). He insists on his identification with his fellow Jews: "I was educated strictly in our ancestral law, just as all of you are today" (22:3). Yet the speech reaches its climax with his vision of Jesus in the temple, when he is told, "I will send you away to the Gentiles" (22:21).

The same duality is found in Paul's defense before Agrippa. He insists that he is standing trial "because of my hope in the promise made by God to our ancestors" (26:6), yet again cites the command of Jesus to him that he is being sent to the Gentiles "to open their eyes that they may turn from darkness to light and from the power of Satan to God, so that they may obtain forgiveness of sins and an inheritance among those who have been consecrated by faith in me" (26:16-18). This statement clearly connects the Gentile mission to Luke's understanding of Jesus' proclamation of good news to the poor: their eyes are opened and they are liberated from the oppression of the devil. Paul will make one final effort to convert the Jews whom he meets in the city of Rome, but when he meets only a divided response (28:24), he applies to them the citation of Isaiah 6:9-10 concerning the blindness and deafness of the people to whom the prophet has been sent, and announces, "Let it be known to you that this salvation of God has been sent to the Gentiles; they will listen" (28:28).

Resistance and Reinterpretation

If the embrace of the Gentiles is the church's radical expression of Jesus' embrace of the marginal within Israel, above all tax collectors and sinners — and this, I argue, is precisely what Luke wants his reader to see — then it is no surprise to discover in Acts the same sort of resistance to this form of prophetic enactment that Luke showed Jesus confronting in the Gospel narrative.

The opposition shown the apostles by unbelieving Jews is for the most part centered on their claims for Jesus as Messiah and Lord and, above all, their working signs and wonders "in his name" as a demonstration of his status as the prophet whom God raised up. Much of the resistance and harassment of the apostles involves dispute over these claims (6:9-10; 9:29; 17:2-3; 18:4-5, 28), the effort to suppress them (4:5-22; 5:17-41; 12:1-19), and the attempt to eliminate the irritant (7:9-14, 54-58; 8:3; 9:1; 13:44-50; 14:5; 17:5, 13; 21:27-36; 23:12-15). Luke characterizes the movement's opponents in terms of "envy" (5:17; 13:45; 17:5), suggesting the rivalry between the competing claims to the heritage of Israel.

Of more significance for understanding the mission to the Gentiles as a continuation of Jesus' own prophetic enactment of the embrace of the outcast is Luke's recognition of resistance and opposition from within the Christian movement. In the Gospel, Luke's presentation of the Pharisees had elements of stereotypical slander, but it also revealed genuine points of conflict between the prophetic agenda of covenant renewal they represented and that proclaimed by Jesus. The Pharisees' position that holiness demanded separation, that free association with sinners and tax collectors went clearly against that demand, and that actually eating with tax collectors and sinners flouted the ancestral (and prophetic) understanding of repentance made perfect sense within the traditional framework of Torah. The Pharisees' position was not outrageous and scandalous within the framework of prior Jewish understanding; rather, it was Jesus' position that had to appear as novel and offensive.

The same flouting of Torah's norms arises when Gentiles are admitted to the people without demanding circumcision and the keeping of the law. Judaism in the first century was completely open to converts (proselytes), and probably even sought them among the God-fearing Gentiles. What distinguished converts from God-fearers, however, was precisely the full commitment represented by circumcision and the observance of Torah. And a corollary of that commitment would be sharing table fellowship only with Jews — this is a reason why such full commitment was difficult. To admit Gentiles into full fellowship with Jewish believers without requiring of them a full commitment to Torah raised serious issues for the identity of the Jewish people and the fidelity of God.

What possible sense could it make to speak of an elect people, of holiness, if table fellowship with uncircumcised and non-law-observing

Gentiles were allowed, much less encouraged? The entire point of being a Jew is not to be a Gentile; without difference, there is nothing: the very people is threatened with annihilation through assimilation. But equally threatened is the authority of Torah itself. If all precedent in Scripture demanded of Gentiles that they enter the people only through circumcision and the keeping of the law, a new practice to the contrary appears to nullify the significance of Scripture altogether.

Luke is acutely aware of these issues, which is why he gives such attention to working them out, especially in Acts 10–15. In his first vision, Peter refuses the command to kill and eat from among all creatures, with the statement, "Never have I eaten anything profane and unclean" (10:14), and is told, "What God has made clean, you are not to call profane" (10:15). At this early stage, God's voice in a vision appears to challenge the entire basis of dietary discrimination and, if so, the separation between peoples. This is the point Peter has reached when he declares to Cornelius's household, "You know that it is unlawful for a Jewish man to associate with, or visit, a Gentile" — this is the traditional understanding found in Torah — "but God has shown me not to call any person profane or unclean" (10:28). He proceeds to proclaim the good news to the Gentile household, and when the Holy Spirit falls on them, he and the other Jewish believers who accompanied Peter saw that the Gentiles had received the same gift as they had.

The "apostles and brothers who were in Judea" heard that the Gentiles had accepted the word of God (11:1). But when Peter came to Jerusalem, he was confronted by "the circumcised believers." Their difficulty was not that Gentiles could respond to God's word. Their difficulty was the observance of separation, or holiness. They charge Peter, "You entered the house of uncircumcised people and ate with them" (11:3). When Peter narrates what God had done, they stop objecting and proclaim, "God has then granted life-giving repentance to the Gentiles too" (11:18). But the issue of table fellowship was not by any measure either dealt with or solved. They had not backed off their position that Gentiles who repented also had to become Jews. The issue emerges more explicitly when some come down from Judea to Antioch and instruct believers there, "Unless you are circumcised according to the Mosaic practice, you cannot be saved" (15:1). It is important to remember here Luke's consistent use of "salvation" language both in the Gospel and Acts. The statement does not refer to a person's status before God — are they righteous — but rather to their status within God's people — are they fully included? Their position is that circumcision is necessary for full membership.

The controversy reaches Jerusalem and requires a meeting of emissaries from Antioch (Paul and Barnabas and others, 15:2) and the leaders of the Jerusalem church, with its apostles and elders (15:4). The opposition is now represented by "some from the party of the Pharisees who had become believers." These strict adherents to the law, who rejected Jesus' ministry of embrace that extended to sinners and tax collectors (Luke 15:1-2), now resist as well the Spirit-directed embrace of the Gentiles, even though they had "become believers." As the Pharisees in the Gospel narrative, they must be recognized as holding the correct theological position, if Scripture alone counts, and the "signs and wonders" accomplished by God do not count. Precisely the recitation of such evidence for God's Holy Spirit at work in the Gentile mission by Paul and Barnabas and Peter (Acts 15:7-12) leads to the decision to free Gentile converts from circumcision and the keeping of the full law, demanding of them — as a compromise and out of respect for the sensibilities of Jewish believers — just such basic observances as would enable pious Jews to join them in table fellowship without being forced to abandon their own prior commitment to the covenant (15:13-21).

That the opposition was not entirely appeased, however, is clear from James's report to Paul when the apostle makes his final trip to Jerusalem: "Brother, you see how many thousands of believers there are from among the Jews, and they are zealous observers of the law. They have been informed that you are teaching all the Jews who live among the Gentiles to abandon Moses and that you are telling them not to circumcise their children or to observe their customary practices" (21:20-21). The reader of Acts (and in fact, the reader of Paul's letters!) knows that the accusation is false: Paul appears to observe the law himself as a pious Jew and never encourages Jews to do otherwise; his only object is to prevent Gentiles from being forced to become Jews in order to "be saved." But those who wanted the church to be "holy" as Israel had been holy continued to resist the ultimate implications of full Gentile inclusion.

Despite such resistance, Luke shows how the church did, in fact, obey God who had urged them forward through the power of the Holy Spirit and had demonstrated the legitimacy of the embrace of the Gentiles by the "signs and wonders" done among them — not least, the reception of the same prophetic spirit from Jesus by these Gentile believers. By extending Jesus' own mission to the outcast in such radical fashion, the church proved to be as prophetic in its enactment as he had been; indeed, the church, led by the Holy Spirit, reached a vision of embrace that was not available even to the prophet Jesus. As I have noted, the church saw this step as a continuation of what Jesus did and said (see 10:38; 11:16).

The fullest expression of this conviction is found in Peter's statement at the council. Having noted how God had given the Gentiles the Holy Spirit just as he had the Jews and "made no distinction between us and them, for by faith he purified their hearts," he declares that placing a burden on the Gentiles' shoulders is "testing God" (15:10; compare Luke 4:2, 13; 11:16; Acts 5:9). Instead, Peter says, "through the gift that is the Lord Jesus Christ, we are believing in order to be saved in the same manner as they are" (author's translation). The statement is altogether remarkable. Peter has come to understand that "being saved" — that is, being part of God's people — is the same for Jews as for Gentiles. It is a matter of faith, not of ethnic descent or cultural location. What he has learned "through the gift that is Jesus Christ" is *not* that "they" are saved in the same way as we are (that is, by being Jews), but that "we are saved in the same way that they are" (that is, by faith). The salvation of the Gentiles reveals to Peter the true grounds of his own salvation.

Challenge to the Contemporary Church

Prophetic embodiment means living in accord with the rule of God announced by the good news; prophetic embodiment means acting in the world to realize that good news. Throughout Luke-Acts, the good news is enacted through exorcisms and healings and through welcoming into God's people those who are marginal or outcast. The two modes of enactment, I have shown, are interconnected: exorcisms and healings find their term in the restoration of persons to community; the embrace of the marginal serves as a healing both of them and of the community.

In the case of prophetic embodiment, we saw that translation from the world of Luke-Acts to the contemporary world is necessary, if the prophetic challenge of that composition is to be engaged. How possessions are to be shared, what itinerancy might mean, and the modes of servant-leadership all require careful consideration of Luke's text in its first literary and social context, as well as a careful analysis of the social realities of present-day Christian communities. Only prayer as a means of disposing individuals and communities to the Spirit of God remains recognizably the same in Luke's world and ours. Such prayer is therefore all the more valuable as a means of seeking and receiving the guidance of the Holy

Spirit and learning to discern how such translations must be carried out, both with respect to embodiment and to enactment.

Exorcism

Luke sees exorcism as the liberation of captives from oppression. In his worldview, the figure of Satan or the devil commands a counterkingdom hostile to the rule of God that exercises its dominion through the unclean spirits that inhabit and inhibit human freedom, alienating them from their authentic selves and from others. In Luke's world, the signs of such oppression and alienation appear above all in manifestations of psychological dissociation and physical violence.

Unfortunately, exorcism has lost much of its powerful meaning for most contemporary Christians. Psychotherapy or drugs are the recommended response to conditions of personal alienation and distress. Exorcism — when not parodied in plays and films that emphasize grotesque special effects — is regarded by the few mainstream communities that practice it as a last-ditch exercise for cases that resist every other sort of intervention. The notion of exorcizing an evil system is mostly the stuff of comedy, as when a hapless worker seeks to drive the demons out of a recalcitrant computer. Indeed, among most sophisticated Christians, language about the devil and the demonic is regarded as an unfortunate holdover of a mythological world exploited by ignorant or unscrupulous preachers to create fear and revulsion in the face of what is strange. Here is a case where appropriate translation is desperately needed.

The language of the demonic is perfectly appropriate for the church to use in order to name evil forces that are real and transcend the realm of individual choice. It is important, first of all, for the church to be able to name evil for what it is and resist the tendency to reduce everything to forms of sickness, for evil is real. It often takes systemic forms, and it does oppress and alienate humans in our world. One of the great contributions of contemporary liberation theology, indeed, is its retrieval of Paul's language concerning the "powers and principalities" to identify oppressive economic and political systems that hold humans in bondage. Racism and sexism are now broadly and correctly recognized as systems of meaning and practice that are inherently evil and have the cumulative power to hold both victimizers and victims captive to a web of falsehood and alienation that destroys those caught within it. Increasingly, the evil effects of behaviors driven by homophobia are also rightly regarded as a form of being "oppressed by the devil."

How can churches practice exorcism against such contemporary examples of Satan's "counterkingdom"? Three steps seem necessary and basic. First, the church must be able and willing to name the demonic evil for what it is. To be blind to forms of human captivity and oppression is, ultimately, to share in them. Naming requires, to be sure, a renewed comfort with mythological language and its value in identifying realities that transcend the empirical. False demonization is itself a form of evil-doing, but naming as demonic that which systemically oppresses and destroys humans is sober truth-telling. Second, the church must resist such demonic systems "in the name of Jesus Christ." To do this, the church must constantly examine the ways in which allegiance to the name of Jesus demands a rejection of all forms of oppressive and enslaving behavior and the ways in which the church's current practice may fall short of that norm: to what extent do racism and sexism and homophobia, for example, hold members of the community captive from within? Third, the church needs to work to provide an alternative to such systems of oppression in its own life, by cultivating the poverty, prayer, freedom (itinerancy), and servant leadership that oppose the hegemonic and oppressive values of Satan's counterkingdom.

Exorcism is an appropriate response as well to a form of captivity and oppression that is increasingly prevalent among Christians in so-called First World countries, a kind of demonic possession that manifests itself in patterns of addiction. Alcohol and drug addiction have been around for a long time, and their manner of holding people captive and destroying both them and their families is well recognized. More recently, addiction to sexual gratification and addiction to gambling appear at least as destructive of individuals and communities as the older manifestations. Is it appropriate to speak of addiction as a form of demonic possession? I think so, for when addiction rages in full force, persons are truly alienated from their authentic selves and from healthy community, driven by impulses beyond their rational control. We know that exorcism is possible in the case of alcohol and drug addiction by the naming, resisting, and providing alternatives — Alcoholics Anonymous has set the pattern for a difficult but successful driving out of such demons — one day at a time — and the reincorporation of addicted persons into community. The church can learn much from the simplicity and directness of this and similar programs and use what it learns to address other forms of addictive possession.

Healing

In Luke-Acts, exorcism and healing are closely linked as the "signs and wonders" through which the presence of God's rule is demonstrated, and with good reason: both sickness and possession are forms of oppression and captivity; both alienate the person who is "different" from those who are "normal"; in both cases, Jesus' healing command and touch leads toward a restoration to full community participation. The way that churches today think about translating Luke-Acts' language about exorcism into contemporary pastoral practice can, therefore, also guide their thinking about forms of healing in the contemporary world.

Cures of physical injury, sickness, and disease happen, today as in the world of Luke-Acts. Most often, they happen as the result of God's working through skilled physicians and surgeons. Sometimes they occur spontaneously in response to prayer and fasting. Sometimes they result from therapy and prayer in harmony. Whenever and wherever cures happen, we recognize that God is at work, though most often we do not understand how or to what purpose. But we know enough to give thanks. It must be stated plainly that there is nothing religiously inappropriate in Christians gathering for prayer and the laying on of hands for the sick. The power of God's spirit to work through the communal body so engaged has been and continues to be revealed. But it should also be stated clearly that such forms of physical healing are neither necessary to nor exhaustive of the church's mission of healing.

Most people with physical distress do not ultimately get healed, in the sense that their symptoms are utterly removed, either in Luke's day or in our own. Luke has Jesus point out, in fact, that Israel had many lepers that were not healed by the prophet Elisha and many widows in Israel whose sons were not raised by Elijah (Luke 4:25-27). Neither the prophet Jesus nor the apostles who had his prophetic spirit healed everyone. And today, despite the amazing advances in medical technique, the world of the sick seems to increase rather than diminish. If cure by any means were normal, it would no longer be a "sign" or a "wonder."

Without dismissing the significance of curing through prayer and fasting, then, I suggest that the church's ministry of healing should above all include three dimensions of the healing accounts provided by Luke-Acts. The church should think of healing in terms of caring more than in terms of curing. The first aspect of Luke's healing stories is the simple *seeing* of the one afflicted. Such seeing requires that the church, like Jesus, must be among those who are afflicted. When the church, in imitation of the dominant culture, seeks to deny weakness and illness through quarantine (formal or informal) — keeping the AIDS-afflicted and the lepers out of sight, the physically disabled in another space, the aged and the dying in segregated enclaves — it fails in its mission of healing. Luke describes both Jesus and the apostles as "gazing attentively" at those who are afflicted. To be seen is already a stage toward being healed.

The second aspect is *touching*. Illness of every sort bears a stigma with it; the ancient laws of purity exacerbate the perception that the weak and afflicted, those "marked" by sickness, necessarily threaten the health of others. Stigmatization, in turn, exacerbates the illness of the one afflicted. The gesture of touch removes the stigma and begins the restoration to human community. The third aspect is *placing in the midst*. When the church refuses to segregate the afflicted, but rather seeks to construct forms of community that place the afflicted at the center rather than at the margins of life, it truly carries out the ministry of healing as a prophetic enactment.

CHAPTER EIGHT

Prophetic Witness

The final dimension of prophecy to consider is witness and how it connects to persecution and death. This discussion is not an afterthought but is rather the culmination of everything said about prophecy to this point, for the prophet is, above all, a witness for God in the presence of others. At the end of the Gospel narrative, the risen Jesus tells his followers, "You are witnesses of these things" — his passion and death, the testimony of the Scriptures concerning him — before promising that they would receive the promise of the Father (Luke 24:48-49). In the beginning of Acts, the risen Jesus again declares to them, "You will receive power when the Holy Spirit comes upon you, and you will be my witnesses (or 'witnesses to me') in Jerusalem, throughout Judea and Samaria, and to the ends of the earth" (Acts 1:8). The term "witness" (Greek *martys*) is Luke's most inclusive term for Jesus' disciples in Acts (1:22; 2:32; 3:15; 5:32; 7:58; 10:39, 41; 13:31; 22:15; 26:16), and he speaks of the apostles (4:33), and especially of Paul, as "bearing witness" (20:26; 23:11; 26:22). For Luke, prophecy and witness are virtually synonymous; thus, the prophets also "bear witness" in their writings to the events in Luke's narrative (see Acts 10:43; 13:22). The prophet bears witness to God in service to other humans. It follows that a prophetic church bears witness to the truth of God in service to the world. Such witness clearly must involve more than merely speaking about God; as I have shown in earlier chapters, it means as well embodying and enacting God's vision for humans.

The Character of Witness

By its very nature, witnessing is a perilous human activity. In bearing witness, a person stands on and by a truth concerning the world as that person sees it and declares what is seen to be, simply, the truth. Because humans are embodied, personal witness must always be particular and perspectival, yet the one witnessing states that, from the place that person stands, what they see (or hear or touch) is true. Inherent in such witness is the risk of personal commitment. This is not a matter of detached analysis or forming an opinion. The witness must decide, "This is the case," and must stand by that choice, no matter what others claim to see and hear. The witness cannot wait upon a permission given by another before witnessing; the witness cannot accept the witness of another as one's own; the witness cannot be directed to a testimony other than one's own — this would be subornation. The witness stands open to the one who "knows the hearts of all" (Acts 1:24), knowing that the truth or falsehood of witness is known always to God even when it is hidden from other humans. The personal risk of taking a stand is supported only by the awareness that one is supported by the God who knows the inner truth.

Bearing witness is perilous as well because no individual's truth is (or can be) everyone's version of the truth. Witnesses, because they each speak from a distinctive and irreducible perspective — rooted ultimately in the necessarily limited capacity of specific bodies to perceive reality — necessarily come into conflict. This is a reason why courts are so hedged about with rules governing the protocol of speech and action: they seek to establish an order to inevitable conflict. A contrary witness automatically challenges one's own testimony and simply by its presence reduces one's witness from absolute to relative status. Because witness is not simply opinion but involves serious personal commitment, furthermore, the clash of witness can easily escalate to other forms of conflict — the very sort of "acting out" that the strict rules of courtrooms seek to preclude. But in the public forum, a contrary witness is not simply "another opinion," it is a personal challenge.

If the kind of witness that involves testifying to the sequence of a car accident is so fraught with the danger of conflict, any claim to bear witness to or for God is necessarily even more perilous. There is no "objective truth" about God, after all, that is not grounded in human experiences, perceptions, and symbols. Subjectivity is at the very heart of religious confession. Christians state in the creed, "We believe in One God," not "There is one God." Paul recognizes the subjective character of confession in 1 Corinthians 8:5-6, when he states that although there are many gods and lords in the world, "for us there is one God and one Lord." But although religious confession is clearly subjective, it also makes a claim about ultimate reality. It is not a witness concerning the time of a crime, or the identity of a burglar, but about the way the world is and the way life is shaped by the unseen power that brings the world into existence. To claim to speak in behalf of God to other humans is itself offensive to others because of its implied assertion of intimacy with the divine and its weighting of speech with divine authority. Rival truth claims in matters of religion stimulate maximum friction precisely because they are made by fellow frail human beings yet involve matters both ultimate and universal.

Being a "truthful witness" with regard to God's word cannot be a matter of accuracy in prediction or analysis — being objectively "right" — but rather a matter of personal integrity. The witness must be faithful to the truth as the witness sees it, must speak consistently with that vision, must embody that conviction in manner of life, and must enact the word in behavior. Witness is valuable, indeed indispensable, to the degree that it truthfully states and embodies a human being's perceptions from that person's limited perspective. In this sense, every witness is needed, for no human perspective can speak for all others. Witness is falsified, therefore, not because it fails to correspond to the objective facts, but because it fails the test of personal integrity, when witnesses speak not of what they see but what others tell them they see (subornation), or change their testimony for personal gain (perjury), or bear witness only when it is convenient and safe, or speak in order to gain notoriety rather than to improve the world.

The character and the cost of authentic witness can be found in the forms that are private and quiet as well as those that are public. It is found wherever persons go against their own inclination and the pressure of their environment in order to be faithful to a higher vision. The soldier who stands guard for comrades while they sleep even though all appears to be quiet; the teacher who reads papers carefully and grades them justly even when the work is poor and grades are inflated; the preacher who exegetes both texts and human lives responsibly and freshly in preparation for sermons even though colleagues and congregations expect less; the mother who faces the hostility of an adolescent daughter and remains in conversation even as her fondest dreams of intimacy are shattered; the pastor who listens attentively for the fourth time to the tale of a little old lady as though he had never heard the story or dealt with a garrulous old lady before. These are all forms of witness, of standing on and for a transcendent truth within the specific circumstances of life. All such forms of witness also carry the cost of suffering: the soldier loses sleep and gains no thanks for simply "doing his duty"; the mother experiences rejection from the one toward whom she had shown all her devotion; the teacher experiences the equivalent of battle fatigue as well as the resentment of colleagues who follow an easier way; the preacher loses free time since congregations do not acknowledge serious study time as real work; the pastor's patience with little old ladies serves only to produce many other little old ladies desiring equal attention.

When the witness is public and political and the prophetic word issues a challenge to the values and systems of society, then the suffering of the prophet who speaks, embodies, and enacts this word is going to be commensurate to the degree of resistance generated by the stakeholders in the society's dominant values. In the case of the prophetic movement initiated by Jesus, we have seen, the challenge was not only to the prevailing "worldly" measures of success and power in Greco-Roman society, but also to competing prophetic programs, represented in Luke's narrative by the Pharisees and lawyers. The greatest and most violent resistance of all, however, is marshaled by the ruling class within Judaism — represented by the chief priests and the members of the Sanhedrin — whom Luke presents as collaborating closely with Roman imperial authority in the effort to suppress the prophetic movement.

The Suffering Prophet

Everyone who has read Luke's Gospel recognizes that, in comparison with Mark and Matthew, he portrays Jesus as a public figure. There is no "messianic secret" in Luke, no private teaching of the disciples in inner rooms. As Peter reminds his audience at Pentecost, the powerful deeds that God worked through Jesus were "in your midst, as you yourselves know" (Acts 2:22). His witness is not the quiet one of the honest workman or the good parent; he is not a teacher who withdraws from society with close followers. Rather, Jesus appears as a prophet, as God's spokesperson to the people Israel. His students (disciples) likewise are prophets in the public forum.

Corresponding to the public character of Jesus' witness are the certainty and the severity of his suffering. Luke places Jesus' witness in the context of the tradition of the suffering prophet — figures such as Isaiah and Jeremiah, who were rejected by authorities and punished precisely because they challenged the assumptions of royal and priestly authority. Luke has Jesus tell his followers to rejoice when they are hated and excluded and insulted and denounced as evil, because "their ancestors treated the prophets in the same way" (Luke 6:23). Similarly, Luke has Jesus attack the lawyers in terms that make the tradition explicit:

> Woe to you! You build the memorials of the prophets whom your ancestors killed. Consequently, you bear witness and give consent to the deeds of your ancestors, for they killed them and you do the building. Therefore the Wisdom of God said, "I will send to them prophets and apostles; some of them they will kill and persecute" in order that this generation might be charged with the blood of all the prophets since the foundation of the world, from the blood of Abel to the blood of Zechariah, who died between the altar and the temple building. Yes, I tell you, this generation will be charged with their blood! (11:47-51)

Stephen likewise evokes this tradition in the closing attack of his speech before the Sanhedrin and connects it directly to the death of Jesus:

> You stiff-necked people, uncircumcised in heart and ears, you always oppose the Holy Spirit; you are just like your ancestors. Which of the prophets did your ancestors not persecute? They put to death those who foretold the coming of the righteous one, whose betrayers and murderers you have now become. (Acts 7:51-52)

The degree to which Jesus is portrayed as a prophet, then, to that same degree his suffering for his witness becomes a certainty, indeed, a "necessity." When warned away from Herod's desire to kill him, Jesus declares,

> Behold I cast out demons and I perform healings today and tomorrow, and on the third day I accomplish my purpose. Yet I *must* (literally, 'it is *necessary* that I'] continue on my way today, tomorrow, and the following day, for it is impossible that a prophet should die outside Jerusalem. Jerusalem, Jerusalem, you who kill the prophets and those sent to you. (Luke 13:32-34).

It is within this framework that Luke's frequent statements concerning the "necessity" of Jesus' suffering are to be understood: suffering, rejection, and death are the consequence of a prophetic ministry that strikes at the core of the world's corruption and calls it to repent. Thus, Luke takes over from Mark Jesus' own predictions of his suffering and death: after Peter's confession, Jesus tells his disciples, "The Son of Man *must* suffer greatly and be rejected by the elders, the chief priests, and the scribes, and be killed and on the third day be raised" (Luke 9:22; see also 9:44). As they get nearer the city of Jerusalem, he tells the Twelve, "Behold, we are going up to Jerusalem and everything written by the prophets about the Son of Man will be fulfilled. He will be handed over to the Gentiles and he will be mocked and insulted and spat upon; and after they have scourged him they will kill him, but on the third day he will rise" (18:31-33). At the Last Supper, he tells them again, "The Son of Man indeed goes as it has been determined; but woe to the man by whom he is betrayed" (22:22).

Corresponding to the predictions are the reminders provided his followers after Jesus' resurrection. The women at the tomb are told, "Remember what he said to you while you were still in Galilee, that the Son of Man *must* be handed over to sinners and be crucified, and rise on the third day" (24:6-7). The disciples on the road to Emmaus are told, "Oh, how foolish you are! How slow of heart to believe all that the prophets spoke! Was it not *necessary* that the Messiah should suffer these things and enter into his glory?" (24:25-26). Finally, the disciples are told how "everything written in the law of Moses and the prophets and the psalms *must* be fulfilled . . . that the Messiah would suffer and rise from the dead on the third day" (24:44, 46).

The open and public character of Jesus' witness is found especially in the part of Luke's narrative devoted to Jesus' journey to Jerusalem (chapters 9–19). As the prophet sets his face toward his destiny (9:51) and travels steadily toward the city that kills the prophets, Jesus prepares his disciples for his suffering and death through a series of passion predictions (9:23, 44; 18:31-33) and speaks to those around him on the way. Luke carefully notes Jesus' audiences, having him turn from the crowds, to the disciples, and to his opponents (the Pharisees and lawyers). He also carefully aligns Jesus' statements with the audience he addresses. To the crowds, he issues calls to discipleship (9:23-27, 57-62) and warnings of judgment for nonrepentance (10:13-15; 11:29-32; 12:49-56; 13:2-5, 24-30; 14:26-33). To the disciples — those who converted to his movement and followed with him (8:1-3) — he addresses his most extensive teachings concerning possessions, prayer, and perseverance (11:2-13; 12:2-48; 16:1-13; 17:1-10, 22-36; 18:1-14, 18-30; 19:12-27).

To his opponents, who hold him under close scrutiny and seek to trap him, Jesus issues direct denunciation (11:39-52) and a series of parables that have a barbed edge (10:25-37; 15:1-32; 16:14-31; 18:9-14). The sequence in 14:1-24 is illustrative: Jesus is invited to eat with Pharisees, but they "observe him closely" as he heals a man suffering from dropsy; Jesus heals the man, then challenges them concerning the legitimacy of healing on the Sabbath, silencing them (14:1-6). He then goes on the attack when he observes how guests sought the best places at table, advocating humility rather than such self-seeking (14:8-11). Jesus next tells the host to invite not friends or neighbors but those who cannot repay — the poor, the crippled, the lame, and the blind. In a word, Jesus challenges his host to follow the prophetic program that Jesus announced in 6:20-49, declaring that he will indeed be "blessed" because of the guest's inability to repay (14:12-14). When another guest, missing the point entirely, speaks of the blessedness of those who "dine in the kingdom of God," Jesus tells the sharp parable of the Great Wedding Banquet, the invitation to which those first called reject for one reason or another, leading to their being rejected in turn, while the "poor and the crippled and the blind and the lame" are included in the banquet (14:16-24). The witness of the prophet Jesus throughout his journey to Jerusalem is both public and provocative.

While Jesus is on the road through Galilean and Judean villages, his public witness can be seen as that of an itinerant philosopher, whose constant movement is accompanied by skirmishes with members of rival schools. But with his entry into the city of Jerusalem, the prophet's witness takes on a new and more ominous dimension. This was, after all, the very heart of the established order: in Jerusalem were the Roman prefect with his troops, the vast temple with its sanctuary and priestly attendants, and the official court of the Jewish people, the Sanhedrin, whose members were drawn from the wealthy and powerful, including the chief priests and the scribes. The shift is more than one of place, it is one of significance. Jesus' witness is now not simply to the country crowds, but to those gathered for festival from all over the world; it is heard not simply by followers and a changing group of villagers, but by the official leaders whose power and prestige are directly threatened by this prophet's countercultural message and manner of life. Contemporary analogies would be a grassroots politician arriving in Washington to confront the power of government or a local Catholic pastor arriving in Rome with a handful of his parishioners to challenge the Vatican. The danger of Jesus' witness mounts as the power of his opposition is more present.

Like Mark's Gospel, Luke has Jesus initiate his Jerusalem ministry by two prophetic acts whose challenge to the political and religious authorities could not be mistaken. Immediately after telling his disciples the "kingship parable" (the "parable of the Pounds") in 19:12-27, which responds to their expectations concerning the immediate disclosing of the kingdom of God (9:11), Jesus enters the city as a royal figure, proclaimed by the crowds: "Blessed is the king who comes in the name of the Lord" (19:38). In response to the Pharisees' rebuke, Jesus refuses to silence his followers, implicitly accepting the acclaim: "I tell you, if they keep silent, the very stones will cry out" (19:40). He then enters the temple area and drives out those who were selling things, declaring, "It is written, my house shall be a house of prayer, but you have made it a den of thieves" (19:45-46).

He enters the city as the Lord's king and purifies the temple of its commerce: these actions are sufficiently provocative to guarantee resistance from the political and religious authorities. Luke has Jesus virtually inhabit the temple area as the new site for his teaching and the place where the subsequent controversies will play out. To recall the contemporary analogies: the political reformer is on the steps of the Capitol building after having scoured the chambers of Congress; the pastor is at the doors of St. Peter's, where pilgrims from all over the world can hear his arguments with the Vatican authorities. Luke sets the stage:

> Every day he was teaching in the temple area. The chief priests, the scribes, and the leaders of the people, meanwhile, were seeking to put him to death, but they could find no way to accomplish their purpose because all the people were hanging on his words. (19:47-48)

The series of controversy stories that Luke takes over from Mark and places in the context of Jesus' teaching ministry in the temple (20:1-47) — his opponents approach him as he is surrounded by crowds in that public place — serves to heighten the tension and provide a transition to Jesus' discourse about the future to his disciples (21:5-36) and then the story of Jesus' suffering and death. Three of the controversies are begun by religious leaders seeking to entrap him: the first is the question of the origin of his authority as a prophet (20:1-8); the second concerns the payment of taxes to Caesar — set to "trap him in speech, in order to hand him over to the authority and power of the governor" (20:20-26); the third seeks to catch Jesus in a quandary concerning Scripture's teaching on the resurrection (20:27-40).

But Luke also shows Jesus as the aggressor: he turns on his Sadducean questioners the question concerning their conviction that the Messiah is David's son, when in Scripture David calls the Messiah, "Lord" (20:41-44), and in the "hearing of all the people" Jesus directly attacks the scribes for their hypocrisy and avarice (20:45-47). Finally, Jesus tells "to the people" the parable of the tenant farmers who rejected all the emissaries of the owner seeking what was owed him and at last killed his "beloved son," with the result that the farmers would be killed by the owner and the vineyard handed over to others (20:9-18). It is a tale that transparently refers to the history of the rejection of the prophets and the imminent death of Jesus, God's beloved son. Luke draws the explicit point: "The scribes and chief priests sought to lay hands on him at that very hour, but they feared the people, for they knew that he had addressed this parable to them" (that is, the leaders; 20:19).

Given the challenging character of Jesus' prophetic actions in the entry to the city and the purification of the temple, this series of confrontations in the temple area that show Jesus striking at the legitimacy of the religious authorities prepare the reader for his imminent arrest and death. There is little surprise in light of such provocation that the official keepers of the dominant system of values, whose place is secured by their willingness to go along with Roman rule, should seek to eliminate this threat through the help of Rome itself. Thus, the cleverness of the charge that they eventually bring before the Roman prefect: "We found this man misleading our people; he opposes payment of taxes to Caesar, and maintains that he is the messiah, a king" (23:2). Jesus' proclamation of God's kingdom that spoke good news to the poor and the sick, the sinner and the outcast, is here translated into the starkest political form as a challenge to Rome.

Ancient critics like Celsus questioned whether Jesus could really be called a sage, since when he was called before authorities he failed to provide a stirring defense of his teaching (in the manner of Socrates) or demonstrate his contempt of tyrants (in the manner of Zeno). But in Luke's narrative, Jesus' laconic responses to the Sanhedrin and Pilate serve to make another point: these are not the ones to whom his teaching and his mission are answerable. He is God's prophet, and when he cannot speak to the people directly, there is no need for him to speak at all. The transition is marked explicitly at the arrest of Jesus in the garden: "Jesus said to the chief priests and temple guards and elders who had come for him, 'Have you come out as against a robber, with swords and clubs? Day after day I was with you in the temple area, and you did not seize me; but this is your hour, the time for the power of darkness'" (22:52-53).

It is useless to speak to those closed to the truth. Thus, when the San-hedrin demands to know if he is the Messiah, Jesus responds, "If I tell you, you will not believe, and if I question, you will not respond. But from this time on the Son of Man will be seated at the right hand of the power of God" (22:67-69). In response to their question whether he is the Son of God, he says, simply, "You say that I am" (22:70). He answers Pilate simi-larly when asked whether he is king of the Jews: "You say so" (23:3). To Herod, whom Jesus had earlier dismissed as "that fox" (13:32), and whom Pilate involved in the case simply to secure local allegiance ("Herod and Pilate became friends [allies] that very day," 23:12), "he gave him no an-swer" (23:9).

The uselessness of responding to those who had already demon-strated their hostility to the prophet's message is confirmed by the treat-ment Jesus receives at their hands. Before Jesus is even questioned by the Sanhedrin, "the men who held Jesus in custody were ridiculing and beat-ing him. They blindfolded him and questioned him, saying, 'Prophesy! Who is it that struck you?' And they reviled him in saying many other things against him" (22:63-65). Jesus, to be sure, had long ago identified such treatment as that given to the prophets of old (6:23; 11:47-48) and pre-dicted that such would be his own treatment (18:32). The reader knows that he is a prophet; playing parlor tricks for his torturers serves no end. The despicable Herod shows Jesus similar contempt when he is disap-pointed in his expectation that Jesus would "perform some signs" for him (23:8): "Herod and his soldiers treated him contemptuously and mocked him, and after clothing him in resplendent garb, he sent him back to Pi-late" (23:11). Finally, even as the people stand and watch while Jesus is on the cross, "the rulers sneered at him and said, 'He saved others, let him save himself if he is the chosen one, the Son of God'" (23:35).

But Luke shows Jesus still bearing witness as a prophet to those whose resistance has not already been demonstrated. He addresses the women of Jerusalem who bewailed and lamented him with words of pro-phetic warning: "If these things are done when the wood is green, what will happen when it is dry?" (23:28-31). He prays that God forgive those who are sneering at him, "for they know not what they do" (23:34). And to the criminal executed with him who asks to be remembered when Jesus enters into his kingdom, Jesus responds, "Amen, I say to you, today you will be with me in paradise" (23:43). Jesus' prophetic voice has not been si-lenced; it has consistently been addressed to those whose hearts are open to a word from God and who are ready for repentance. Thus, when he breathes his last, with the words, "Father, into your hands I commend my spirit," those who had gathered as for a spectacle, return home beating their breasts — they are ready to receive the word of repentance that comes to them at Pentecost, because they see in Jesus at the end what the centurion sees, "a righteous man" (23:46-48).

Jesus also foresees that his prophetic witness will be continued by his chosen followers. As the tension grows around his open confrontation with authorities in Jerusalem, Jesus speaks of the tribulations that will occur in the future (21:7-36). In contrast to Mark and Matthew, Luke has Jesus provide a three-stage prophecy. Before the final stage, the coming of the Son of Man (21:25-36), there will be a long period of Gentile dominance that begins with the destruction of the temple (21:8-9, 20-24). But even before the war with Rome that will lead to that destruction, Jesus tells his disciples, they will face tribulations of their own caused by their allegiance to him:

> They will seize you and persecute you, they will hand you over to the synagogues and to prisons, and they will have you led before kings and governors because of my name. It will lead to your giving testimony (Greek *martyrion*). (21:12-13)

Jesus assures them that he himself will give them a wisdom in speaking that their adversaries will be powerless to "resist or refute" (21:14-15). But he warns that they will be handed over by those close to them, and, in a deliberate echo of the Beatitudes (6:22), "will be hated by all because of my name" (21:17). This discourse anticipates the role that will be played by the disciples in Acts and explicitly connects what they do "in the name of Jesus" with the prophetic witness that Jesus gave throughout the Gospel narrative.

The Church's Witness in Acts

Throughout the Gospel narrative, Luke shows that Jesus' prophetic witness was more than speaking God's word; it involved, indeed demanded, the embodiment of that word in his own character and the enactment of that word in his actions. Jesus' poverty displayed the good news to the poor and also challenged the dominant assumption that wealth equaled worth. His prayer opened him to the guidance of the Holy Spirit and challenged the world's premise that honor from other humans rather than truth before

God was important. His itinerancy showed the freedom that followed from obedience to the Spirit's prompting, and challenged the conventional wisdom that security comes through control. His servant leadership revealed the true nature of authority and threatened the patronage-client system of antiquity. In the same way, his exorcism of the possessed, his healing of the sick, and his embrace of the marginal both demonstrated the full meaning of "good news to the poor" and threatened the tendency of all societies to seek identity through sameness and health through the expulsion of what is deemed weak.

The witness of the church in the narrative of Acts likewise must be found not only in the apostolic proclamation of the exaltation of the crucified Messiah — although this is clearly important — but also in the manner of life and the ministry that the church can carry out "in his name" precisely because he is the source of the Holy Spirit that empowers them. We return once more, then, to the critical importance of Luke's description of the first community of believers in Acts 2:41-47 and 4:32-37. He shows the restored Israel living according to the prophet's program — sharing their possessions and praying — and in this fashion winning favor with the people and drawing those willing to repent as adherents. A single line in the second community description captures the close connection between the proclamation of Jesus as the prophet whom God raised up and the community's life according to the prophet's message. Immediately after stating that the believers held everything in common (4:32), Luke notes, "With great power the apostles bore witness to the resurrection of the Lord Jesus, and great favor was accorded them all" (4:33). He then continues with his description of possessions being placed at the feet of the apostles and distributed to each according to need (4:34-35). The "witness" (Greek *martyrion*) that the apostles gave to the resurrection was the proclamation of him as raised, to be sure (2:22-36; 3:13-18), but it included as well the healing they carried out "in his name" (3:6, 16; 4:10) and their participation in the common life (2:41-47).

Luke also shows the apostles fulfilling Jesus' prediction in the Gospel that they would bear witness in his name (Luke 21:12-13). The opposition to the apostles' preaching and healing comes from the same authorities that resisted Jesus. After the healing of the lame man in the temple area and Peter's announcement that it was in the name of the resurrected Jesus that the man had been restored to health, "the priests, the captain of the temple guard, and the Sadducees confronted them, disturbed that they were teaching the people and proclaiming in Jesus the resurrection of the dead" (Acts 4:1-2). Peter and John are brought the next day before the "leaders, elders, and scribes, with Annas the high priest, John, Alexander, and all who were of the high-priestly class" (4:5-6).

To appreciate this and the following scenes, it must be understood that these followers of Jesus were being arrested and called to account by the highest religious authorities — the religious authorities of the tradition that they themselves affirmed. Peter is "filled with the Holy Spirit" (4:8) and restates in their presence what he had declared to the crowd: it is through the name of Jesus that the man was healed (4:10). Luke nicely links the apostles' testimony to that of Jesus with this observation: "Seeing the boldness of Peter and John, and perceiving them to be uneducated, ordinary men, they were amazed, and they recognized them as the companions of Jesus" (4:13). When ordered to stop teaching in the name of Jesus, Peter and John respond, "Whether it is right in the sight of God for us to obey you rather than God, you be the judges. It is impossible for us not to speak about what we have seen and heard" (4:19-20). Their reply summarizes the essence of witness.

Peter and John are equally bold when they are arrested a second time and brought before the Sanhedrin — not least because in response to prayer they had been freshly empowered by the Holy Spirit (4:23-31) — replying to the charge that they stop teaching in Jesus' name, "We must obey God rather than men" (5:29), and after reciting again the basis of their proclamation (the resurrection of Jesus, 5:30-31), declare, "We are witnesses of these things as is the Holy Spirit that God has given to those who obey him" (5:32). Persuaded by Gamaliel not to put the apostles to death, the Sanhedrin has them flogged and again orders them to desist speaking in the name of Jesus (5:40). The response of Peter and John is to continue preaching and teaching the Messiah Jesus in homes and in the temple area, "rejoicing that they had been found worthy to suffer dishonor for the sake of the name" (5:41-42) — language that echoes Jesus' blessing in Luke 6:22. Herod subsequently has James the brother of John killed and imprisons Peter, who escapes only by means of an angelic intervention (12:1-19).

The pattern of prophetic witness is demonstrated fully by Stephen, whom Paul refers to in prayer as "your witness" (22:20) and whose ministry and death both imitate Jesus. Filled with the Holy Spirit, Stephen worked signs and wonders (6:8) and was confronted by Hellenistic Jews, but in fulfillment of Jesus' promise, "they could not withstand the wisdom and the spirit with which he spoke" (6:10; Luke 21:15). They bring false accusations against Stephen and bring him to trial before the Sanhedrin

(6:12-14). Unlike Jesus when similarly accused, Stephen's speech is a full-fledged response to the attack as well, as we have seen, a reading of Scripture that provides the prophetic framework for Luke's entire two-volume work. When he concludes with the charge that his hearers always refuse to hear prophets and have rejected the righteous one, Jesus (7:51-53), the members of the Sanhedrin throw him out of the city and stone him (7:58). The strong connection between the witness of Stephen and that of Jesus is indicated in three ways. At the moment the Sanhedrin grows enraged at him, Stephen is filled with the Holy Spirit and sees Jesus standing at the right hand of God (7:55-56); as he is being stoned, he prays, "Lord Jesus, receive my spirit" (7:59; compare Luke 23:46); and before he dies, in imitation of Jesus, he forgives those who put him to death: "Lord, do not hold this sin against them" (7:60; compare Luke 23:34).

Above all, Luke identifies Paul as Jesus' chosen witness. Fearful of welcoming Paul after his conversion, Ananias is told by the Lord in a vision: "This man is a chosen instrument of mine to carry my name before Gentiles, kings, and Israelites, and I will show him what he will have to suffer for my name" (Acts 9:15-16). The statement directly links Paul's public testimony with his suffering. Paul recounts the vision he had of Jesus in the temple, in which the Lord tells him that those in Jerusalem will not accept "your testimony about me" and that he is being sent "far away to the Gentiles" (22:18, 21). And after the dispute that arose in the Sanhedrin because of Paul's declaration that he is on trial for "the hope of the resurrection of the dead" (23:6), Jesus appears to Paul in the compound, saying, "Take courage. For just as you have borne witness to my cause in Jerusalem, so you must also bear witness in Rome" (23:11). In Paul's speech before Agrippa, he reports Jesus' commissioning of him in these words: "I have appeared to you for this purpose, to appoint you as a servant and witness of what you have seen [of me] and what you shall be shown" (26:16). Finally, Paul reassures his frightened shipmates in the midst of storm and shipwreck with the words spoken to him by an angel during the night, "Do not be afraid, Paul. You are destined to stand before Caesar; and behold, for your sake, God has granted safety to all who are sailing with you" (27:24).

Like Peter and John, then, Paul's witness is in obedience to "what he has seen," and he carries that testimony wherever he goes. Luke shows him preaching in the synagogues in Damascus (9:20) and among Hellenistic Jews in Jerusalem (9:29); sent out by the church in Antioch, he preaches in the synagogues of Antioch in Pisidia (13:13-42), Iconium (14:1-7),

Thessalonica (17:1-9), Beroea (17:10-11), Athens (17:16-17), Corinth (18:4), and Ephesus (18:19; 19:8). In his first synagogue sermon, Paul draws direct connections between the prophecies in Scripture, John the Baptist, and Jesus (13:17-25), before linking the apostles before him and himself: "For many days he appeared to those who had come up with him from Galilee to Jerusalem. These are now his witnesses before the people. We ourselves are proclaiming this good news to you, that what God promised our ancestors he has brought to fulfillment for us their children, by raising up Jesus" (13:31-33). Paul carries out this witness before his fellow Jews with prophetic zeal: he and Barnabas "spoke out boldly for the Lord, who confirmed the word about his grace by granting signs and wonders to occur through their hands" (14:3). Paul bears witness also directly to the Gentiles in Lystra (14:8-18), Philippi (16:28-34), Athens (17:16-34), Corinth (18:7-10), and Ephesus (19:10). And he bears witness to fellow believers in the assembly: he tells the elders of Ephesus, "I did not shrink from telling you what was for your benefit, or from teaching you in public or in your homes. I earnestly bore witness to both Jews and Greeks to repentance before God and to faith in our Lord Jesus" (20:20-21).

His testimony, in turn, stirs resentment and resistance, because Paul was seen (as he is still seen in some quarters) as disloyal, a renegade who has turned on his own people. In Damascus, where he first proclaims Jesus as Son of God, he narrowly escapes being killed by a daring escape over the city walls (9:20-25); resistance to him grew so strong among Hellenistic Jews in Jerusalem that they also seek to kill him and the church must send him to Tarsus (9:28-30). The Jews in Antioch stir up a persecution against Paul and Barnabas in that city (13:50); so also do the Jews (and Gentiles) in Iconium (14:5). Jews from both cities pursue Paul to Lystra, stoning him and leaving him for dead (14:19). He and Barnabas rightly report to their new churches, "It is necessary for us to undergo many hardships to enter the kingdom of God" (14:22). The conflicts continue in Philippi (16:19-20), Thessalonica (17:5-9), Beroea (17:13), Corinth (18:6), and Ephesus (19:9). When Paul tells the elders in Ephesus that he had "served the Lord with all humility and with the tears and trials that came to me because of the plots of the Jews" (20:19), he does not exaggerate.

That Paul's witness will take on a new shape is intimated in his farewell speech — "Compelled by the Spirit I am going to Jerusalem. What will happen to me there I do not know, except that in one city after another the Holy Spirit has been warning me that imprisonments and hardships await me" (20:22-23) — and prophesied by Agabus in Caesarea (21:10-12).

The warnings are fulfilled when Paul's presence in the temple incites the Jews to riot and seek to kill him (21:30-31; 22:22). When the centurion rescues him, forty Jews form a conspiracy to kill Paul (23:12-15), and he is only rescued from death through the intervention of his nephew (23:16-22). What the Jews fail to accomplish directly, they seek to achieve legally in the series of hearings before the Roman prefects Felix and Festus (24:1-8; 25:19, 24). Only Paul's appeal to Caesar enables him to escape their grasp (25:11-12; 26:32).

Through his series of hearings and trials, Paul fulfills Jesus' prophecy that he would be "a servant and witness of what you have seen and what you shall be shown" (26:16). His speeches are not in service of securing his release but of speaking the truth concerning what God had accomplished in the resurrection of Jesus. His concluding words to Agrippa can stand as a fitting summary both of his witness and that borne by all those filled with Jesus' prophetic spirit in Acts:

> I was not disobedient to the heavenly vision. On the contrary, first to those in Damascus and in Jerusalem and throughout the whole country of Judea, and then to the Gentiles, I preached the need to repent and turn to God, and to do the works giving evidence of repentance. That is why the Jews seized me when I was in the temple and tried to kill me. But I have enjoyed God's help to this very day, and so I stand here testifying to small and great alike, saying nothing different from what the prophets and Moses foretold, that the Messiah must suffer, and that, as the first to rise from the dead, he would proclaim light both to our people and to the Gentiles. (26:19-23)

Challenge to the Contemporary Church

Luke shows the church in Acts continuing the prophetic witness of Jesus in the Gospel: the church is filled with the spirit, speaks God's word, embodies that word in prayer, itinerancy, sharing possessions, and servant leadership, and enacts that word through a ministry of healing and embrace. All of this constitutes its witness at the most fundamental level. Because the church's prophetic profession and practice necessarily run athwart the power and privilege vested in conventional values, such witness is expressed also through "speaking truth to power" and through bearing the suffering that follows inevitably from a clash of fundamentally divergent visions. In every respect, Luke shows the early church to be just as prophetic as Jesus himself. The most pertinent question for the contemporary church that reads Luke-Acts is whether it can be called prophetic in anything like the same manner.

The church today has certainly not lost completely some senses of the term "witness" as it is found in Luke-Acts. The act of preaching, especially missionary preaching, is legitimately thought of as an expression of witness, and especially in some Protestant churches there is a strong tradition of personal story-telling that is called witnessing: individuals relate their experience of Jesus and how it has changed their lives. These uses are well grounded in Luke's work: the apostolic preaching is a form of witness, and story-telling — whether Peter's tale of Cornelius's conversion or Paul's story of his own calling — serves as "testimony" before judges. The connection of witnessing to suffering, above all suffering to the point of death — as in the case of Stephen — has also been preserved in the church's particular reverence for the martyrs through the ages. Such witness continues to be given throughout the world. The day I write this, newspapers report the death of Christian medical missionaries at the hands of the Taliban because (it is claimed) they mixed religious teaching with their care of the sick. Like Peter, they healed "in the name of Jesus Christ."

The church's reflection on what it can learn about witness from Luke-Acts should not begin by repudiating these understandings and practices, but by deepening and broadening them. It can broaden them by thinking about witness not simply in terms of individual speech — preaching, story-telling, apology — but also in terms of communal activity, how the church as church bears witness to the world. It can deepen its understanding by thinking about witness first of all as embodiment and enactment of God's vision and secondarily as speaking about that vision.

Proclaiming Resurrection

The part of the prophetic message that distinguishes the church from Jesus is the proclamation of Jesus as the prophet whom God has raised from the dead and exalted to his right hand. The resurrection of Jesus is more than God's vindication of him, though it is also surely that; for Luke as for Paul in his letters, the resurrection of Jesus is the source of the gift of the Holy Spirit that empowers his followers and inaugurates a new age. The reality of the resurrection runs through all the speeches of Acts, from Peter's first sermon at Pentecost to Paul's last defense before Agrippa. Luke's narrative expresses the same conviction that Paul stated to the Corinthians: the resurrection of Jesus is of first importance, the good news by which they are being saved, and the shared message of all the earliest leaders: "Whether it be I or they, so we preach and so you believed" (1 Cor 15:1-11).

The church today should examine itself with respect to the integrity of its proclamation of the resurrection. It must ask first whether it continues to proclaim the apostolic faith or whether the corrosive effects of modernity have softened the hard edges of the resurrection truth in the church's preaching and teaching. The church needs to consider the slow collapse of creedal commitment among its members, and even in its leaders. The popularity of the "historical Jesus" as a touchstone for many communities needs careful analysis and criticism. Certainly, the learning of history in order to be better readers of the Gospel is to be applauded; but a reconstruction of Jesus' ministry by historical means cannot replace the Gospels, which are written from beginning to end in light of the resurrection — that is, in light of the faith shared by the church of the evangelists, and the church today, if indeed it is.

But the resurrection is more than a perspective on Jesus' ministry in the past: it is the perception of Jesus' exalted rule over the world in the present. Precisely this aspect of the resurrection faith — the way it announces the good news of God's rule — is most corrupted when Christians act as though recovering the "historical" teachings of Jesus sufficed for Christian faith. The irony in Luke's report of Gamaliel's advice to the Sanhedrin is frequently missed. Gamaliel compared the Jesus movement to those of other messianic figures who stirred a movement that then disappeared with their death (Acts 5:35-38); but what has confronted Gamaliel, the Sanhedrin, and the world today is not a movement that stopped with the death of its messiah, but came to new and more powerful life. What was required of Gamaliel and likewise of Christians today is not historical analysis but the obedience of faith: as Peter declared, "We must obey God rather than men. The God of our ancestors raised Jesus, though you had him killed by hanging him on a tree. God exalted him at his right hand as leader and savior to grant repentance and forgiveness of sins. *We are witnesses of these things, as is the Holy Spirit that God has given to those who obey him*" (5:29-32).

More than doctrinal fidelity is required, however; the church must ask itself about the passion and the urgency of its proclamation of the resurrection as the heart of the good news. The degree to which the resurrection has become a day in the liturgical calendar that is preached only at Easter, rather than the premise and theme of all preaching, points to the decline in Christian proclamation. At issue here is the manner in which the church presents to the world how the resurrection matters, how the gift of the Holy Spirit enables a manner of life that is distinct from the values of the "twisted generation" that is the world's steady offering in every age. How convincingly does the church press its case that the resurrection of Jesus, which is made powerfully present by the outpouring of the Holy Spirit, demands and enables repentance unto eternal life and the deeds that demonstrate such repentance?

Embodying Witness

It does not matter much what the church declares to the world concerning the resurrection if its common life does not embody the truth of the resurrection. The church's manner of life needs to display the power of the Holy Spirit that comes from the exalted Lord. The manner of life suggested by Luke is that of the good news first proclaimed, embodied, and enacted by the prophet Jesus. The character of the church's common life is its first and most important witness, its most public and persuasive form of politics. The church "speaks truth to power" in the world first, not by making speeches, but by living in a manner that is consistent with the prophetic word. Indeed, if the church's own power arrangements simply mimic those of the world, it offers no challenge to the world, no good news. If the church measures success and prestige in the same way the larger culture does, then the larger culture has nothing to learn from the church. If the church's own sexual mores are disordered, then nothing it says about sexual morals is convincing.

But when the church lives in prayer, faithfully seeking to discern the movement of the Spirit; when it is itinerant in the sense that it responds to such movements freely rather than seeking to control them; when it shows that authentic power displays itself in a servant disposition that empowers others; and when it lives out of the poverty of the Christ, sharing its possessions with the world's needy, then when it speaks about "good news to the poor," the world actually can find meaning in the message. Likewise, when the church offers an alternative to the demonic powers of addiction in the contemporary world, when it heals the sick by restoring them to full humanity, when it is a community of reconciliation that is holy by means of embrace rather than by exclusion, then its message of "good news to the poor" can be heard by the world, because it is made powerfully present in communities gathered in the name of the Lord.

The church that so embodies and enacts the prophetic word can also expect to experience the suffering that Luke suggests is the logical consequence of authentic prophecy. Many in the world will want to hear the good news and seek repentance; the world is as hungry today as it has ever been for healing and embrace, for a manner of life based in God's gift of grace more than in the competitive hostility and self-seeking offered by contemporary culture. Such are the poor and the sick and the excluded and the demon-possessed around us. But the real wielders of prestige and power — those with the greatest stake in the maintenance of a system of competition rather than collaboration, stealing rather than sharing, exclusion rather than embrace — those "leaders of the people" will resist and reject the church's prophetic vision in the same manner they rejected the good news announced by Jesus. The more forcefully the church expresses God's vision for humanity, the more violent are the responses of those who deny God and despise the notion of God's vision. The more the church is authentically prophetic, in short, the more it can expect to experience suffering and persecution. Popularity and success are the marks of false prophecy; when the church truly lives in God's kingdom, the more it can expect rejection from the kingdoms of this world.

Witness to the Church

Such integrity of communal witness is extraordinarily difficult in itself. Even when the power of the Holy Spirit is active, shaping a coherent community character must overcome the internal resistance of individualism and all the subtle ways in which each church member is deeply affected by the values of the world. Achieving a genuine prophetic embodiment is made even more difficult by the long history of Christianity's enmeshment in culture and the multiple ways in which leadership and membership alike only weakly embody the prophetic word, only partially enact the prophetic mission of embrace, perhaps even fail to express the prophetic spirit at all. Because of this, the church as a community must also hear God's word from prophets in its midst and be called to repentance by those who call the church to its own best identity.

Prophets within the church should be heeded. But those who seek to express God's prophetic vision for the church must also be aware of the demands and the costs of this role. If their criticism is to be heard by the church, they must also loyally embody the message they proclaim. They above all must seek through prayer to discern the working of the Holy Spirit in human lives; they must respond to the movements of the spirit rather than human reward; they must express leadership through service. If they are to "speak truth to power" in the church as Peter bore witness to his own religious leaders in the Sanhedrin, then they must not only state with Peter (Acts 5:29) the necessity of obeying God rather than humans — even ecclesiastical humans! — they must also bear the responsibility of living in accord with the prophetic word. Such prophets within the church can, moreover, expect to be unpopular in direct proportion to the degree they challenge the corruption of power and prestige. They must, like Peter and John, "rejoice that they have been found worthy to suffer dishonor for the sake of the name" (Acts 5:41).

One of the invaluable roles that prophets can play within the church is to help it remain in touch with the margins. The church can, and does, become all too preoccupied with upkeep and maintenance, with keeping faith with tradition, with preserving the bounds of orthodoxy. These are legitimate and even necessary concerns. But they are also precisely the concerns of the Pharisees in Luke-Acts, and the lesson Luke teaches is that such preoccupation can hinder the perception of what new things God is doing in the world and block an openness to the work of the Holy Spirit in the actual lives of humans. The powerful message of the church's ministry of embrace in Acts is that the way in which God works among the marginal has a critical revelatory function for those who presently occupy the "center": the Jewish believers come to understand the real basis of their own salvation as faith through the gift of Jesus Christ only because of the way in which God has purified the hearts of the Gentiles through faith (Acts 15:11). Because prophets within the church do not bear the responsibility for making ecclesiastical machinery run in accord with tradition, they are uniquely positioned to allow the challenge of God's work outside the boundaries of the church to be heard within the community of faith, offering it also the chance to repent.

Scripture Index

Scripture Index